"In *Held Hostage*, Ken Cooper describes the absolute horror and despair of prison life as well as any writer I have encountered. More importantly, however, Ken points his readers to the only Light that can penetrate the darkness of prison—or the darkness of the human heart. This is an amazing testimony."

—**Chuck Colson**, founder, Prison Fellowship

"Since I was a boy, I have been influenced by stories about one-time criminals who made a radical conversion to Jesus Christ while they were imprisoned—molding my conviction of the transforming power of the Good News Gospel. In this book, Ken Cooper vividly displays that power and sustainable truth. He is living out what 2 Corinthians 5:17 clearly states: 'If anyone is in Christ, he is a new creation; the old has gone, the new has come!'"

—**Luis Palau**, evangelist

"Ninety-nine percent of us have never robbed anyone, much less numerous banks. But, like most of us, the 'gentleman bank robber' had no clue what was really missing in his life. He was convinced that, given the right circumstances, he could find it. And he blamed God for what *He* did to him. Cooper finally found, in the most unlikely of places, what had been missing all his life, and confronts us eloquently and powerfully with an inescapable reality: The only thing that can satisfy our deepest, most intense longings is a personal relationship with God. Cooper lays it all out in this fast-paced, easy-read page-turner you cannot put down."

—**Ben Kinchlow**, former co-host, The 700 Club; bestselling author

"I strongly recommend Ken Cooper's gripping life story, which describes his criminal life as 'the gentleman bank robber' dramatically transformed by God. Ken was sentenced by a 'hanging judge' to 99 years in prison, where he survived cells ruled by gang rapists and, in those cell blocks, became a Christian. Then he started working with other Christian inmates to create cells of transformed prisoners, and in turn to transform cell blocks, until he was surprisingly released from prison. On the outside he created an organization to help inmates reform their lives when they got out of prison.

"Ken's life story is an inspiration. It also helped me understand what life is like in a maximum-security prison (near where I live in Florida). Truly, as a Portuguese proverb states, 'God writes straight with crooked lines.' *Held Hostage* reveals the compassion of Jesus in a marvelous way."

— **Francis MacNutt**, Ph.D., co-founder and director, Christian Healing Ministries; bestselling

"Ken's transformation is a living witness to the timeless healing power of Jesus Christ. His story serves as a reminder that God's light can never be put out by the darkness. He will shine His timeless healing power on us when we call on Him, especially in moments of deep despair. Ken's book points the way for others to tap into life, joy and transformation based in the love of a living God."

—from the foreword by **Robert H. Schuller**, founding pastor, the Crystal Cathedral, Garden Grove, CA; bestselling author

"We're all junkies, addicted to what makes us feel good. Adrenaline junkies race cars, jump out of planes, live on the wild side. My friend Ken Cooper got high robbing banks. He was addicted to the adrenaline rush of crime until a cop's bullet ended that career, and a prisoner named Jesus who was executed on death row captured his heart. Ken is now addicted to sharing the exciting truth of God's love. A must-read, and excellent encouragement for people tired of madness and dead-end addictions."

—**Jack ("Murf the Surf") Murphy**, international director, Champions for Life

"Ken Cooper has written a shocking book that looks into the emotions of people running from God. Ken was obsessed by the thrill of the robbery as much as by greed for money. He experienced the high achieved in the wild excitement of wrongdoing and leading a double life. It was only in complete brokenness that Ken finally came to Jesus Christ and was freed from an addiction no different than the addiction to alcohol, drugs, sex or power. He discovered that the only true satisfaction is found in the grace of God through the Person of Christ. Ken Cooper's story is a must-read for Christians as we attempt to evaluate our lives, living in the world as citizens of a higher authority. Cooper and I challenge you to be satisfied in Jesus—and nothing less!"

—**James P. Gills**, M.D.

"What a privilege it is to endorse Ken Cooper's book *Held Hostage* and to know that our prison ministry freed him from his own bondage in prison. God set him free and Ken no longer is being held hostage by the adversary. Since then, his work in the prisons has helped thousands of prisoners accept Christ. This book is powerful and those who read it will certainly be set free."

—**Abe Brown**, founder, Abe Brown Ministries, Inc.

HELD HOSTAGE

HELD HOSTAGE

A SERIAL BANK ROBBER'S ROAD TO REDEMPTION

KEN COOPER

Chosen
a division of Baker Publishing Group
Grand Rapids, Michigan

Published by Chosen Books
A division of Baker Publishing Group
P.O. Box 6287, Grand Rapids, MI 49516-6287
www.chosenbooks.com

Printed in the United States of America

Library of Congress Cataloging-in-Publication Data

Cooper, Ken, 1937–
Held hostage : a serial bank robber's road to redemption / Ken Cooper.
p. cm.
ISBN 978-0-8007-9456-9 (pbk.)
1. Cooper, Ken, 1937– 2. Christian biography—United States. 3. Prisoners—Religious life—United States. 4. Criminals—Religious life—United States. 5. Bank robberies—United States. I. Title.
BR1725.C678A3 2009
277.3'082092—dc22 2009002779
[B]

Scripture is taken from the King James Version of the Bible.

Music lyrics on page 217 taken from Roger Miller, "You Can't Roller Skate in a Buffalo Herd," Copyright 2002 STLyrics.com.

Music lyrics on page 252 taken from W. D. Cornell and W. G. Cooper, "Wonderful Peace."

In keeping with biblical principles of creation stewardship, Baker Publishing Group advocates the responsible use of our natural resources. As a member of the Green Press Initiative, our company uses recycled paper when possible. The text paper of this book is comprised of 30% post-consumer waste.

To the bank tellers, my mother, my daughter
and all the other victims held hostage by my depravity.
I continue to pray for their healing and forgiveness.

FOREWORD

I have lived long enough to look back on my life—through hard times, trying times, hard luck times. But when it was all finished and God was done with the whole thing, it was blessing that came out of it all.

So I preach a positive message. We have hope and fullness and every blessing in Christ. Yet to take hold of these blessings so that they take root in our lives, we must make a choice. Just by looking up, we see the hand of God at work in our lives. He loves us dearly!

That's the secret that Ken Cooper knew. He has been down to the darkest places a man can go, both in his soul and in his life. Yet God was there with him all the time. God called Ken to Himself and kept him there, and He has used every failure and every flaw for the perfection of His plan.

What can we learn from Ken and his story?

Believe in the God who created you. Believe in the One who will not let anything happen to you unless He can pick it up, turn it around and make a blessing out of it. That is the transforming power of Jesus Christ.

Ken's transformation is a living witness to the timeless

healing power of Jesus Christ. His story serves as a reminder to all of us that God's light can never be put out by the darkness. He will shine His timeless healing power on us when we call on Him, especially in moments of deep despair.

I have often said, "It's not necessarily how strong you begin, but how you finish that counts." Ken's book points the way for others to tap into life and joy and transformation based in the love of a living God.

—Robert H. Schuller

ACKNOWLEDGMENTS

I am thankful to my beloved wife, June, for her support and encouragement throughout the publishing process.

I am deeply grateful to scores of people God used to redeem me, but I want to especially thank the following for helping me along the road to redemption: Dr. Syd Barrett led me to Jesus Christ, who delivered me from destructive addictive behavior. Raymond Duncan and James L. Whyte orchestrated my release from prison.

I also would acknowledge those who helped with the telling of my story:

Raymond Walker, my weekly prayer partner since 1988, prayed the book from my heart onto the printed page.

Raymond Murray encouraged me to begin the project and supported me the whole way.

Rev. Doyle Harper, Dugger Jamison, Ron Oglesby and Rev. Ernest Setzler backed me as the KCPM Board of Directors.

Author Tom Noton served as publishing consultant and assisted with self-editing and rewriting the drafts.

Jeff Peck, director of communications for Prison Fellowship, provided initial editing and guidance.

As the project progressed, authors Lavada Haupt, Dale Recinella, and Bob Terrell gave editorial assistance.

Jimmy Crosby, Shirley Jeup, Michael Hamm, Donna and Earl Porter, Alex Taylor, Katherine Taylor and June Cooper contributed invaluable proofreading to prepare the manuscript for publishing.

1

On a steamy Florida morning in July, I was in grave danger.

Grave danger. Those were Jim's words in our latest phone conversation, and they gnawed at me. My brother warned me plenty about living in the fast lane. But he'd never said it like that before.

As I walked toward the Carrollwood Exchange Bank in North Tampa, Florida, perspiration trickled down my sides, but maybe I was sweating more from the relentless hammering words in my brain.

I defy death each time I rob a bank. Why is today any different?

Jim doesn't know how dark my dark side really is, yet he tends to call just as I am getting ready to pull a bank job. He doesn't know that today for the first time I'm working with a partner. Today Jonathan is watching my back.

The bank came into view—North Del Mabry Boulevard branch. It was like others I'd robbed through the years. Ten minutes from the nearest police precinct, a safe distance.

Two minutes from the apartment complex where I'd left my car.

Typical deep-South Spanish design, beige stucco with red brick veneer, surrounded by southern oaks. Four steps from the door to the first teller gives easy access. Easy escape routes through front or back doors to parking lots.

It's a simple mark, but my hands are clammy. It's time to be cool, to shift into automatic drive and leave this hovering doom behind.

I touched my leather watchband and saw that my hand was trembling. *How disgusting. It's 9:25. We're right on schedule, and there's no need to be shaky, but I am. Now in the parking lot and still no good stuff, no rush to thrust me into superman mode. What's wrong with me? Where's the juice? It can't be the plan. The plan will work. It always does.*

Jonathan appeared in the rear parking lot and eased toward the building. He took his position in the shadow of the bank.

Jonathan and I are playing cops and robbers, just like when we were kids together.

Stop! Turn back! Run! How can I involve Jon in my felonious lifestyle? He's like a kid brother to me. Stop it now while there's time. No, I can't turn back. It's too late.

Jonathan will stand by the front door until I send a hostage to him. That will buy us the time we need. He'll take her to the getaway car and wait the extra thirty seconds required for me to grab the money and get to the car.

It's a good plan. We've rehearsed it a dozen times.

Now is the time to swallow my emotions, take a deep breath and force myself to shift into high gear. My reflection in the dark glass of the front door doesn't look like me. Where is the suit and long-sleeved white shirt with cuff links, like a gentleman on his way to the office? This casual dude with his shirttail hanging out and his eyes masked with dark glasses doesn't fit. He looks like a beach bum.

It's not too late to flee.

My hand touched the shirttail covering the .9mm handgun tucked under my belt. *I am cool. I am in control. I am invincible.*

Dismissing the reflection in the glass, I pushed through the double doors into the lobby.

The young lady at the courtesy desk looked up and smiled. After two months of casing the bank, this woman was marked to be the hostage.

"Good morning."

"Good morning," I said, forcing a pleasant expression. A quick scan of the lobby showed that everything was normal. No crowd of people, no kids, no one in a wheelchair, no guards. It was the perfect setup.

With a sigh, I stepped to her desk. The young woman's smile broadened. "How may I help you, sir?"

I nodded and pulled my shirttail back to show her the butt of the gun. "Don't say a word. Just stand up and step around here."

My tone was gentle and my words soft. As she moved around the desk, I checked the fear in her eyes. A hostage could panic and go haywire. Her glazed pupils showed that she was in shock but would cooperate.

I'm in control. My hands are not tingling, though the A-rush is rapid. Finally, I'm in the zone.

"I won't hurt you if you do what I say."

All continued to be normal in the row of tellers, the customers. The woman was trembling, so I touched her arm for reassurance. She drew back, swallowed and licked her lips but didn't speak or cry for help. The bank has trained her well. She will cooperate.

Holding her upper arm with my left hand, I pulled the pistol from my belt and held it high.

"This is a holdup!"

Every person in the bank turned to look at me, but no one seemed to grasp the words. No one fainted. They stared at me with their mouths agape. The door to the manager's office swung open, and he stepped out.

That's a surprise; it's his day off.

I glared at him, turned and held the weapon above my head. I let go of the girl's arm. Clutching the firearm in one hand, I released the cartridge with the other. The metal case holding the bullets dropped into my hand. When I rammed it back into the cartridge chamber, the clanking sound of metal against metal shattered the silence.

In all of my holdups, I've never done that.

The manager turned pale and immediately obeyed the demand to go into his office and shut the door.

My heart jumped into my throat and pounded so hard it throbbed.

I've lost control again; this job has gone haywire. I am in grave danger, and my body knows it.

I knew the choking in my throat was an adrenal blockage that had prevented adrenaline from reaching my brain.

Despite all that, my mind must regain control and press my body into action.

I gripped the gun, waved it in the air and repeated, "This is a holdup! Put your hands above your head and don't move." A few scowled; some smiled as though they still couldn't believe what was happening. Others were frozen in place.

These are the usual reactions. Ah, this is better. I'm back in control.

My body relaxed.

"Cooperate and nobody gets hurt! Put your hands down and go back to your business."

There was a titter of nervous laughter and some customers actually turned back to the bank officers who were helping them.

I love it. Things are going as planned.

The adrenaline flow resumed, and my senses became razor sharp. Taking charge of the first teller, who was five steps away, I shouted, "I want the money in your top drawer. Just large bills." After pulling a cloth drawstring bag from my belt, I pushed it into my hostage's hand and said, "Take this to her and come right back." The trembling young lady followed my instructions. She handed the bag to the teller and returned to my side.

I glanced at my watch. *Only thirty-four seconds have passed.*

"C'mon! Hurry up!"

It takes the teller less than a minute to fill the bag.

That gave me the time to direct the hostage toward the door. Turning to her, I nearly whispered, "See the man in the blue shirt waiting out there? Go with him, and nobody will get hurt." Watching her go through the glass doors, I again noted how different this was from my past robberies.

I always have my hostage with me. Can I still control the bank lobby?

Without her at my side, I feel naked and alone. And what is the bank manager doing behind that office door?

I refocused on the teller. The bag was full, but people were getting fidgety.

"Bring it here." With faltering steps she obeyed.

"Just hold steady," I instructed everyone. "I don't want *your* money! You just go back to business." They laughed. I grabbed the loot and checked my watch. *Sixty seconds. Time to go!*

With the bag of money in one hand and my weapon in the other, I hurried across the lobby. Two sets of plate-glass doors stood between me and the getaway car. There also was a strange man outside. He stood with feet apart in a solid stance. His weapon was pointed at me.

The hair on the back of my neck bristled.

What's he doing here? No cop could have gotten here that fast.

Should I stop? He's taken the stance of a trained shooter. No problem. He'll fold when I rush him.

Lunging through the first set of doors, I noticed that Jonathan was taking off in the getaway car.

I'm stuck!

Goose bumps popped up on my arms and hair all over my body stood up in static electricity as a supercharged jolt of energy prepared me to face death. The ogre inside me took over and sneered at the man through the glass. In that moment, it seemed that I disconnected from the monster in me.

As if in slow motion, fire flashed from the shooter's pistol. The plate glass exploded into fragments, coming at me like glistening darts. A slug slammed into my chest, knocking me backward. Shards of glass pierced and sliced my skin. Fire burned in my chest. Someone screamed, the sound bouncing around in my mind like an echo. Everything faded to black.

I awoke to feel the thrust of a heavy knee in the middle of my back.

"Don't move," he snarled. No question about moving with all that weight flattening my face against the glossy marble floor.

Slivers of glass dug into my cheek and neck. I tasted blood.

Gasping for breath brought a whiff of gunpowder. The cold steel barrel of the pistol pressed hard against the back of my neck. *Wonder what happened to my gun?*

The weight shifted to between my shoulder blades.

"Move a muscle and I'll blow your brains out!" came a growled warning.

Move? Wouldn't dream of it. Mister, my life is in your hands.

The senses remained heightened. Surreal. Horrifying. Cuffs rattled. Both wrists were pulled together at my back, grinding my shoulder and face into the glass slivers. I clenched my fists.

Obviously, the shooter is a plainclothes cop.

Through the shock, and the descending fog, I heard the hum of voices as customers rushed to the inner door to see me facedown. Humiliation drowned me in despair as the adrenal drug wore off and I slipped from the A-zone back to earth.

An invincible man has been shot down. My breathing is labored, heavy, my gut wrenching.

I was hurt badly and suffocating under the weight of the officer's knee.

"You move just one muscle!" he dared once more.

Things were becoming fuzzy. Out of focus. The pain in my chest was excruciating, but something was warming my gut. I winced. Blood was pooling under me. My mind ran through pictures of my life. I smiled. *I'm not in the A-zone, but this must not be hell.*

It was a crazy thought, but at that moment my life seemed totally insane.

With rough jerks the policeman snapped the final cuff into place and called for backup. It seemed that only seconds later, Tampa's uniformed policemen arrived, along with an ambulance. I was still lying in my blood on the floor of the entryway. I was groggy with shock but still aware of the paramedic cutting off my shirt to examine the wound.

"Look at the size of that hole!" he exclaimed. "He's a goner."

A female attendant's voice answered, "The slug must've missed his heart by an inch. When we turned him over to see where the bullet went, there was no hole, no blood on his back, but he sure is bleeding a lot."

She's wearing nice perfume. It reminds me of my first-grade teacher.

They carried me out of the bank on a stretcher. "Blood's dripping through the canvas," observed a woman in the crowd. A deep voice said with finality, "He's dead." I raised my head to show that this was not the case. People gasped. I noticed a man with a television camera, capturing the moment of infamy. I turned my face away from its lens as they loaded me into the ambulance. Someone in the crowd shouted, "The hostage is back; she's safe; she's okay."

The people cheered.

I'm glad the hostage is okay, but I'm worried about Jonathan.

On the way to the hospital, the fog in my head cleared a bit, enough to hear a man in the front of the ambulance talking. "This one's not gonna make it. His vitals are good, but he's losing too much blood."

"It's over," I muttered aloud.

They probably think I mean my life, but I don't. It's the end of a weird way of living. Yeah, the end.

I got another whiff of the attendant's perfume, and Miss Buckley's shrill voice echoed through the corridors of time.

2

My rebellion began with Miss Buckley in Revelo, Kentucky. Maybe it was just my feeling of inferiority, but it seemed Miss Buckley scorned me because my mother was the daughter of a coal miner and my father *was* a coal miner.

Miss Buckley decided to crush any seed of rebellion before it grew beyond the first grade. One day I was daydreaming and caught a glimpse of her out of the corner of my eye. She lunged toward my desk, yanked me up by the hair of my head and screamed, "You *will* do your work in my class!"

The sudden attack filled me with terror. My arms flailed as I attempted to get my balance. She let go, and I plopped back into my seat. "You're not applying yourself," she snapped. "You're trying to make me look like a bad teacher. You're not going to get away with it here, young man!"

Before that fateful day I really had tried to learn. After she jerked me around by the hair, I stopped applying myself. The seed of rebellion was watered, and I was determined to water it some more.

It wasn't until near the end of the year that another unhappy student and I organized the class in open rebellion.

When Miss Buckley left the classroom to go to the principal's office, Johnny and I lined up all twenty kids and stamped each one with the teacher's red ink date stamp as they passed by her desk.

I was aware of the teacher's every move as she came through the door and glanced our way. Every child had "May 14" imprinted above their eyebrows. She did a double take, threw her hands up, shrieked, whirled around and vanished into the hallway. I could hear her bellowing all the way to the principal's office, "I'm gonna kill those kids!"

Johnny and I enjoyed a two-day suspension, and Miss Buckley changed professions. I flunked the first grade while developing my penchant for rebelling against authority and nurturing my distrust of women.

I was born near Sharples, West Virginia, in Camp Number Two and brought up at Camp Number Six and Camp Number Nine. Coal camps there had numbers rather than names. This numbering system seemed demeaning, and it intensified my determination to be somebody.

"Being somebody" demanded that I break out of the mold, and that meant rebellion controlled me from the first grade.

Even at home I was called Lil' Abner after a gangly comic page hillbilly because of my appearance and the nasal twang with which I spoke. There was one bright spot: I was protected by Jim and Ted, my tough older brothers. The bullies didn't lay a hand on me.

The summer following my run-in with Miss Buckley, my family moved two miles south of the school in Revelo to Pine

Knot, my dad's birthplace. Despite having five children, he volunteered to serve our country in the Navy.

If he had been home, I might not have met "Old Man Brewer," owner of one of the town's two country stores. He was a rotund man, whose girth could not be covered by overalls. His chin was stained brown with tobacky juice. Though he had never done anything to me, I loathed his sloppy appearance and disliked the beady eyes set under his dark, bushy eyebrows.

It came as a real shock when he approached Jimmy Worley and me. "Boys," he said, "I could use a little help around the store."

We stood speechless.

He spat a stream of tobacco across the room into a spittoon. "I'll pay you to do some work for me."

It was 1945. For those fortunate enough to have automobiles, gas cost the high price of fifteen to twenty cents a gallon. Like my dad, Jimmy's was off fighting the war. Nobody had much money.

I strolled past Mr. Brewer and spat into the brass bucket.

Mr. B guffawed.

"Mister Brewer, you've got a deal. Just tell us what you want done," I bragged.

The next day we showed up at Old Man Brewer's door, and the day after that. A job! For eight-year-olds, a few pennies to buy candy or ice cream was grand. If the job was hard enough, we were paid a whole dime.

One day Mr. Brewer asked us to bring Jimmy's wagon to the store. The balding man peered down at us over his belly, displayed a silver dollar as big as our fist and said, "You boys can earn a dollar's worth of sweets at my store if you'll do a special job for me."

Jimmy and I gasped as we looked at each other with wide eyes. I chirped for both of us in my nasal twang. "Sure, Mr. Brewer! Wha'da ya want us ta do?"

"I just need you to haul some goods in Jimmy's wagon for me. You know the biggest oak tree yonder where ya'll play sometimes?"

We both squinted and shaded our eyes from the bright sunlight, following his pointing finger down the path. The tree seemed to be a mile down that rough path, but it couldn't have been more than two hundred yards. Jimmy and I looked up at the rotund man. "What about it?" I asked.

"Follow me," he commanded. He took us around the corner to a rickety shack where he stored canned goods. "I got peaches and pears—things folks like."

He dumped wood shavings into the little wagon. After he put in the shavings, Mr. Brewer picked up a gunnysack and put it on top of the soft pile and made it secure. Mason jars could be heard clinking against each other. The gunnysack was full and heavy.

Mr. Brewer put his hands on his hips and glared down at us. "You do this job right, you hear? You break one of my jars and I'll tell your mamas. They'll skin the hide off your boney backsides."

Carefully we eased the wagon down the path, sweating every bump. The sack was full and heavy, and it took all our skill to ease it from the wagon to a level spot under the tree. Little did I know that I had broken the law for the first time, running jars of white lightnin' for Mr. Brewer.

I thought we were in really good with Mr. Brewer. But the next day after the special job we did for him, he seemed sort of different. He didn't give us any jobs that day or the next. In fact, he never asked us to work for him again.

We were mad. He'd offered a taste of easy money, then snatched the dream of it away. The more we missed the treats, the deeper our bad feelings toward the store owner.

"Jimmy, it ain't fair. We did jist what he wanted."

"I'm with you, but there ain't nothin' we can do about it."

"Sure, there is. If Old Man Brewer won't give us money to buy candy, I say we hep ourselves."

We called it sneakin' the goodies. After school, a bunch of kids gathered in the store, buying if they had a penny or more likely looking because they didn't. This was plenty of distraction as we cautiously snuck some candy off the shelf and into our pockets.

Outside the store, I giggled nervously and enjoyed the thrill.

"I was skeered ta do it," Jimmy said, pulling a jawbreaker out of his pocket.

"Me, too," I giggled. I was feeling the thrill of sneaking something right in front of the authority.

After that, I got brave and pushed closer and closer to the edge of disaster. Each time I stole, I did it more openly, making it easier for him to catch me. When he didn't, I felt the rush of adrenaline, until I craved it. I was getting as much out of the thrill of stealing as I was out of eating the goodies. The sensation was always there, but it was just too easy to sneak all kinds of stuff from Mr. Brewer's store. Jimmy and I broadened our criminal career to the auto service station on the corner. We hit all the places that were available to us, though Mr. Brewer remained our favorite target. It was easy, and it still felt good to get back at him. I got a bigger kick out of sneakin' there than anywhere else, especially when I took what I wanted right from under his nose.

At age thirteen, I saw Dad fall on his knees at a mourner's bench at Ball Chapel Methodist Church. I ridiculed him, appalled that my hero, a rough, tough mountain man would show such emotion, weeping and wailing as the minister prayed with him. It wasn't the mountain way. Besides, how could someone dying on a cross save my dad from the hellfire the preacher preached that night?

To my surprise, becoming a Christian worked for him. Following his salvation experience, Dad became a much better father. But he had always been my hero.

Despite my wayward ways, I knew the way to get ahead was to do well in school. I worked hard for top grades on my report card, and by the time I reached high school, I was an honor student motivated to attend college. No one in my family had graduated from college, and the idea filled me with pride.

To make it, I sacrificed my own family and went to live with Aunt Edwina and Uncle Ernie in Tucson, Arizona. Ernie was a kindhearted man who worked as a switchman for the railroad, and my aunt stayed home and took care of Jeannie, age ten, Georgia Ann, six, and Kathy, two.

Aunt Edwina and Uncle Ernie were amused by my hillbilly ways but treated me like their own son. I felt like a part of their family and liked the role of big brother to the girls, though I missed my two little brothers, Paul and Gene, back home.

I understood when Aunt Edwina told me I had to earn my way through school and college. That meant I couldn't play on the basketball team as I did in Kentucky, but it also meant I would have my own spending money and maybe even a car.

Within days of my arrival, I landed a job at a nearby car wash, where I worked after school and on Saturdays. Mr.

Fitzpatrick liked my work ethic and soon promoted me to serve as cashier and assistant manager. That was a serious mistake. A seventeen-year-old kid who had always gotten his kicks from stealing could not handle the temptation. It bothered me, especially at nights when I went to bed, that I was stealing from Mr. Fitzpatrick, the car wash owner, to save up to buy an old 1948 Desoto from a neighbor.

I got high taking money from the cash register right under his nose. To make up for the shortfalls, I sold more wax jobs, the primary source of income for the business. I was motivated to help him feed his twelve children, but even my love for him and the kids didn't match the adrenaline addiction that drove me to steal from him.

Washing cars was my first real job, and I fit in with the older men working there though they were mostly Mexican-American and black alcoholics at rock bottom. I didn't have to drink with them to be accepted, and the racial differences meant nothing since I had grown up with blacks in the mining camps. I was intrigued with the strange accent of the Hispanic workers. They all called me Ken Tucky and teased me about my nasal twang.

After a few weeks, I grew tired of being put down to bottom rung of the pecking order, vowed to change my way of speaking and enrolled in radio and television broadcasting, a special reading and writing class at Tucson High School. The guys at the car wash poured on the sarcasm about the class. "I wanta be a newsman like Edward R. Murrell," I explained.

"It's Murrow, not Murrell," someone corrected. They began calling me *Edward R*, rolling the *R* on their tongues into a Spanish trill forced through their noses to form a nasal tone. It tickled me to hear them, and it brought tears of laughter when my black friends tried to roll the *R* through their noses. At the same time, I was made even more self-conscious about how I spoke. It made me more determined than ever to rise above my backwoods ways.

With my slow drawl and limited writing skills, it was more than evident from the very first class that I was out of place studying broadcast journalism. The first time I served as the news anchor taping a high school newscast that would be broadcast throughout the city of Tucson, I began, "Today, one of our very own at Tucson High School was named Miss Arizona. Barbara Hilgenberg, a member of this broadcasting team, will represent the state of Arizona and Tucson High School in the Miss America pageant. Here's Ed Morgan with an interview of Barbara."

Ed and Barbara laughed. I was confused until the instructor played the tape. Hearing my nasal twang and hillbilly drawl brought tears to my eyes. That couldn't be me. Every vowel was drawn out and every word projected through my nose.

The moment I listened to his recording of my voice, I realized why I was called "Lil' Abner" and why my car wash buddies teased me. My voice had the whine of Chester, Matt Dillon's sidekick on the TV series *Gunsmoke*. I dragged out the words more than even Chester did.

"Mr. Broyles, I'm just too bad a talker. It's hopeless," I said sadly. "I'll just drop the class."

"You can speak normally. You just need a little help," argued Mr. Broyles. "If you are willing to come back to the classroom after school, I'll show you."

He met with me after school. Pinching his nostrils together with the tips of his fingers, he whined, "No need to be whining your words through your nose like this." He took his fingers away and boomed like Edward R. Murrow, "Despite dragging your words out through your nose, you have a resonant voice, like mine, for broadcasting."

"I can't ever sound like that. You heard the tape. You are just putting the shuck on me to make me feel better."

He noted my downcast look and added, "I'll stay late with you to give you extra speech coaching."

It took six or eight lessons to learn how to do what seemed impossible. I began to project my voice through my mouth. The twang disappeared.

I swelled with pride at my accomplishment, something essential to my self-image. Mr. Broyles spent a lot of time and effort with me. To my amazement and delight, I developed a smooth baritone speaking voice and after several months of hard work joined the school's broadcast team. I made A's down the line on my report cards.

In May, I was graduated with the Tucson High School Class of 1956. I grinned like a big-eared mule eatin' saw briars. "Aw shucks, I thank ya kindly, Mr. Dillon," I whined in my most nasal-like hillbilly twang when Mr. Broyles congratulated me.

3

The letter came; I was accepted by the University of Arizona.

My new family and the car wash gang cheered me on. Everything ahead looked bright. No one guessed that an inner darkness held my future captive and already threatened to destroy me. A compulsion to do something extreme took control. It was my birthday, and my acceptance into college called for a dual, double-whammy celebration.

For months, I had been free from the strange addiction that drove me—the crazy feeling that shot through my body when daring danger to its limits. *Only adrenaline can jolt me to the max for this day. But what would really turn me on? Getting drunk would be a downer. Partying with the gang is not an option. No, I've got to shock my senses with a natural adrenal gland zap, not numb my brain with booze.*

That evening, to work on my dilemma, I consulted with a friend named Lester Puckett. He was an expert on such matters, a part-time daredevil who did outlandish things for the thrill of it. We met to talk at a neighborhood park. I smiled as he approached. Like me, he carried a lean 165 pounds on a six-foot frame and stretched his legs and arms into a full swagger when he walked. We were both the identical size of Elvis Presley and sported wild mops of dark brown hair. We tried to sing like him and called each other Elvis.

"Elvis, I'm tired of gearing down my urges for the sake of going on to college," I told Lester. "I'm revved up to fly, man, higher than a kite on my birthday."

"I dig it, Birthday Boy; you're talking about joy juice."

"Exactly. Remember that time we stole a car on Congress Street?"

"Yeah, at rush hour, you drove it the wrong way on the main drag on purpose." Lester's large blue eyes beamed.

I laughed. "You've got the picture. Just like a chase scene in the movies, cars darting every which way."

"Man, that was a high old time. Elvis, I'm game if you are. I can just see it now, the cops right behind us. That'll give us both the juice!"

"Yeah, but I don't want to get locked up, Hound Dog. So, let's just go joyriding."

"Excuse me, sir, but getting that sheepskin has turned you into Mary's little lamb."

"No, I'm still mama's black sheep, but I just gotta get high without screwing up my chance to go to college."

"Okay, okay, I'll settle for a low-key rush. We'll do a spot and steal."

"Bird dogging and taking our ride in broad daylight feels just right."

"Okay, if we steer our mark to La Fuentes for a noontime fiesta."

At nine the next morning Lester and I left my jalopy at the car wash and high-stepped it through traffic to the El Rancho Supermarket parking lot across Speedway Boulevard. It was a hot day and the place was packed with early shoppers trying to beat the heat.

The parking lot was busy with row after row of cars and customers coming and going. We eyed each other to see if we wanted to go through with it around so many people. Both of us shrugged; it was the perfect setup. Danger was what it was all about, and the crowded parking lot started our adrenal glands flowing.

We stalked the target car. Ten seconds later, Lester yelled, "This new Olds '88 has the keys in it!" His voice carried all the way across the parking lot. It seemed to me a hundred people must have heard him.

I smiled at the incoming customers nearest the intended car and yelled back, "Wait there, I'll go inside and find the owner."

As several other customers walked by, I used my best radio voice, "Welcome to El Rancho!" I pushed several shopping carts together. The shoppers smiled and continued on into the store. Then one lady turned back.

"You boys are doing such a fine job. Let me give you two a dollar to show my appreciation."

"Oh . . . thanks, ma'am," said Lester, reaching out to take the money before I grabbed his arm.

"We aren't really supposed to take tips from customers, though we sure appreciate your kind offer. We are just happy to serve you."

When the elderly woman disappeared into the store, I breathed a sigh and got on Lester's case. "Man, don't bring attention to us. We need to play it low-key." I was excited but cautious. "I don't wanna get locked up a week before college starts."

He laughed with me as I checked out the Olds.

It was new and sported a University of Arizona staff parking sticker. A devilish grin stretched my lips into a crescent shape as I wondered if the car's owner would be one of my professors. I enjoyed the irony of that. But then, thinking of my family and Mr. Broyles brought me down a bit. I didn't want to disappoint them, but I still wanted the rush we'd get from stealing a few cars and joyriding the whole day.

The lot was relatively clear. "C'mon, let's get outta here," I said.

We jumped into the sleek Oldsmobile and took off for our fiesta. Soaring through the skies on a magic carpet could not have given us a greater high. We beamed like the car's new paint and all too soon arrived at La Fuentes, a Mexican food restaurant near the university.

We parked the car out front and marched into La Fuentes like mariachis summoned to entertain the lunch crowd. We ate our chili verde burritos with frijoles and rice in a very mannerly fashion, left the waiter the handsome tip of a silver dollar, smiled at our neighbors and walked out the front door without paying the tab.

We belly laughed like two drunks. Lester asked, "Now, where are we goin'? Congress Street?"

I smiled, ignored his insinuation and said, "Since this used car's got a university sticker, I figure we can go there and trade it in on a newer one." Lester bellowed and I pointed at the corner of the windshield. "It's a staff parking sticker."

I drove to the university and parked it legally in its lot to heighten the fun of our riding. I was beaming. "The owner's gonna be flabbergasted to find his car here where he parks it every day."

"Yeah," Lester agreed. "The absentminded professor will wonder how it got moved across town from El Rancho's."

We laughed like hyenas and strutted down the aisle of vehicles to find our next free ride with the keys in it. Our "mark" turned out to be an old dirty-yellow Studebaker. The driver's window was down and the keys were dangling from the ignition. Lester didn't want to take it. "Man, this thing's a bomb! Let's jus' do the Olds again."

"Uh-uh. We're gonna take this buggy. Nobody'll think *this* is a stolen car." I slid in and started it up.

Lester snorted, "It's a piece a junk like yours." Even so, he jumped in and off we flew.

Neither of us did drugs or alcohol that day. We got high on natural rushes. Our clean binge lasted for six hours.

We drove west on Speedway and spent the afternoon taking in the sights and sounds of Old Tucson, a movie set and tourist trap. Lester and I loved the staged gunfights, including a bank robbery. Of course we cheered for the robbers. We were disappointed to see all the bad guys gunned down on the dusty street in front of the bank.

On the way to a movie house to watch one of the Westerns filmed there, I whispered in my buddy's ear, "Lester, I wanna rob a bank someday, Jesse James style."

Lester frowned at me. "Get outta here. You ain't serious." He eyed me again. "Man, you're crazy for sure." He chuckled. "If you did, you'd get killed for sure."

I laughed with him and agreed. "You're right. I'll probably get shot down just like the dupes in the fake robbery we just saw."

We savored the thrill of the experience for days. It was a super adrenaline high, and it wouldn't leave me alone until it was satisfied. My mind needed another fix of inner juice, but I kept it in check and behaved myself. Two days later I enrolled in college, majoring in psychology.

I picked up on the college scene, started drinking a lot and hooked up with a fellow named Wally. We partied together and had a blast. One Sunday evening Wally picked me up for a ride. I was several sheets to the wind. We'd drunk about half a bottle of corn whiskey in one afternoon. My half was much larger than his. Wally appeared to be sober as a judge as he watched the road.

"Where we going?"

He smiled at me. "To my favorite place in Tucson to find females."

I leaned back and relaxed until he pulled into the parking lot of a Baptist church.

"This is a church!" I jerked a quick glare at him. "What's up with this?" I was still high and my speech carried an exaggerated slur.

"Chicks, you drunk!" he said.

"You gotta be kidding!"

Wally waved a hand at the red brick building with its white steeple. "This is the place."

I slumped down in the seat. "I'll wait in the car with my real friend, my good ole Kentucky bourbon buddy, Mark Makers."

"C'mon, you shouldn't be calling the best corn squeezin's in Kentucky by anything but its proper name, *Maker's Mark*. Remember, I brought you here to get you saved from yourself." He chuckled. "Hey, you ever see the girls who go to church? Man, there are lots of good-looking chicks."

I lifted a skeptical eyebrow. *Oh, why not. We are here to find some women after all.* I eased out of the car.

The ushers weren't friendly, but when I got situated in the back pew I scanned the place and saw that Wally was right—there were several fine-looking young women. The choir cranked up to sing, and I spotted the most beautiful girl I'd ever seen and sat up to get a better look. She was a petite blonde with large, bright eyes and a slightly tilted nose. She was in a prominent spot in the front row of the choir. I nudged Wally and nodded toward her. "Hey, good buddy," I whispered. "I'm ready to get saved."

He eyed the blonde and nodded.

Later I found out she was the choir director's daughter. She didn't notice me staring at her from the back, so I was forced to return to church.

This time completely sober, I introduced myself to Jennie Regal. I held her dainty hand in mine and told her she fit her name; she was a royal princess. She blushed and her hazel-green eyes twinkled. Court had convened. The verdict was a life sentence pounding in my heart: love in the first degree. She was the girl of my dreams.

We went on double-dates at first to please her parents more than anything else. Jennie was good for me. I stopped drinking and carousing. Over several dates we grew inseparable. By the time I was a junior, we were married.

The laughter we shared lit up a room. We loved each other passionately. She was my earth angel. There seemed to be a halo around her head.

Well into a glorious honeymoon at a nearby dude ranch, I noticed a lump on the side of her neck. I checked it out with the tips of my fingers. It was a bulging lymph node.

A picture of cancer in her neck darkened my mind. I had seen loved ones succumb to the dreaded disease. To hide my death thoughts from Jennie, I said, "I've heard that all singers, especially the great ones, get these things from straining their windpipes."

My bride smiled at my attempt to comfort her. "It's nothing, but to be safe, I'm going to get a checkup when we get back home."

I took Jennie for an examination, and too soon we heard the verdict: Jennie had lymphosarcoma, an incurable and invariably fatal form of cancer. Horror rose up.

"No, doctor, no!"

Jennie's large green eyes became pools of tears that spilled out. I took her in my arms. "He's wrong, honey; he's wrong," I whispered.

Instantly my mind was caught in a whirlpool of black water that sucked me into its depths. The prognosis could not be true. I looked at Jennie. Her bright eyes and ruddy cheeks spoke of life, not death. *She's barely twenty years old.*

Within days, the doctors operated and removed as much of the cancer from her neck as they could. When they said they could not get it all and the disease would spread, our dreams for a fantastic life together faded. Although I had controlled the compulsion to get high from stealing throughout our courtship and my college days, at this point anger sank deep into my gut. I wanted to lash out at our unseen enemy, but there was no one to fight.

By the time we reached home that day, I had decided to fly away from it all. I told Jennie we would take a grand vacation. She didn't question where the money would come from.

Over the next six months, I stole a thousand dollars from my employer, grabbing ten to twenty dollars a night from the catering truck I drove that served the university's sororities and fraternities. When the owner assigned a "shotgun rider" to stop thievery, I stole all the more and enjoyed it to the max, especially when I lifted the loot from under the nose of the guard sent to stop me.

I felt justified. And as planned, when I had reached my thousand-dollar goal and while Jennie's health remained good enough, we took a monthlong vacation. We drove home to Kentucky to visit my relatives throughout the mountains and then motored to hers in the flatlands of Ohio. During our thirty-day escape, we had the time of our lives, though sometimes at night, guilt pangs stole my sleep. I dreamed the catering company had gone bankrupt because of me.

When we returned to Tucson, Jennie's health remained stable, and the cancer had not spread beyond the lymph nodes in her neck as feared.

The doctors warned us over and over, though, to make certain she didn't go through a pregnancy. The cancer in her lymph glands would then spread at an accelerated rate. We were taking precautions, but Jennie wanted to have a baby despite the doctors' warning.

One night, as we prepared to go to bed, she told me what was on her heart. "Ken, I want you to keep a part of me when I'm gone. Let's make a baby."

I turned away so she couldn't see my tears. Then taking her in my arms, I said, "Sweetheart, you're not going to die, but if you want a baby now, let's go for it."

Two months later when she became pregnant, the doctor ordered her to abort the child to save her life. She refused. We were overjoyed when the cancer did not immediately spread. It seemed we had cheated death with the new life in her belly. On June 24, Jennie presented me with a baby girl we named Rebecca.

During the first weeks of Becky's life, Jennie remained strong enough to care for our precious little girl. We lived in our own apartment and clung to each other every moment of every day like there was no tomorrow. Life was good. I stopped stealing from the catering company. Then, for no apparent reason, the cancer began to course through Jennie's blood from one lymph node to another as the doctors had warned. Various treatments were tried, from chemotherapy to injecting her arteries with a form of mustard gas. At times, they stopped the spread of cancer, but her strength waned and she could not care for Becky. Mom and Dad Regal, along with several of their church friends, took care of our infant. Then one dark day, at her parents' insistence, Jennie and Becky moved into their home. They both needed care I couldn't give. I despised my helplessness and loathed myself for not stepping in and taking over, but I couldn't handle the thought of Jennie's impending death, along with the responsibility of the child. A war raged in my mind, but, as usual, there was no one to fight and no one to blame.

Strangely enough, shortly after Becky's first birthday, just when all seemed lost, things turned for the better. A new type of chemotherapy worked, and Jennie's health improved enough for her to reassume Becky's care.

What a day of celebration we had upon their return to the apartment. Jennie decorated the supper table with fresh-cut flowers and fixed a favorite poor folks meal of pinto beans and turnip greens with biscuits. I stuck my chest out like a king as I sat down at the head of the table. Feeding Becky with one hand and talking with the other, Jennie said, "I'm really thankful to God for our blessings; why don't we close our eyes for a moment and thank Him before we eat?"

My face flushed as I bowed my head and mumbled, "Honey, I haven't said grace for years."

"I know. That's all the more reason you should."

"You're right. Here goes: Lord, we Thank You for these beans and greens and everything."

When I looked up, Jennie had the happiest look on her face. It puzzled me. I didn't know whether she was beaming over my sense of humor or was elated that I had said a childish prayer.

"Ken, this is the way we should live because I'm expecting God to bless us even more."

Ironically, within a week, the local juvenile court hired me to supervise juvenile delinquents. I laughed like a madman all the way home the day they hired me. Jennie wept tears of joy, and I vowed never to return to my evil ways and began to attend church with Jennie and her family. She was a person of strong faith, who couldn't understand my lack of faith. It amazed her that I couldn't accept the crucifixion of Christ as the way to salvation. Still, going to church with her and Becky on Sunday mornings was good for me. The compulsion to steal subsided, and I realized some peace of mind. Though the urge was there, and even strong at times, most of the time I refrained from living on the edge for eight years.

During Jennie's nine-year battle with cancer, though she was near death many times, there were some months when she felt well enough to sing. She possessed a wonderful lyric-soprano voice and sang with the Tucson Symphony Chorus. Her music was like a call to the angels, and she was just that beautiful. I loved to see her in an evening gown surrounded by men in tuxedos as she sang a solo.

She was in and out of the hospital through those agonizing years, but six months before her death I moved my wife and daughter back to her parents' home. Being home alone nights, I slipped back into a funk of anger and resentment. I couldn't function well enough to work with delinquents, quit my job with the court and took a traveling job as a management trainer for a pyramid sales program called Bestline Products. I didn't care that training people to promote greed was simply another form of stealing and slipped back into darkness. Working three or four days a week out of town helped me escape the truth that my wife would soon die.

There were times when Jennie seemed to be slipping away, yet death wouldn't come. She begged me to help her, to give her extra sleeping pills, but I refused. Then I felt great remorse that I was not giving in to her pleas.

As she weakened, I took a break from working and stayed at her bedside day and night. When her time came, I was sitting next to her bed and watched her give up her last breath. I held her tiny pale hands in mine until they turned cold. I couldn't let go of her, though I was relieved that she was no longer suffering. I no longer had to deal with whether or not to help her die. I felt guilty for feeling relieved.

Angry, despondent and restless, I blamed God for taking her.

My desire to get back at God in rebellion made me stagger at the edge of a black abyss. The draw of the bottomless pit beckoned me to take the plunge into hell.

Held hostage by a death wish, I leaped.

4

"Why? Why, God? Why?" I screamed as I stood at Jennie's grave.

Jennie's parents were there to support Becky and me, but I turned away and shook my fist at God. I needed the comfort of my mother or father, but not one family member was around. Father was ill and two thousand miles away in Kentucky, but to me no excuse would do.

I needed them.

Following the burial, we returned to my in-laws' home. Holding Becky on my lap and swinging in a front porch swing, I talked to Dad Regal. "You realize I can't take care of my precious little girl without your help."

Tears glistened in his eyes. "We know, Ken. Isabel and I are still in our fifties; we want to take you and Becky in to live with us."

I looked at him. Walter Regal was a kindly little round man who loved his family and home as much as any man could. "When I get home from work each day, I'll give Becky a piano lesson and help her with her homework."

"I wish I could be here, but I can't quit my out-of-town job now with all the expenses."

"Don't you fret about that; Mom and I will take care of both of you until you can get on your feet."

I couldn't accept the offer of Jennie's family to take me in and returned to the apartment that night. I wanted nothing to do with God, and they were godly people. By the weekend, however, I allowed them to take Becky home with them. I returned to my place alone and once more escaped into a shell of hatred and anger. I refused to grieve Jennie's death.

In the following months, I masked my horrific emotions and tried to lose myself in work, traveling with the Bestline promotions team. I couldn't concentrate and was let go. Returning to Tucson, I struggled to live. I was not winning the battle. Death held my mind in its grip.

Two of our married female friends came at separate times to offer sexual intimacy, and I readily agreed. I wanted the release only the feminine touch gave me. I was hurting, confused. These women wanted to have sex in my bed—the bed I had shared with Jennie. I led them to another room.

After these encounters, I felt contempt for them and for other women as well. I felt more contempt for myself.

One day, I called the Veteran's Hospital in Nashville to see how my ailing father was doing. After finding out who I was, the nurse switched me to social services. At that moment my heart sank.

"His heart failed," said the disembodied voice.

The phone fell. "Mr. Cooper . . . Mr. Cooper . . . Are you there?"

Tears blurred my vision as I reached down to grasp the receiver. "He's gone." I moaned with agony. "He's gone."

Like Jennie, he was too young to die. Only fifty-seven.

At his gravesite in Kentucky, whatever scraps of life remained in me shriveled. Once again, God was to blame. *Go to hell, God! You go Your way, and I'll go mine.*

Back in Tucson, anger became depression. I stopped looking for work. The living room became a tomb. Sitting alone sucked me into death, and I slipped beyond the veil separating me from sanity. Utter darkness engulfed me until I couldn't sleep, eat or even drink to escape. All I could do was think about Jennie and Dad.

I wanted to be with them, wanted to die, but couldn't. Becky needed me now, though she would have to live with her grandparents. Besides, I owed more than I could make in three years, just to pay medical bills.

Although my daughter wasn't there, I talked to her. "I'll take care of you, Becky," I blubbered. "But I have nothing to give you, baby."

Straining to objectively consider my mental state and what I might do to hold on to at least a thread of lucid thought, I thought about my study of depression in college psychology classes. I had encountered severe depression when working with emotionally disturbed delinquents. Then it hit me: Sometimes the sick mind has to be shocked back to reality.

If I do something crazy enough, or even totally insane, it'll shock me back to life. I hesitated, then jumped up and shouted, "I refuse to remain dead. I will live."

I considered several zany ways to experience that gigantic zap to get my heart pumping again. My mind raced. I pictured Lester and myself joyriding, and the surge I got when we drove back into the El Rancho Store parking lot and saw a cop parked there.

"That's it. Adrenaline. I need a massive jolt of joy juice. That'll do it." I laughed as I remembered the crazy, fun things Lester and I had done. Back then there was life in me. I sobbed as I relived Lester's death during his freshman year in college. He had been electrocuted by touching a power line as we sneaked up onto a roof to get a better view of a parade. I went limp remembering Lester, but then I threw my arms into the air.

"I will not die like Lester. I will live. I'll live for Becky. She needs me. It'll take lots of dough, baby, but I'll get it."

A moment later the image of Jesse James robbing a bank surged into my mind. I placed my fingertips on my temples and laughed like a deranged man. "I'm gonna do it!" I screamed between cupped hands. "Just like Jesse James, I'm gonna rob a bank."

Laughter roared, and a strange energy flowed into my body. It stirred me to feel fully alive for the first time in months. It was a superhuman force, shooting vigor into my veins. I ran out to the car and pulled my old handgun from under the front seat. It was only a .22 caliber but was modeled after the larger and more powerful German Luger.

With the pistol shoved into my belt, I paced back and forth in front of the sofa. "I can feel my feet in my shoes," I shouted. "I can feel them each time they touch the floor. I'm not dead anymore. I'm gonna sure enough rob a bank. I'll wipe out my debts and get some real kicks. This is great!"

Still raving, I went into the kitchen, sat down at the table and pled my case to the empty flower vase Jennie once kept full of fresh cuttings. "Yeah, I know I'm crazy, and I don't care. I'm as empty as you, little vase, but I'm not going to be stupid like you and just sit there and do nothing about it."

The vase remained silent.

I took a few minutes to start thinking rationally. Then I spoke aloud again: "I've got to be cool and plan out this bank robbery."

After shutting the venetian blinds, I prowled from room to room. A plan took shape as I walked and talked. It seemed like a person outside my body was doing the speaking. "You can't go barging into a bank with your gun blazing. Somebody's liable to get hurt."

I pulled the pistol out of my belt and held it with both arms extended, one hand under the other, pointing it at an imaginary banker. Then I dropped my arms to my sides. *I can't shoot anyone, and I don't want to get shot.* My brow furrowed. *I have to plan this thing out and learn how to do it.* I conspired and schemed until I devised a plan to rob a grocery store as practice.

Arranging a robbery practice run was easy enough. It had always been fascinating to watch TV and movie holdups. However, my boyish looks, good manners and soft baritone voice took away from the persona of a bad man. A good act was what I would need to pull it off. I would have to transform myself into a tough guy. If I didn't, I could be laughed right out of the place. I said into a mirror, "I gotta act and look mean, like a bad guy." Then I smirked at my image. "But I can't even point a gun at anyone." I stuck my pistol back in my belt.

Turning away from the mirror, I suddenly stopped in my tracks. "I'm different." A smile tugged at my lips. "I'm not depressed." For the first time in months, I was excited and raring to go. Even so, my emotional state was tottering, and I laid the gun on the kitchen table in the shadow of the empty vase. I took out a sheet of lined paper to put my plan in writing. My mind was blank, so I stared at the ceiling. The faces of Jennie and Dad appeared as if they were looking down on me through a darkened window. I dropped my eyes. "I know you two don't like what I'm about to do," I blurted. "But I'm gonna do it anyway. I promise I'll take good care of Becky. You don't need to worry about her."

Across the top of the page I scrawled, "How to Rob a Store." I realized this was an asinine thing to do, but I had to start somewhere. I listed the steps from "Choose the store" to "Do it."

Pacing the floor, I rehearsed my plan. On the second day I screamed into the bathroom mirror, "This is a holdup!" When I saw my reflected image, it occurred to me that I hadn't considered disguising myself. I put on sunglasses and pulled an old Cincinnati Reds baseball cap down over my eyes, checking the image again.

You're ready, Coop.

Somewhere inside, an eerie voice whispered, *Oh, no, you're not. You're not ready.* I ignored it, smiled and saluted myself in the mirror.

A couple of days later, I rehearsed the robbery, step-by-step, for the last time. A blast of heat hit me as I hurried out to the car for the ride to the chosen store. When I opened the car door, the hair on my neck stood up and goose bumps popped out on my arms, even in the heat.

On the way to the store, a strange feeling came over me; it was almost as if my mind left my body. I knew it wasn't from drugs or alcohol. No substances of that nature had entered my system for a week. My hands gripped the steering wheel, but my fingers were numb. I muttered, "Maybe I'm *not* ready, but I'm gonna do it. I'm really gonna do it." I tried to hype myself. "Wow, this is fun."

As I eased into the parking lot in front of the little adobe store, the battle continued to rage inside. *I can't do this.* I glanced up into the Arizona sun and shook my head. *What am I thinking about? This isn't me.* Even as I argued, I poked the pistol into my belt and covered it with my shirttail. At that moment a surge of something spiked my blood. *Yeah, I know I can't do this, but I gotta do it. I have to do something.*

In the end it was adrenaline-driven anger that forced me into the store. Hate, rather than my legs, carried my body from the car toward the front door. My mind was still dragging behind.

I'll do it. I will do it.

I yanked the plate-glass door open. The place was empty except for the little woman behind the counter who ran the place. I felt relieved and sighed.

She glanced up. "Good afternoon," she said.

To my astonishment, as I heard her voice I thought of my mother. Instead of immediately showing her the gun and shouting, "This is a holdup!" as planned, I said, "Good afternoon." My heart sank. After a moment's hesitation I headed over to the soft drink box to regroup. It took some time to get over the shock of the unexpected development. I pulled out a cold drink. My mind went into high gear as I took the bottle toward the counter where she would open it with an opener hanging from the wall near the cash register.

When she took the bottle, I used my most macho voice. "This is a holdup!" I pulled my shirt up to show her the butt of my gun. "Just open it up and gimme the cash."

The old woman looked at me like I was crazy and let go of the soda bottle. It crashed to the floor and exploded. She pressed her lips together and then screamed, "Does your mama know what you're doing?"

I froze. Her voice sounded like my mother's, but the words made no sense. My hand was on my pistol, but I couldn't grip it to pull it out.

She bellowed, "Get out of here, and don't you . . ."

My mind was suddenly confused, and I didn't hear her finish the sentence. I was gone. I beat it to my car and burned rubber out of the parking lot.

I drove back toward my apartment slumped over the steering wheel like a dead man. I didn't know what to think. I was baffled—completely floored—by her response. A few blocks from the store, I sat up, and the same weird laughter burst out that came when I considered the robbery.

Back at the apartment, I laughed at myself. What had happened was downright funny. I cackled the old woman's question into the mirror: "Does your mama know what you're doing?" Then, in the same breath, I answered, "No, my mama doesn't know what I'm doing." I hesitated and looked at myself. *And I don't know what I'm doing either.*

5

What a wimp. You are a gutless wonder. You sure weren't ready. I considered what went wrong and resolved, *No, I wasn't ready, but I will be next time.*

The more I thought about the old lady ordering me out of her store, the madder I got. It was the debacle of the century. I was embarrassed and humiliated. The incident should have eased the obsession to rob anything, but it didn't. I should have realized I was not made of the stuff it takes to strike fear in the heart of a victim. My nature was too gentle.

The day after my attempt, my self-image was less than zero.

As I relived the incident over a beer at a local pub, it irked me. I was too soft spoken or softhearted to scare even a defenseless old lady. Turning tail and running meant I was gutless, or it may have indicated I cared more about her welfare than I did the money. It seemed I was nothing but a wimp. My stomach was a rumbling boilermaker, and I chased the beer with a shot of bourbon.

After slugging down the hard liquor, I stared into the mirror behind the bar. A grin softened my scowl as I remembered the indignation etched on "Mom's" face as she ordered me out of her store. She showed no fear of the gun tucked into my belt, or of me. I shook my head and chuckled, knowing I didn't have the makings of a robber.

The thought shocked me and I muttered low enough so the bartender couldn't hear me, "I'm no pushover. I'm a man. I've got what it takes. Nobody is ever going to make me back off again."

There were lessons to be learned from the experience:

First resolution: Never try to rob a place run by an old woman.

Second resolution: Follow the plan to the letter, no matter what.

After that day's fiasco I was determined to do it right the next time. I would plan every move, rehearse with dry runs and anticipate the unexpected.

I had to find a way to strike fear in the heart of the next victim if I was going to walk out with the cash. My acting out the robbery in front of the mirror hadn't worked, so I was determined to come up with a better approach.

After two more beers and another shot of bourbon, I stared at my sad reflection and whispered, "Look at you: hollow eyes, sunken cheeks. You look like you're made of paste, a dead man." I answered myself, "The dead man in the mirror is not really me."

I laughed at the thought and then glanced at the bartender washing glasses at the far end of the bar. I checked the mirror again and muttered, "Coop, it's not you, not the old you." My head sagged and I continued, "You're not the man Jennie married."

I raised my head and checked the pale reflection again.

Then it hit me: I couldn't do normal things like normal people to bounce back from the deaths of Jennie and Dad.

"Another one?" the bartender called.

I waved him off and continued to study the face in the mirror. It scowled at me, and for a split second, I saw the reflection wearing a mask. I blinked and the mask was gone. My mouth tightened. "That's it!" I muttered. "I'll wear a mask and use my gun at the next holdup. It'll get me some respect." I laughed, formed a pistol with my hand, pointed it at the man in the mirror and shouted, "Ka-blam! You're dead, but you ain't gonna be broke."

The bartender called, "Hey, fella, you want something?"

I shook my head.

"You had enough to drink?"

I wobbled off the bar stool, pointed at him and said, "No! I'm just getting started." I noticed my hand was still in the form of a gun and added, "But I'm not after your money."

He shook his head and mumbled, "Crazy drunk."

I turned and staggered out to my car.

While driving toward the apartment, I told myself I was glad to be drunk. It gave me a good excuse to sleep at *our* place, if not in the same bed where Jennie used to sleep.

I slept all right, but morning brought a huge hangover. My head throbbed and it seemed my body was separated from my mind, and my eyes didn't know which to follow. I was miserable and wanted to die but made it to the bathroom and faced the mirror. I told my reflection, "The rage boiling in me will erupt like a volcano during the next robbery." I got real with myself. "If people won't fear me as a bad man, they'll fear me as a dead man. Either image will do." I leaned in close and peered at my bloodshot eyes. "I sure look bad enough today."

In the afternoon, I picked up my old "buddy," Mark Makers, my pet name for my favorite Kentucky bourbon, Maker's Mark. Back at the kitchen table, I looked from the empty flower vase to the half-empty whiskey bottle. The whiskey spoke louder with each drink. "I should use a nylon stocking or a ski mask for the next robbery. And I won't go into a store with an old woman behind the counter, that's for sure."

My eyes closed and I imagined the next hit. "It's gotta be a young store clerk, a guy who has sense enough to give up the cash." In my stupor I saw the empty flower vase laugh with me when I tried to envision what the old lady would have done if I'd have stormed her wearing a nylon stocking. I held up my drink and toasted, "Well, man-with-the-gentle-voice, I'll bet she would have screamed at you for wearing her stocking and made you give it up."

I chuckled again and thought maybe I should do something about my voice to make it rough. But, I didn't know how to do so and just let it go.

Knowing Becky was safely tucked into bed at her grandmother's house, I left the apartment. "Another night out of the House of Death," I muttered. I missed Becky terribly and wanted her to return home, but I was in no shape to take care of her. I had to keep her out of the war zone. High from two days' drinking, I drove directly to a friend's home and climbed in a bedroom window that had been left open for me by arrangement. I lay with his wife until my pal was almost due to come in from his swing shift.

Somehow, having sex with her made me feel more alive than I'd felt in days, yet I was racked with guilt. What a buddy I was, a real pal, taking care of my friend's wife while he worked. As I drove away from their home, Jennie's face appeared in my mind, and I wept. I was sorry for taking advantage of the situation. The four of us had been great friends. Deep remorse clawed at my mind and nearly drove me crazy. Flashes of Jennie, my buddy, his wife and me doing things together and being true friends, continued to plague me. "Why did I ever start going to bed with her?" I agonized.

Rather than drive home, I headed for the foothills of the Santa Catalina Mountains overlooking Tucson. I parked, reached under the seat and brought out my gun. I placed it beside me and eyed the huge saguaro cacti, standing like sentries, looking down on me. The bright desert moonlight cast shadows of their giant arms across the car.

I lowered the driver's side window, gripped the steering wheel and took in a deep breath of dry air. The scent of scrub chaparral evergreens filled my nostrils, and I realized its pleasing aroma would be my last sensation before I blew my brains out. Tears ran down my cheeks, and I rubbed the smooth surface of the gun handle lying next to me. My mouth felt like cotton. With my finger on the trigger, I picked up the pistol and I raised the weapon to eye level. I wanted to put it against my temple, but instead I stopped and stared at the blue steel in the moonlight. A picture of Becky riding her bike flashed before me, and the pistol dropped between my legs. I sobbed, "Becky, my sweet Becky, I can't do it." My knuckles turned white as I gripped the steering wheel with all my might. I groaned as though there was no life in me.

But for Becky's sake I had to live.

A week later, I pulled a nylon stocking over my head, leaped out of my car and burst into a convenience store. It was empty except for a young man behind the counter with his hand in the cash drawer. I shouted, "This is a holdup!" He jumped back from the cash register and threw up his hands. His face contorted and a dark spot grew on the front of his pants.

As I lunged toward the counter, he fell to the floor facedown, covered the back of his head with his hands and screamed, "Don't shoot me! Please don't shoot me!"

Looking at the pitiful young man with a yellow puddle forming around him, I muttered, "Good grief, this isn't working. I just came to take the money. I've scared this guy to death." I recovered my senses and hurried around the counter to the open register, emptied it into a pillowcase, ran out to my car while tearing the stocking off my face and sped away.

After a few blocks, I slowed down, and glanced in the rearview mirror. I could still see the scared young man lying on the floor in his own urine.

"What have I done?" I muttered. As I drove, I kept asking myself the same question, but no answer came. I shook my head all the way to the tavern.

I was disturbed, considering the mental anguish of the man I left behind. I could not believe what had happened. In my wildest flashes, I had not thought that wearing a nylon stocking would strike such terror in the heart of the clerk. I was devastated by his horror and couldn't wait to wash the memory away with booze.

Causing trauma of such a high degree made me realize that robbing stores was not worth it. The victims of the two jobs I pulled were whacky; one was not afraid at all and could have shot me. The other was so crazy from fear he might have died. I whispered, "I could be wanted for murder."

I decided then and there to be my gentle soft-spoken self and vowed, "I'll never wear a mask again. I'll go into a bank looking and acting like a gentleman, show the butt of my gun, politely ask a bank employee to serve as my hostage, take her and the money and leave." I liked my plan. It meant I could be myself and yet make it work.

After finally counting the money and discovering the measly sum of $280, it was settled. "I'm going to stick to my original idea. Just like Jesse James, I'll rob banks!" I vowed.

6

I was determined to work out a good plan before I launched my banking business. I wanted to be prepared. My first priority was to pick up several sets of clothing, wigs and mustaches to disguise myself when I pulled a job. I stole a .45 caliber pistol from a security guard and bought three pairs of dark glasses.

However, when school let out for the summer, for Becky's sake and my convenience, we moved into my Uncle George's home. He and his wife, Vera, lived across town from Becky's grandparents. Becky still was drifting back and forth between Jennie's parents' house and mine since her death. I wanted to bring some stability to her life, so I put my bank-robbing plans on hold.

I didn't like it, but the move worked out well for both of us. Becky spent quality time with me, and I stopped the heavy drinking and looked for work. I didn't find employment right away. When I paid the second month's rent with money from the convenience store robbery, George and Vera became suspicious. They knew I had no income.

Vera searched my car and discovered my gun and other tools of the trade, including the nylon stocking I used at the convenience store. "Ken," Uncle George threatened, "the source of the rent money is apparent."

I started to respond, but he cut me off with an upraised hand.

"We don't need an explanation either. We'll call the police."

"No, don't! Becky and I will be out tomorrow. We'll move back to Mother's home in Kentucky."

Vera didn't want George to call the cops. "What about Becky? How is this going to affect her?"

Uncle George was silent for a moment, then said, "Now, Vera, he's not going to continue this crazy stuff—are you, Ken?"

Again, he didn't let me answer, but jumped back in before I produced a lie.

"Going back to live with Grandma Irene is the best thing for Becky."

My mother was clamoring for us to live with her. Though I wanted no part of it, for Becky's sake and to save myself a trip to jail, we moved back to Mother's home in Revelo, Kentucky. To keep my secret obsession alive, I carried a locked toolbox of "banking tools" with me, stashed in the trunk of my car. Robbing banks was on temporary hold, while I looked for work and got Becky settled into a daily routine.

We were miserable at Mother's place. Though she would soon turn nine, Becky cried continually when I left her. Jennie had died only months before. Becky missed her mama when I was gone and feared I would not return. I felt like dying and turned to Mother for help. She did her best to cope with Becky's anxiety.

Making things worse, my mother treated me as if I were Becky's age. She tried to impose an eleven o'clock curfew and couldn't deal with my staying out late and "running around with wild women."

Within a month, Becky's anxiety let up, and I got a job as a caseworker with the Kentucky State Welfare Department. But I wasn't satisfied. I detested the work, though I relished playing with single women employed by the department.

However, since I traveled throughout the region, my work gave me the cover I needed to live a double life. I was able to case prospective banks and began developing the style of the gentleman bank robber.

Deep-seated urges split me into two persons, a good guy and a bad guy. The good one was determined to support Becky in her new world, but the other bolstered his self-image, distorted though it was, through an occasional robbery. And he pursued other, rewarding, interests. That included a relationship with one of the prettiest girls in Kentucky, a state known for its fast horses and pretty women.

Anne was a twenty-nine-year-old beauty from Somerset, a town twenty-five miles north of Revelo. Though she trained caseworkers like me, off the job she lived at high speed, and was not about to slow down. We ran with a fast crowd, including many "thoroughbreds," the rich horse crowd of Lexington and Frankfort. Anne accepted Becky, and I hit it off right away with Lee, her fine ten-year-old son from a previous marriage. Lee was the red-haired boy I'd always wanted. Although he wasn't my biological son, I loved him as though he were. We became great pals.

So much change had happened in my life during the ten months since Jennie's death.

Anne and I were both control freaks with short fuses. Our temperaments produced one conflict after another for the first year. Even so, in many ways, we were good for each other, especially where our careers were concerned.

Thanks to my early experience in radio and television, I found employment with a motion picture production company, and we moved to Lexington. From there, my public relations career blossomed. I served as publicity director for Cumberland College in Williamsburg, Kentucky, and as director of advertising and tourism promotion for the state of Kentucky. Anne became a professor of social work at Union College, Barbourville, Kentucky, during our first year of marriage.

All the while, I continued my banking business when an irresistible urge hit me.

In my tourism director capacity, one day I went to a travel show in Toronto with the director of the Kentucky Derby. During our trip I made a legal withdrawal at a bank, though the account contained several thousand dollars from my illegal career.

When I came out with a fistful of money, my friend jokingly asked, "Coop, how do you always have so much money?"

"You like horses and I like money," I said evasively.

"No, really, what are you, a bank robber?"

I laughed. "Yes, and you ought to try it; it's more fun than betting on horses."

Of course, he didn't believe me. Somehow there is an urge to spill your secrets and end the double life.

I had produced television specials on educational help programs for Appalachian youth with Cumberland College. Representing the state of Kentucky I became a high-profile person. As my name got out in articles and television news,

I was held up as a role model for underprivileged kids from the mountains. I felt like the state's biggest hypocrite. At the same time, other cities in other places dubbed my hidden side *the gentleman bank robber*.

It was hard to face my wife and kids when I returned home from banking business trips. They didn't know I was living a double life. The "other Ken," whom I personally referred to as "Kenny," never came out when I was with Anne, our family or our friends.

Anne knew something wasn't right, not so much due to the easy flow of money as through her intuition. She suspected I consorted with other playmates, though she never confronted me with her suspicions. Although I was faithful to her so far as women were concerned, and I curbed my appetite for other lovers, she was right in the sense that I had a divided heart. While I was on the road, banks were my first love.

Satan's deception was so deep that I did not consciously fear apprehension. I did shudder when I heard a police siren or saw a squad car. I was indeed a hostage to evil but didn't know it. For the most part, I was having a great time getting high on an A-rush.

7

It was brisk, clear and very cold when I booked myself into a local hotel in the target city. I was in the area on legitimate business, something to which I looked forward. But I was a lot more excited about the extracurricular business I planned to conduct while in town.

The mark was a rich, aristocratic downtown bank I'd visited for several months. I couldn't help smiling every time I cased it. It was one of the easiest, safest hits of my career. Located in an old section of town about ten minutes from the police station, it seemed too good to be true. I would follow my method of operation to be in and out in two minutes.

A beat cop patrolled several blocks on foot. I studied his routine. On cold days like this, he ducked into warm coffee shops. The bank was two miles from the auto rental business where I leased my getaway car with a fake driver's license and a bogus credit card fashioned for me by a crooked friend from the racetracks with underworld connections.

The bank was vulnerable. Like all banks in the region, it didn't have a security guard. The layout was wide open, with all the employees in the lobby. The targeted teller window was about five steps from the front door. Even better, the manager's office was upstairs.

The day before my "appointment," given the frigid temperature and vicious wind howling from the north, I stopped at a clothing store to buy myself a pair of lined gloves. I wanted to keep my hands warm, and, of course, I didn't want to leave fingerprints.

On the way out of the store, I passed through the women's department. A stylish coat caught my eye. It occurred to me to buy it for Anne, but I opted to purchase it for the female hostage who would be at my side as I left with the money. She would be in dress clothes, so her new coat would be waiting for her in our getaway car. She might try to elude me while going into the closet to get the one she wore to work.

The next day I stood in front of a mirror, appraising my reflection, and said, "Coop, you look like a million bucks." I created characters for my jobs. Sometimes, I sauntered into the target bank disguised as a common laborer. At other times, I became a country boy dressed in working clothes. My favorite getup was that of the distinguished businessman, the gentleman bank robber that got media attention. I liked that image.

Because of the cold weather, I wore an Oxford wool tweed fit for a king. Although it wasn't my usual black suit, I admired it, and with thumbs in lapels, bragged, "Duke Coop, this is just right to wear to a *bank*quet."

While driving toward the downtown area, I slipped my old German Luger into the belt under my vest and reviewed the plan from the beginning. The woman's coat was in the backseat.

After pulling to the curb, ten parking meters from the

bank's front door, I grabbed my black briefcase and eased around the car toward the bank. I scorned the parking meter and didn't deposit the coin it demanded, knowing I'd only be two minutes. I was surprised by a dozen cars parked on the street in front of the bank. They made me uneasy, so I touched the handle of the Luger under my vest to trigger my mind into robbery mode.

Body function slowed as I conditioned myself. I verbally assaulted my own ears with the plan. "As I step through the door, I am in control. I am calm. I am invincible." I glanced up at the pewter-laden sky. Although I knew it wouldn't snow, I thought about how cold it was.

Donning a huge smile, I strolled through the double doors into the lobby. To free me to shed my overcoat and gloves, I placed my briefcase on the marble floor. The customer service girl nearest the inner door welcomed me with a warm handshake. "Good morning, sir. I see you're dressed for the cold. How may I help you?"

"And good morning to you," I intoned, pressing my fingers into the vest pocket over my gun and glancing around to see if it was indeed a good day for a robbery. It was. I felt good about it, quickly eyeing the situation. There were three tellers behind their windows and two other floor workers.

"I like the looks of your bank," I said honestly as I continued to size up the situation. No elderly folk and no women with children. There were only two male customers. They each faced the teller waiting on them. I studied those individuals for a millisecond and was immediately wary of the one farthest from me. He was a large, lumberjack-looking guy. His hands and head stuck out of a blue mackinaw with brown leather work gloves peeking out of its pockets. I thought he might regard himself a hero. I wasn't concerned about the other one. He didn't look very tough. In fact, he looked like me in his topcoat and expensive shoes. I didn't consider him a threat. But I didn't want any hero-types adjusting the plan. As I appraised the situation, I stared at his back.

"Sir, how may I help you?" the young lady repeated.

I smiled and said, "I want to see the manager."

"He's upstairs at the moment, sir. Perhaps I can help you."

"Yes, you can." I showed her the handle of the gun tucked into my belt.

She gasped and it escaped like a little squeak. Her brown eyes enlarged, and her face was suddenly ashen. I could see a quiver in her lips. It appeared she was trying to say something. She wouldn't be calling for help in the face of this catastrophic turn of events. Bank employees were trained not to resist, not to call for help, and not to make a commotion. I relied on it.

I sympathized with her and touched her on the shoulder. "I'm not going to hurt you. Just do as I say, and do as you have been instructed by the bank."

She flinched and looked up at me like a little lamb, tears filling her huge brown eyes. I wanted to stroke her hair and tell her everything would be fine, but my two minutes were ticking and there was no time left.

"Good girl," I said. "Take this briefcase over to the first teller. Place it on the counter and come back to me immediately."

"Yes, sir," she said. When she took the attaché case, she nearly dropped it as a whimper escaped her lips.

With my hand still on her shoulder, I held her back for a moment. "Open it for her." I stared straight into her eyes. "You come right back to me. Okay?"

She managed a weak response as she took faltering steps on her way to the teller.

While watching her I pulled out my pistol, raised it in the air and shouted like a tyrant drill sergeant, "This is a holdup! Everyone—hands up!"

Everybody obeyed instantly, including the lumberjack and the teller who would fork over the money. I stifled a grin. "Not you, Miss. You fill the case. Big bills only. Nothing marked." Some of the people chuckled.

Everything went exactly as planned. I was in control. My helper came back and stood with me, trembling, as her colleague filled the satchel. I was relieved. I knew the manager had not been alerted or he would have scrambled down the stairs. In about a minute and a half the briefcase was full and back into the hands of my helper. As she handed me the money I was in my glory, but didn't let it show. My voice was low, almost a whisper. "Now cooperate as you've been taught and come with me."

As if in a trance, she turned toward the door and accompanied me.

She looked scared but not panicky. Perfect, I thought. "Our car is waiting right out front."

She snapped out of the daze just long enough to hesitate and plead with me. "Please don't take me with you."

I lowered my voice. "Don't argue. We don't have the time." I stared into her eyes. "I won't hurt you; I promise." She seemed to believe me and relaxed.

I scanned the people watching us and announced, "Lower your hands and get on with your business." The customers and employees laughed, lowered their hands and then stood gawking at me rather than returning to what they were doing.

"Go ahead. Get on with your transactions." I waved the

gun toward my hostage. "She's okay." I hesitated. "Don't try to follow us."

I put my gun back in my belt, jerked on my topcoat and gloves and with my little helper beside me, I walked out of the bank to the car. The young lady shivered in the cold as I rushed to open the door for her. She scooted into the passenger's side. I took brisk strides around the two-door sedan, got in, threw the money on top of her coat in the backseat and drove two blocks to the spot where I would leave her. I grabbed her coat and got out, hurrying around the car to open the door and said, "Take this." I pushed the coat at her.

With hands quivering, she couldn't hold on to it. I felt terrible. "Are you okay?" I asked. She didn't take the coat and appeared to be in shock, so I repeated, "Are you going to be okay?"

Finally, she said, "Y-yes." I pushed the coat at her. She was able to hold on to it. The cold wind tore at us as we stood by the car. She thanked me for the coat like she would have responded to her big brother, and then put one arm through a sleeve. I helped her with the other arm and thanked her for cooperating with me.

"Now start down the street and don't look back."

After turning away, the young woman wobbled slightly, moving back toward the bank, two blocks away. She pulled the coat tighter as the wind whipped down the street.

I didn't take time to see her reach the corner. I got in the car and drove off, checking in the rearview mirror. She was still walking without turning to see if I'd left. I smiled. The job went without a hitch. I tilted the mirror to eye my image.

"You are truly invincible, sir." My smile widened.

8

After the robbery, I checked into a motel room to disappear for a couple of days and flipped on the television. A large black man pointed his finger like Uncle Sam on a recruiter's sign and demanded, "God wants you." The next thing he said nearly knocked me back on the bed. He declared, "You're running from God. You know what you're doing is not right. You're living a double life, and you'll never find your true identity until you make peace with God."

I changed channels and tried to ignore what Ben Kinchlow said on the Christian television program *The 700 Club*. However, his image and voice burned into my mind. I continued to fight the nagging message. It seemed unlikely that God would speak to me personally through a man on television. I questioned how anyone could find peace with a God who took his wife and father at such an early age. I held contempt for Kinchlow's theory.

After a fitful night I inched my way over to the restaurant to eat breakfast. As I brought a forkful of eggs to my mouth, I noticed a well-dressed man with his head bowed and his eyes closed. He was actually saying grace in public. I looked down at my food, attempting to ignore him.

As I ate, I couldn't keep from glancing at him. He wore a cross on a small chain around his neck. This businessman wasn't ashamed of his faith. After he prayed, I distinctly noted a peaceful expression on his face. I attempted to shrug it away, making light of it in my mind. But he smiled at me and nodded. Nervousness made my mouth twitch, and I feigned a smile and went on eating. As soon as I gulped the last drop of coffee, I slipped by the man without further eye contact and got out of there.

Back in my room, I sat on the edge of the bed and took long drags on a Kent cigarette. I stared at the stained carpet under my feet. My life was as messed up and as dirty as the rug. I didn't deserve Anne, the kids or my public-relations job with the Christian college. I walked into churches, newspapers, and radio and television stations to promote the college in the same shiny black shoes I wore to rob banks.

Staring at those shoes through the smoke reminded me of a walkathon I promoted for Project Concern. It was a charity event for medically indigent children of Appalachia and other parts of the world. I involved Colonel Harlan Sanders of Kentucky Fried Chicken fame, Miss Kentucky, wildlife artist Ray Harm, the mayor and city council and other celebrities. For a town the size of Corbin, Kentucky, with a population of less than seven thousand, we drew two thousand walkers and raised over seven thousand dollars. It was proclaimed the most successful walkathon in the nation in 1970.

Sitting on the motel bed reflecting on my life gave me the desire to accept Project Concern's offer and move, whether Anne got a job or not. I wanted a change. At least I hoped being in a new location would empower me to resist the demons driving me to rob banks. I eyed the briefcase. For the first time in my three years doing holdups, I didn't want to touch the money. In fact I didn't even want to count it, much less plan to use it as a down payment on property or blow it on the horses.

Instead, I slumped back on the bed and my thinking processes exploded into paranoia. The agony of it nagged at me, so I lit up another smoke. My unstable thoughts knew there would be a loud knock on the door at any moment. If I didn't answer, the police would kick the door in, burst into the room with guns blazing and I'd be killed or seriously injured. The images were vivid. I could *see* them bursting in, and I hoped I wouldn't resist. Maybe I would live through it all, but they would cuff my wrists behind my back and drag me away to jail.

The torture in my mind held me captive as I squirmed on the bed and could find no rest. Torment punctuated every heartbeat. I pulled on the cigarette, drawing the smoke deep into my lungs before exhaling. Peace eluded me. My college psychology training let me know that I needed help. Again, Ben Kinchlow's words slammed me—I was not just running from the law; I was running from God. The thought hit me hard.

I snuffed out the Kent and admitted my desire to move to Florida might be a result of wanting to run from the reality of my addiction to robbing.

After suffering for a few more minutes, I turned on the television but couldn't find the man who'd hit a nerve earlier. I thought about chasing down the guy in the restaurant who had prayed over his breakfast. The picture of me knocking on motel room doors asking for a peaceful-looking Christian man seemed stupid. Yet, I wanted to find peace—escape from my craziness. For awhile I was stuck, hiding. The robbery was fresh news, and they would be looking for me. At least my paranoia told me so.

I ran through the electronic monster's channel selector again. I was desperate, yet I was relieved. I couldn't find the black man. A mixture of relief and wonder churned in me as I turned off the television and closed my eyes. A part of me wanted to change, but another part feared the consequences of leaving my old lifestyle.

In my troubled state I left the motel room after one day, plunked the robbery paraphernalia and loot in its box in the trunk of the car and headed home. My briefcase was once more an attaché case full of promotional materials about the college.

The drive was not an easy one. I would soon resume the role of family man, businessman and community good guy. My mental images seemed to be split down the middle. On the dark side of my brain, I saw the bad guy as I robbed another bank and played the horses. Then there was the light side where I was Mr. Good Guy. Anne, my family, friends and business contacts all thought I was squeaky clean. That made me nauseous. I was a sham. My façade was whitewashed, but behind the mask of cleanliness I was dirty.

As I pulled into the driveway, the relief I felt helped me come to grips with the fact that I was out of control. It made no sense whatsoever for me to rob a bank and hide out in a motel while on the lam. I didn't need the money, and I would not even count it for several days, if not weeks. The thought disturbed me deeply and made me try to analyze the reason for doing the bank job in the first place. It was some ethereal, surreal event, making no sense at all. Too, I was bothered over not being able to share my problem with anyone, especially not with Anne.

While I was dwelling on my problem, she burst out the front door, ran up and hugged me as I stepped out of the car. Her arms felt absolutely wonderful. Suddenly I was thrust into what was real and what mattered. I was home and I was glad to be in her arms. As we walked toward the front door, it was like stepping back through the looking glass into reality. I bent down and whispered in her ear, "I've missed you, babe. It was a tough trip."

She squeezed me, then stopped and pulled back.

I could see a glow on her face. Her eyes sparkled. I smiled and asked, "What're you up to?"

Her lips spread into a saucy grin as she peered up into my face. "We can move to Florida; I'll be teaching social work at the University of West Florida."

"Wow! That's great news!"

"The administrator called today. They want me to come to work there as a full professor."

"Congratulations, honey. Will I have to call you Doctor Cooper now?" I laughed and pulled her close for a kiss.

Her eyes beamed and she asked, "What do you think about the move?"

"Let's go!" I shouted, danced a little jig and added, "I can just see it now. We'll be introduced to the university set as Doctor and Mister Cooper. I love it!"

"Are you serious?" she countered. "Do you really want to go?"

I reassured her, "Yes, I've wanted to move back to the sunshine ever since I left Arizona. I'll go to work for Project Concern." I would be away from the banks I had cased, and moving way down south would put some distance between our mothers and us.

Two days later was Mother's Day. We spent the holiday with Anne's mom in Somerset. I didn't want to go because her mother was a Christian who forever talked about God and always wanted us to go to church with her. I remembered the strange feeling I experienced at the motel and tried to talk Anne out of going to her mother's place. But I knew we had to tell her mom about our decision to move to Florida. At one point I would have asked Anne to just call her mother and tell her, but I considered her feelings in the matter and relinquished mine. Yet, my inner man loathed the thought of being under the same roof with somebody who preached at me.

Even so, I relented, and on Sunday morning we went to a worship service with the family at Anne's home church, where her father had once served as pastor. I squirmed in my seat when the preacher delivered a message about the love of our mothers. It seemed the pastor knew I could hardly wait to put a thousand miles between our mothers and me. I didn't feel very close to my mom, but Anne and her mother were like twins. I dreaded telling Mother Carlson about our decision to move so far away.

Following dinner we told her about our plans, and Anne asked her blessing. She looked at us across the table for a moment and started in saying, "Now children, I wouldn't do anything rash. You've got wonderful jobs at the colleges and it would be so far from home—"

I interrupted her. "That is our main problem with it. But you can come and spend the winters there with us, Mother." I knew she would never leave her deep roots for even a week.

"Now kids, this is what I'll do. I'll pray for you and ask God to give you a sign to confirm the move."

"Mom," Anne countered, "God has already given us several signs, including a big promotion for me from associate to full professor."

"I know, but you shouldn't do something this drastic unless God gives you a definite sign." She wasn't listening to us.

By midafternoon we hugged Mother Carlson and headed for home. As we rounded the last curve and came down the hill toward home, we spotted a wisp of smoke rising from the vicinity where the frame house stood. When we came around the bend we both gasped. The house had burned to the ground and disappeared into dunes of white ash. Immediately, I thought of Mom's statement about a definite sign. This was as definite as you could get!

Even so, Anne was sick and I was shocked out of my mind at the cards fate had dealt. An old anger boiled up that I hadn't felt for a year. The bitter taste of bile surfaced and I swallowed. Becky and Lee cried over their lost possessions and asked where we would live.

For help we turned to Anne's sister, Nancy Jane, who lived in town. We spent the night there, but before going to bed Anne called her mom to tell her what had happened. After they talked and cried for a little while, she told me Mother Carlson wanted to speak with me.

I picked up the phone, laughed and said, "Mother Carlson, you definitely got your sign."

"Now Ken," she declared, "don't jump to conclusions."

"Mother C, you and I both know if there ever was a definite sign, this is it."

A few days later we moved to Gulf Breeze near Pensacola to begin our new life in the sun. I carried the banking tools, still locked in the toolbox, but stored the toolbox in the attic, vowing never to use these things again.

I loved my new challenge with Project Concern, and from the start I was able to raise a considerable amount of money for the indigent kids we served. Traveling throughout the Eastern United States and meeting with community leaders to raise money put me in the company of many bankers who supported the cause. I made friends with several, including one who became a golfing buddy.

One day while riding down the back nine of his country club, he shared his dismay with me. He was concerned about the regional directors forcing him to train his people to cooperate with bank robbers, and not offer any resistance at all.

"What's wrong with that?" I asked, smiling deliriously over our conversation, unable to resist the urge to spur him on to talk about bank robberies.

"I'd shoot 'em all down," he raved. Then he added, "I'd throw the corporate training junk in file thirteen and train my people to cooperate my way—with a slug."

I agreed but couldn't focus on golf the rest of the game. I kept thinking about how much fun it would be to rob his bank. Associating with him and being thrown into the path of many irresistible banks brought the old urge back and got the juices flowing. I did not return to rob his bank, but on the next trip I carried my tools with me. It was like a drunk hauling a truckload of booze around while vowing never to touch another drop.

9

I gave in to the old urge on that run, cased a bank and then robbed it on the second trip. I lied to Anne about my schedule so I could buy the time to do my banking business.

Meanwhile, our lives were taking us in separate directions, and it became clear to both of us that our marriage was not working, though we shared a home in Florida. I was surprised we stayed together for twelve years, but when the time came we divorced as friends.

By then, Becky was away in college. At twenty-two, Lee chose to continue living with me when his mother moved out. My red-haired stepson and I became like brothers over the years and shared much more than a party house with a huge swimming pool and matching Jacuzzi. I taught him to be a macho male and provided him with a license to live it up with his young friends while I traveled.

One night when I was home, Lee was attending a party at an apartment building just a few blocks away. At midnight the ringing phone woke me. In the haze of half-sleep, I could hear a voice scream, "Lee's hurt, bad! Real bad!"

"Who is this?"

"It's Jeremy. I'm not kidding. Lee's hurt. You gotta get over here."

"What happened?"

He didn't answer my question and nearly screamed into my ear, "Come over here now, man; this is for real. It's serious!" And he was gone.

My mind triggered what felt like electrical impulses as I attempted to picture what might have happened to Lee. I jumped into my Caddy and wheeled out the driveway, headed for the apartment where Jeremy lived. The five-minute drive seemed like thirty minutes.

At the scene, Lee was laid out on a stretcher beside the pool. I fell by my son's side as paramedics attended to him. His head was split so wide open I could see his brain through the ooze of blood that formed a puddle at his head.

Paramedics whisked him away.

I stood there in deep shock, weeping. I turned to Jeremy. "How did this happen?"

He was defensive. "It wasn't my fault. We were all just having fun. I guess Lee got into an argument with a guy named Tony. I didn't see it happen, but some of my friends told me Lee fell over the railing."

I looked up toward the balcony, three stories above me, then back to Jeremy. "What does this Tony have to do with it?"

Jeremy shrugged. "I don't know any more than what I've told you."

I was in a rage as I got back into the car and headed for the hospital. Lee was in the emergency room. I was carried into a hell of guilt and despair.

Lee was in a coma for weeks, and I visited him every day I

was in town. Though he could not respond, I told him I was going to rob a bank in his honor to get out of my depression. It seemed to help me to vent my anger to someone who could only listen. However, his situation produced a rehash of my emotional state after the deaths of Jennie and my dad. In a matter of days, the doctors told us Lee would never recover. His brain damage was too severe. I felt my wrath rising, as it had years before, and I knew it was just a matter of time before I cased my next mark and robbed it, but this time I was in for a huge surprise.

Robbing banks was usually very stressful—especially for the two minutes in the bank. But the holdup dedicated to Lee turned out to be downright hilarious. I was high and happy, filled with optimism, as I parked a stolen getaway car at an apartment complex immediately behind the bank I planned to rob.

Before I got out, I pulled one of Lee's baseball caps low over my dark sunglasses, then stuffed a .45 long barrel pistol and a cloth bag in my belt. My gaze darted around to make certain no one was watching as I covered the tools of my trade with my loose shirttail. Within seconds, I took a deep breath and started down the block, around the corner and into the bank. I almost whistled as I pushed the door open.

My heart pumped hard when the heavy glass door closed behind me. The usual mixture of fear and exhilaration rushed through my veins in waves. This addictive rush heightened my senses; nevertheless, I was able to go about my business calmly, mechanically, as I had trained myself to do. I could have turned around and walked out, and no one would have been the wiser. Instead, I scanned the lobby and chose the teller I would force to hand over the cash. She would be my hostage as we left the bank in her car.

Maybe it was my fantastic mood making me choose this particular teller, but I should have known better than to pick a blonde who was decked out in a bright red dress. However, it fit the way I was feeling. Compared with the plainly dressed tellers, she grabbed my attention. What a picture she was, standing behind the first window. Even in my distracted state of mind, I noticed that her long blonde hair framed a very pretty face.

I approached and smiled politely as I said, "Good morning." She smiled and returned my greeting as I leaned in across the counter and pushed my money bag toward her, whispering, "Honey, I'm not gonna hurt you. Just fill up this bag with your biggest bills. No marked money."

At first there was a flash of unbelief, then, with sudden comprehension, her money-green eyes lit up. The smile on her face reflected genuine appreciation for what I proposed. I was taken aback as I heard her purr, "Why, it's no trouble at all, sir." She began stuffing large bills in the bag. "And how are you doing today?" she chirped.

She was so unlike any of the tellers I'd approached previously, my mouth dropped open and I grumbled, "Not so good." I was confused by her lighthearted response and snapped my mouth closed. Her smile and the delight in her eyes were disarming. I glanced to the side. No one seemed to be paying any attention to us, so I relaxed a little as I watched her put the bills into the bag.

With a soft voice I gently ordered, "Don't worry about filling it up." I took another glance at the two customers being served by the other tellers. No one knew a bank robbery was in progress. My eyes met those of my elated teller. "Just gimme all the big bills—no little ones."

As perky as ever, she responded with a wispy voice, "That's no trouble at all, sir. I'm delighted to do it." She didn't look up from the drawer where she picked up the big bills.

Another sigh rippled through me as she worked. It took about a minute but it seemed like ten before she raised her head and peered at me. "Will that be all?"

I nodded down toward my belt and showed her the dark handle of my pistol, and then pointed to the front door and said, "Thank you for doing a great job. Now grab your purse; you're coming with me."

Her eyebrows shot up as though the news delighted her. She smiled. "Okay." Without wasting a second, she moved around the end of the counter into the lobby. "Where are we going?" It was like I'd stopped by to pick her up for a brunch date on her break. She was bright, almost effervescent.

No doubt about it, we were a matched pair. As though we didn't have a care in the world, we strolled out of the bank. I was in shock. No one noticed us leaving. The large bag of money in my hand didn't even receive a nod.

As instructed, the blonde took me to her car. It was a sporty little thing, just like her. I asked for the keys and opened the driver's door for my hostage. A fleeting thought ran through my mind. *Who's the hostage in this caper?* I shook off the question and got in.

As I handed her the keys she begged, "Please take me with you." She tossed her long hair into the air with her left hand. The keys were poised above her open right palm and our eyes locked in a questioning stare. "Take me with you?" Her voice was sultry and inviting.

It took a moment for me to consider the option. I blinked and chuckled. "That's what I'm doing, girl." I shrugged her off and pointed toward the apartments behind the bank. "Take me back there."

She started the sleek little car. Her large eyes begged as she eased the car out of the parking lot. "Please."

My mind exploded with the concept. She liked what I was doing. It was giving her a rush just like it did me. Right then I figured she was a whacko who wanted to go for a thrill ride without regard for the consequences. I made a determination.

"Please. I mean it, mister. I won't be any bother."

We were out of the bank's parking lot and moving toward the hidden getaway car. Still, I just glanced at her and didn't reply. I was trying to take care of business and my mind was being invaded with unnecessary extras. My life was on the line here.

I reviewed my plan. Everything was going by the book except for this blonde. I knew I'd have to leave her in her car, scoot around the corner of the building to the hidden automobile and slowly drive away.

I stared at her again and momentarily my resolve wavered. She was a knockout. I considered what a trip she would be and how much fun she could add to my life. Then I shook my thoughts into reality and realized she would be nothing but trouble down the line.

After turning her forbidden body toward me, squirming like a schoolgirl, she pleaded one last time, "I mean it!" Then she bubbled, "I haven't had this much fun in . . . I don't know when." Her hands waved with excitement. "We could have a lot of fun together," she tempted.

I could see she was very serious, and I had to do something quickly. "Look, girl, you're out of your mind. There's no way!" I caught myself giving her a nervous chuckle. "No,"

I repeated and got out of her car. "Sit tight until I'm gone," I ordered.

I threw away my chance for the blonde and me to become a modern-day Bonnie and Clyde. Just before I rounded the corner of the apartment complex, I glanced back at her, sitting in her car, and was almost persuaded to motion for her to come with me. I forced the tendency back and turned away, but not before I noticed her hand go up. She waved as though I might be the sailor she loved who was shipping out to sea. It was strange, and it made me see a new facet of womanhood. I'd thought they all wanted total security, not adventure or daring.

10

The beginning of the end was a local bank job. It was a hot, sultry summer morning. Since Lee had been a painter, I wore one of his uniforms, complete with billed cap, decorated with blue and yellow splashes of paint. The cap was pulled down to the dark glasses over my eyes. I wore scuffed-up black shoes.

This time I poked a toy .45 in the front of my belt. The butt sticking out looked like it belonged to a real gun.

I sucked my gut in, covered my robbery paraphernalia with my shirttail and strolled through the apartment complex parking area adjacent to the bank.

On the sidewalk in front, I conditioned my mind, repeating power thoughts. I was cool, in control. *No one will get hurt. The hostage will cooperate with me, but she won't be like that blonde.*

I reminded myself, "I am invincible."

The holdup went as planned. With the money in one hand and the receptionist's arm in the other, I left the bank and hurried around the corner to her car. She seemed to be doing okay.

That made me feel better about forcing her to provide my ride, but it was a new red convertible. The top was down. I laughed. Leaving a bank robbery in a red convertible was a first.

At my instructions, she gave me her keys. I opened the driver's door for her. She got in as I tore around the rear of the car to get in. There was a child's car seat in the front, so I squeezed into the backseat. I handed my hostage the keys and told her to drive out. She did. I apologized to the poor thing for making *her* go with me. "Ma'am, I didn't know you had a kid. I hope you're doing all right."

With an air of indignation she said, "I can't believe you're doing this."

Grinning, I said, "I can."

I poked my pistol back into my belt while she accelerated out of the parking area. "Slow down now, honey pie, you're going a mite too fast! We don't want you gettin' a ticket now, do we?" She let off the accelerator, slowed down and laughed as she glanced into the rearview mirror at me.

Her sense of humor surprised me, and I relaxed. Within seconds we were at the apartment complex where I'd left my stolen getaway car.

She parked as I instructed.

I got out and took her car keys. "These here keys will be on the second doorstep 'round the corner, yonder. You wait five minutes before you go get 'em. Okay!"

She agreed.

I scooted around the corner and dropped the keys as promised. When I reached the stolen vehicle I jumped in, jerked off my robbery getup, put on a fresh shirt and drove slowly toward the station. I resisted the urge to wave at the cops when a police car passed me, siren blaring. They were speeding to the bank to catch the thief. I smiled and drove on.

When the story about the robbery came out in the paper, the woman described how she was held hostage. Deep regret sunk into my gut. *It's like they're talking about a crazy man I've never met, and an unseen force is driving me from bank to bank.*

Though I suspected I had gone over the deep end and knew it was insane to continue robbing banks, something inside wouldn't let me stop. I formed a gun with my hand and touched my temple with the index finger. "There's no gun to my head, but I'm as much a hostage as those poor women I took."

Really, nothing about it made sense. The little bit of money accumulated from the banks wasn't much good. I used three thousand dollars from the last holdup as a down payment on a piece of property, but generally, cash was stashed in a briefcase and dribbled out a little at a time. It was like having a part-time job without pay. Flashing too many bills, I feared, might lead to being turned in by a well-meaning family member or a self-appointed citizen crime stopper.

Maybe I was tired of running and ready to chuck it all. I had never told anyone about my dark side, but the next time I was with Jonathan, a lifelong friend, I spilled my guts and told him I had been robbing banks.

When I revealed the secret that fear had kept locked up for years, Jonathan's eyes bulged, and his face turned red. All he could come up with was, "You've had too much money for it to be clean."

The shocked look on his face brought regret that I had uncorked the poison boiling inside. That poison was ready to spew out on a childhood buddy. We had grown up together in the mountains. Like us, our fathers were best friends, and my gut told me I could trust him. He would not betray me.

With Lee now in long-term care, he was hanging out at my house but had no idea of my dark side.

"You've always lived on the edge, but you've got too big a heart to hurt anyone."

"Pulling holdups is about that adrenaline rush—staring down death. It's not in me to hurt people, and it's really not about the money."

Jonathan nodded, but I could tell he didn't understand.

"It's about the big kick. That's what I'm hooked on, but sometimes I take a hostage in order to grab control and get away. I don't like to scare women, so the thing I regret the most is taking hostages."

"I've always looked up to you as a big brother," Jonathan said. But then he chuckled, "Let's do a bank together."

Now it was my turn to be shocked. I turned away from him. My stomach churned and my face flushed. I felt I was going to be sick. I'd already ruined Lee's life; Jon's was next. I raised my voice like a father. "I'm only gonna include you one time, Johnny boy."

He shrieked with glee, ready to take the plunge into hell.

My shoulders sagged. He had no idea what he was getting into. "I can't allow you to get hooked too, but for some crazy reason, I'll allow you to do just one. You got it?"

He didn't seem to hear my warning and pressed me for more information. "How do you go about robbing a bank?" Pointing at me, he added, "Uh, case the place, right? Isn't that what you do?"

I fought the urge to tell him how I robbed banks while he kept right on talking about how exciting it would be.

Finally my willpower broke down, and I squinted at Jonathan. Despite the horrible consequence of his involvement with me, this venting had been a long time coming, and I loved reveling in his admiration.

"Okay, okay. I'll take you through one robbery I've done."

The next time we got together, he pressed for more information about how I'd done the local bank job.

"Through the years I have usually dressed like a gentleman, but at the last bank I played the role of a laborer, dressing like a workingman on his way to the job. I used a hillbilly twang like we used when we were kids in West Virginia."

My mind drifted into the scene as I unraveled just what had gone down. Jonathan hung on every word. I ended by telling how I had parked my car about a block from the police station to heighten the risk of being caught.

Jonathan slammed his fist on the desk. I was jerked back from my dream state. He shouted, "You sorry dog—you were just showing off." He gave me a high-five. "Man, you've had a lot of fun, haven't you? You've gotten away with it for a lot of years."

He put his nervous hand on my shoulder. "Ken, thank you for including me in your business," he chortled.

Over several weeks I trained Jonathan to become my partner in crime.

A day before the planned robbery, I rehearsed the preparation with Jonathan and took him through the steps one last time. "I walk into the bank at 9:26 tomorrow morning. As usual, I'll wave my pistol, take control and get everyone to cooperate."

"Okay," he jumped in, "I'll be outside near the getaway car."

"Yes. You wait just outside the glass doors, but close to the car, parked for a quick takeoff. I'll take a teller hostage and instruct her to step through the atrium, where you'll escort her to the car."

Jon blurted, "I know it by heart. I reassure her everything will be all right. She won't get hurt, and she'll be free in a few minutes."

"You can't know the plan too well," I said, "because you'll get juiced up—really hyped—so you must be able to operate on automatic without having to think about each step."

"I know, I know. I put her in the front passenger seat, and I sit in the back and wait for you."

"You left something out."

"Oh, yeah, I have the keys in my hand, and toss them to you when you jump in behind the wheel," Jonathan said. "But what about the money?"

"Take it easy." He was overly excited. That concerned me. "I'm taking you through the process as it goes, so stay with me." I put a hand on his shoulder. "After bagging the money, I'll follow with the cash."

"Man, this is gonna be fun."

I said, "Okay, we're set to go tomorrow morning, so let's party."

It was a hot July Sunday afternoon, a great time for a poolside party with some playmates. My girl for the day was Barbie. She was shapely, intelligent and fun. Life was filled with revelry as I tried to forget Lee and acted as though I didn't have a care in the world.

Jonathan and his girlfriend, Sally, were lying near the pool when the telephone, next to my Jacuzzi, rang. I excused myself and answered on the third ring. It was my brother Jim. The sound of his voice freaked me out. Here he was calling again just before a bank job. How could he know when to call? It was eerie.

After the usual greeting he said, "You're in trouble this time. Your life is in grave danger. I've got an overwhelming feeling—"

I lost it, turned away from my friends and softly cut him off. "Jim. You're letting your imagination run away with you. You're way off base."

"No, I'm *not* off base!"

Although he pushed, I pushed back. I turned again so my companions could hear me declare, "I'm great!"

"No, you're not. Not this time."

Even though I was unnerved, I downplayed it. I smiled at my lady over the mouthpiece as I chirped, "I'm on my way to Acapulco with Barbie tomorrow evening. Business is going great, cash flow is outstanding and things couldn't be better right now." I winked at my Latin beauty as she sipped a tequila sunrise.

Jim's voice rose and took on a deadly tone. "This time, hardhead, I'm telling you that things will be very different."

I couldn't listen to another word. "Thanks for calling, big brother; I'll call you from Mexico on Wednesday."

I hung up, but could still hear his warning. *This time* things will be very different? That was amazing. He couldn't have known about the *other times*. Yet his calls usually came just after I completed my plans and was ready to put them into action. I felt sweat run down my side and soak into my swimming trunks. Though I wouldn't admit it, his call soured my stomach, and the party was over.

Long after Barbie, Jon and Sally were gone, I sat by the pool, gazing into the moon's shimmering reflection on the troubled water. A sense of imminent doom hovered over me. The specter of trouble—even death—was not a figment of

Jim's imagination, but I was addicted and couldn't stop, no matter how strong the warning or the consequences.

It was almost midnight. I was by no means drunk, but Jim's face appeared again and again in the moon on the surface of the water. I couldn't erase his warning.

A cloud from the south drifted overhead and blocked out the moon. The hair stood up on the back of my neck. In the dim light, I considered the warning, and thought of skipping this next job. I dismissed the thought as impulsive. I put a lot of work into preparing this deal, and I was confident it would go off without a hitch. There was no way I was going to let Jonathan down. The deal was on, no matter what Jim said.

The cloud blew over, and I returned to my conversation with the moon and came to an agreement with my thoughts. Jim didn't know I was a bank robber. But the timing of his phone calls was uncanny. Every time I heard his voice, it gnawed at my guts. The calls expressing his concern about my lifestyle *always* came just before my next bank job.

So this call was a kick in the teeth to my paranoid mind. I felt like he was checking up on me, even though he knew nothing about my bank withdrawals—only that I was living fast and free. Jim knew I had a problem with alcohol and suspected I was a two-fisted drinker and womanizer. He was a professional engineer, but I always carried more cash than he did. Even so, he never commented when he saw me lay down a whopping tip at a restaurant. I figured Jim was concerned about where the money was coming from and what I was doing to bring in so much cash.

I told the moon that the next bank was a perfect target. I wasn't going to let it slip out of my grasp. I had gone into this bank several times. The first time in I took a fifty-dollar bill to the nearest teller and asked her to break it for me. She was a mere three paces from the front door. While she was busy counting the smaller bills, I studied the upper drawer she worked out of. I estimated that this drawer held about ten grand. After leaving the teller's window, I went to the courtesy counter and pretended to write a deposit slip. There was no armed guard, and the young woman whose desk was near the front door so that she could greet the customers would be our hostage. The Carrollwood Exchange Bank in North Tampa was an easy mark. The moon agreed, and I went to bed.

The next morning, at 9:26, as planned, I walked through the front door of the bank. Pausing in the "no-man's-land" between the double glass doors, I heard Jim's voice warning me, "You're in grave danger this time!"

I cursed under my breath and burst through the second door into the lobby.

11

Less than two minutes later, on my way back out, with a .9 mm in one hand and a heavy bag of money in the other, I was dropped between the same doors by a single shot from a .357 magnum. By the time the emergency medical team had delivered me to the hospital ER, I'd lost a lot of blood. They began an IV and transfusion. I could hear them mumbling about the gaping hole in my chest, but my mind was not working well, and I only got bits and pieces. After I was stabilized, I noticed a uniformed cop at my bedside. My left hand was cuffed to the steel frame. Time didn't mean much to my fuzzy mind, so I had no concept of the length of my stay in recovery.

Having spent countless agonizing hours with Jennie and Lee in a hospital, as soon as my wounds were bandaged, I insisted that the sheriff take me immediately to the jail. When I arrived in the medical unit at Hillsborough County Jail, the man in the next bed introduced himself as Danny.

I really wasn't interested in conversation and kept my eyes

closed. Pain drew me inward and images of my life were like a mental slide presentation.

"Hey!" Danny persisted. "You awake, man? You're bleeding."

I sighed and rolled my head toward him. He was a young, decent-looking black guy with about a week's worth of stubble on his face. "I'm awake. I have a hole in my chest," I moaned.

"In pain?"

I didn't answer and said, "Cooper. I'm Ken Cooper."

He smiled. "Yeah, I saw it all on the news." His chin jutted up toward a suspended television. "You're the man they call the Gentleman Bank Robber." He gave me a blow-by-blow of the arrest details he had seen on the news.

Sick pain racked my body, and I didn't want to talk, but Danny's persistent inquisitiveness drew me out of my shell. I was there with him for several weeks. He told me his story, and I gave him a little of mine. As we talked about my early thefts, I noted the interest in his eyes. I asked, "Does this make any sense to you? Did my need to get high on excitement put me here?"

My new friend cracked up. It made me angry until he stopped laughing and said, "Sounds like you're wrestling with the same issues I am. I'm a sneak thief burglar." He appeared to be reflective for a split second and then admitted, "I get high, especially when the people are right there in the room I'm robbing. But, dig this, my questions are about things you don't care anything about."

"Like what?"

"Life and death. You don't seem to care if you live or die." He pointed at my chest. "You got a bloody slug in you and missed dying by inches. Yet, it don't seem to matter to you none. You should still be in the hospital!"

I admitted to myself that he spoke the truth, but defying death was my way of life. I grimaced. "Funny thing is, this is not my first close call with death."

"Huh?" Danny grunted. "What do you mean? Did you get shot before?"

"No. There were other times. I nearly drowned when I was a kid." I reflected on that time. "My father was always my hero. After he pulled me out of the water, I knew there was no one like him in the entire world."

"What happened? You fall out of a boat or something?"

I laughed and told him how, as a ten-year-old, I had left the shallows where I was supposed to swim and dared to play on the edge of the deep rapids. Without warning I had slipped into the swirling waters. "My dad got to me after I went down the third time. He carried me ashore and got the water out of my lungs and saved my life. . . . I loved my father with a passion. Whenever I considered being like someone, it was always my father."

Danny said, "I didn't have an old man. At least I never met him."

Danny's head rested against his pillow, and when I finished rattling on, he muttered, "Nice family."

I reflected on my loss and added, "But loving somebody can be painful."

Danny's mouth pinched together. "Give me a break!" He threw his hands up.

"I mean it." I explained how Jennie's death and my father's death had made me so crazy with grief and anger. "I didn't care if I lived or died."

"My mom died early . . . never knew what it was to have a family. When my grandma died, it was one foster home after another," he said, wiping his nose with the back of his hand.

Hearing him talk made me realize how much my family meant to me as a young man. Yet, even with all the warmth and love I was afforded, it never seemed to make the difference that would keep me out of trouble. Now the warm hugs, the sense of being loved and the encouragement from those who cared for me were gone. Nothing but stark coldness froze the atmosphere.

I felt sorry for myself, but then I glanced at Danny. That poor young man agonized over his wretched existence without love or family. As a child I had both. My life was rich with relationships, and when they should have meant the most to me, I didn't even count them as anything worthy of my concern.

My mind whirled, and in the hours I laid in the darkness of the medical cell, I thought about my teen years. Back then I was full of pride and thought I was smarter than the rest of the world. I lived on the cutting edge of disaster. That's where my rebellion really surfaced. But thinking of my teenage buddy Lester and our joyriding capers brought a grin, nevertheless.

I told Danny about Lester and eating free steaks, stealing cars and wheeling into the supermarket parking lot to see a cop car there. He pulled as much of that story out of me as he could. I finally said, "When I was doing crazy stuff, I was also getting ready for college."

The sound of the chow cart rumbling down the jail's passageway interrupted us. I thought about how I'd wasted my education, and a deep sigh shook my body.

Danny sat up on his bunk and pulled a gray blanket around his shoulders as protection against the cold dampness. He seemed befuddled. "I ain't been to college. I stole a lot of cars, but I ain't been joyriding like you." He smiled ruefully.

"I stole a lot of food from supermarkets, but never thought about eating no steak in a restaurant and then walking out without paying for it. That's really dumb, man."

The chow cart was almost to our cell when he added, "If you don't die from your gunshot wound, or this cold place, the food's gonna kill you."

In the month we were together as my wounds healed, Danny and I shared a lot of life. We became good friends, and I missed him when I was sent to a regular eight-man cell. It was a good thing Danny wasn't transferred with me, though, since 22 guys were packed into it. Most of us slept on the floor. I wanted to bond out to escape this hell. Although I had money, I couldn't do it. The feds had a hold on me, and if I bonded out I'd be transferred right to a federal holding cell. I decided to stay put and take my chances with a state charge.

A few afternoons after getting out of the medical unit, my brother Paul came to see me. We were always close when we were growing up and then when we were young adults, but we certainly weren't close that day. All we could do was peer at each other through the plate glass separating us, but it was evident there was much more than the heavy glass keeping us apart.

Even so, I was glad to see my little redheaded brother, and I picked up the handset on my side of the partition. I smiled and lifted my brow to let him know I was glad he came.

He hesitated, then grabbed the phone and snapped, "You idiot!"

I was jarred by the hostility in his voice. He punctuated his outburst with cursing. "This isn't a family visit. I only came here to make sure you aren't going to commit suicide." He cursed again.

To my surprise I laughed. I suppose it was a way of dealing with the tension and embarrassment. My laughter infuriated him as he screamed into the tinny microphone. "You've already ruined the family name." Again he cursed. "Now all we need for you to do is take your own sorry life. That'd end it all."

Again, my shock and embarrassment made me respond by smiling and fastening my eyes on his. "You're right, Paul." I widened the grin. "And I'm glad to see you too."

My flippant approach didn't set well with my brother, and his ruddy face grew purple and his blue eyes bulged. He shouted, "You're not even sorry for all this." He shook his head.

I winced. I wanted to tell him how sorry I really was for what I'd done, but he blurted his harsh judgment.

"It's not that I care! You're not worth the rope it would take to hang you." Another curse darkened the air. "I'm thinking about Mother and the rest of the family, not about you!" A snarl curled his upper lip.

I sobered and sighed, "You're right."

"You're damn right I'm right!" Paul glared at me. He slammed the phone into its cradle, jumped out of his seat, whirled around and stomped out of the visiting area, figuring he had made his point.

I sat there gripping the black telephone until the officer came to get me. I truly was sorry for my crimes. I deeply regretted hurting Paul and my family, and now I was upset with myself for not telling Paul I was completely remorseful.

But he was gone. I couldn't tell him how much I regretted what I'd done. If only I could take back the frivolous words uttered out of nervousness and shock, I would cease the lighthearted antics, wipe the smile off my stupid face and begin again. The time for that had passed, and I couldn't recapture the words, the smile or the moments before he left. I should have been making memories, not regrets. But it was too late.

12

Even though I was in jail and facing harsh punishment, my mother did not give up on me. I knew she never would. Mother had always been on my side. When I was ten, playing under a large tree, I felt something telling me I would preach someday. I ran in the house and told my mother what happened. She nearly fainted and said she would be praying for me. I knew she had done so for many years.

One answer to her prayers may have been the visits I now received from a jail ministry volunteer. As part of the Abe Brown Prison Ministry Team out of Tampa, Syd Barrett came to the Hillsborough County Jail every week and talked to me about spiritual matters. I told him that I had been searching for peace of mind for a long time and that when I was arrested I felt like God had rescued me from the insanity of my double life.

He responded that most people are caught up in a double life until they find their true identity in God. "Most people may not have experienced the extremes you did, but most are always at odds with themselves," he said. His statement switched on a light in my mind and gave me hope that I might not be as different from other people as I feared.

His approach to life impressed me, and my interest intensified. After a few visits, something about the twinkle in his eyes and the glow on his face made me look forward to more time with him. I had another reason for accepting his visits. No one else was coming to see me, and I needed to get out of the cell for a few minutes. I guess there was a third reason: Syd made me feel more like a normal human being than I had in a long time. I grew to enjoy the man and really looked forward to seeing him. Through all of his visits, he never condemned me.

One day, when he attempted to talk to me about Jesus and the cross, I balked and said, "Come on. I've never believed the story about someone hanging on a cross two thousand years ago making things right for me today."

Syd's love for me didn't falter. He must have realized God would have to deal with me on this issue of the cross. That may have been the reason he excused himself and left early.

I went back to my bunk and put my head on the flat pillow. The noise around me faded, and I remembered Ben Kinchlow pointing his finger at me from the motel television. I'd thought it too farfetched to think anyone could find peace through an event that had taken place so long ago. I still held contempt for Kinchlow's theory, but I felt no peace, and it troubled me. I couldn't sleep.

The noise of the cell brought me back from my spell. I was amazed at the memory and realized God may have reached out to me even while I was on the lam and lying low following that holdup. In the dark, damp cell I thought about it.

Syd came to visit on a Wednesday. I was glad he returned despite my bad manners. I told him God apparently had been reaching out to me for years, but I was reluctant to face certain issues that were plaguing me. Syd asked me to open up and let out my deepest concerns. Before I knew what was happening, this man of God reached down into my depth and kindled a desire to ask God for help.

My immediate response was, "I can't be forgiven. I've done too much, hurt too many people. Taking bank tellers hostage is unforgivable."

Syd was humble and careful as he spoke. "Ken, my dear friend, we've all failed. No matter how terrible those sins were, Jesus died for all your sins, my sins, and the sins of the whole world. He paid the price for redemption. Remember, Ken, that redemption means to buy back, and that's what Jesus did by dying for you and for me. He bought us back from this sinful existence to offer us eternal life with God."

His statement freed me to reveal something I had not shared with anyone, yet it was one of the problems keeping me locked up in my own personal prison. "The thing is, Syd, I don't think I can be forgiven for what I did to my stepson."

"God forgives *all* sin," he responded.

"You don't understand. To this day, Lee is in a coma. A guy named Anthony Jordan slammed him in the head at a party and knocked him over the railing of a three-story balcony. He's my second wife's son, and I cared about him.

"But here's the problem. When he was a teenager he made a profession of faith in God, and I . . . well, I shot down everything he told me he believed in when he shared his faith with me. I scorned the cross of Christ and his trust in God. Instead of encouraging him, I told him he needed to live like a man and not to take any junk from anybody. I encouraged him to scrap for himself. My lifestyle led him to get into the fight that put him in a coma. And now he's as good as dead."

Syd touched my hand. "God will forgive you, Ken. Have you forgiven yourself or this man named Anthony Jordan who hit your stepson?"

I couldn't believe his question and shrugged. "I don't know."

Syd didn't press me. "You see, you were dead in your own sins and didn't realize what you were doing. You were driven by your sinful nature, so you were fighting God. He'll forgive you if you'll only ask Him to."

I swallowed hard and confession spilled out. "I need to confess the failure in my marriage to Anne as well."

"I can see God is working on you, Ken." He stared at me. "There's a different look in your eyes. The hardness has gone."

My heart nearly stopped. "I feel different." My eyes moistened. "I'm ready to listen to you. I don't know how, but . . . maybe I can find peace of mind."

With tenderness and reverence, Syd took me through a spiritual journey and gave me the biblical direction to the cross. Faith rose in me, and I accepted the truth. Instantly, I knew that Jesus suffered and died for my sins. Even the rebellion I expressed against God could be erased if I would just let Him do it. I would be totally and permanently forgiven. Sobbing, I knelt on the cold concrete floor and surrendered my life to God. As Syd instructed, I prayed out loud. It was through faltering words that I said, "Oh God, have mercy on my soul. Please forgive me for not believing in the death of Your Son, Jesus." Great tears flowed from my eyes and splashed on the floor.

"Jesus, I'm a horrible sinner; please come into my heart and change me. I've made a terrible mess of my life—and the lives of others."

Syd was silent.

I felt misery rise up in my throat. "I'm tired of living a double life, and I'm sick and tired of being out of control and crazy. Please come into my heart and give me peace."

At that moment, though I didn't see flashes of lightning or hear thunder, I knew that Jesus had come into my heart. I relaxed, opened my eyes and dried them with the short sleeve of the blue jail uniform. Kneeling there for several moments after prayer, I finally lifted my head. Syd beamed, and we hugged.

I felt different. Relief and peace wrapped around me. For the first time in years I felt good about myself.

I cleared my throat and asked, "Do you know what date this is? I want to remember it."

Syd smiled and said, "You will easily remember this date. It's Halloween—the devil's day."

"Not for me it's not," I said and embedded October 31, 1982, in my memory, the day a Holy God reached down to me. I stared at Syd and said, "Thank God, I've found peace. I feel free. Isn't that amazing? I'm free."

I gazed at the concrete and steel. "Here, behind bars, facing a prison sentence, I'm free. Wow!" What an awesome, heartfelt sense of peace flooded through me.

Syd confirmed my feelings. "Yes, Ken, you don't have to understand it, but you've been set free through receiving the Prince of Peace, Christ, into your heart."

Syd lowered his glasses and looked at me with upraised eyebrows. "Hear me now, and hear me well. You *will* be tested. Be prepared for something unexpected to happen to test your commitment to Christ."

I felt like a child in Sunday school but didn't care.

Although I didn't take it seriously, I acknowledged his

warning. "Okay, my friend, I'll be ready." I left the visiting cell feeling like I could fly. My feet hardly touched the floor. I was light, alive and clean. A heavy burden was taken off my shoulders. Even in the grungy, smelly jail cell, there seemed to be a new, bright light—one only I could see. I was a changed man.

Although this newness purged me of the old way of seeing and hearing, within days some of the darkness crept back in and my faith was tested, just as Syd said it would be. It took several weeks of intense discipline and humbling confessions to convince me that I was not crazy and that the peace of mind I felt was genuine.

I didn't know that the trial Syd warned me about was just around the corner.

13

As Syd predicted, the trying of my faith came suddenly and without warning. Within a week after that encounter with Christ, a ghost from my past raised his ghastly head. He appeared as a messenger of death through Danny, my young buddy from the medical cell.

Danny was transferred to my unit. He was a welcome sight. I had really missed him. Rather than greeting me, however, he rushed toward my bunk and shouted, "Anthony Jordan is here, Coop. Yeah, right here in *this* jail! Jordan is in *this* cell block."

I grabbed his arm and questioned him, "Anthony Jordan is here? What are you talking about, man?"

"Jordan is here! He's right down the catwalk in B-fourteen."

My bones told me it was true. A rage I hadn't felt since giving my life to Christ rose up and took control. I cursed. "He took Lee's life, and now he's dead meat!" I roared. "His days are numbered."

Danny nodded and smirked.

I blamed Jordan for Lee's death. Although Lee wasn't really

dead, he was to me. Danny knew the depth of my hatred and wanted to help me retaliate.

"He's ours for the taking, Coop. Just give the word and . . ."

I winced and held up my hand to stop him. "No! This is mine, Danny. You leave it alone. I'll handle this. I know just the man for the job."

"Okay, Bro. Whatever you say. I can't believe he was put in your hands like this. You got your chance for *get back*. Know what I'm saying?"

"Yeah, God must have dropped that son of a . . ." I stopped in midsentence, and blurted, "Oh, God, forgive me. I know You're not into this."

Danny frowned.

I glared at him. "I've gotta think about this. Before last week there was no question, I would'a fixed Jordan for what he did to Lee." I tried to clear my mind and repeated, "I've gotta think about this."

Danny may not have understood, but he retreated and left me to my thoughts.

With an overactive adrenal gland stimulating my mind, I couldn't shake the thoughts of vengeance that transfixed me throughout the day. Oblivious to everything else, I paced back and forth in front of the catwalk bars and continued to vow, "He's dead! He's dead meat!"

After chow I returned to my perch on the top bunk. A new Christian friend who was back in Tampa for an appeal hearing saw me that evening.

He smiled at me. "What's up, Bro?"

"Hey, Mark," I muttered. The brightness on his face reminded me of how I must have looked before the news of Jordan came, but now my peace of mind was gone. I felt like

I had before Syd Barrett led me through the prayer that gave me peace. "Not so good. Something's come up."

"Yeah," Mark admitted, "Danny told me, and I watched you stalking *something* all afternoon. That's why I came over. Anything I can do?"

"I don't need your help with this, unless you can transfer me to B-fourteen."

Mark smiled and shook his head. "I can see you're not ready to talk. How about praying tonight, and we'll talk tomorrow?" With that he was gone, and I was glad.

From lights-out to breakfast, I wrestled with my guilt and relived the part of my life I hid in a mental closet. When I broke the seal and opened the door, I was carried back to the angry, dismal days following the deaths of Jennie and my father.

An officer on the catwalk banged his nightstick on the bars. It jarred me out of the nightmare, but I continued to think about Jordan being right where I could fix him for good.

The shame from my past returned, and I was torn in two. One part of me burned to have Jordan wasted. Another part vehemently opposed it. Inner struggles were nothing new to me, but this battle was so intense I thought I'd lose my mind. These opposing forces were equally relentless. My mind was the battlefield, peace would not come, and I didn't sleep all night.

Following breakfast, I approached Mark. "Hey, man, I need to talk to you."

We found a place by the catwalk bars and stood side by side facing the thin steel columns. "What's up, brother?"

It made me feel good to hear him call me "brother." Something special about it offered warmth and friendship. Word had it that he had served as a chaplain's assistant for ten years, so I looked up to him. This helped me open up to him and share my heart. "I'm really struggling with this Jordan thing."

Mark smiled. "I'm glad you're asking for help. I'd be skeptical of your commitment to the Lord if you didn't look to a brother who wants to lend a hand." He touched my shoulder. "Now I'm convinced. You really did become a Christian."

"Yeah, well, maybe I'm a Christian all right, but I'm still struggling with wanting to kill the bas . . ." I wanted to curse him, but I held it back out of respect for Mark.

"Let me tell you something. First, you're still Ken Cooper in the flesh. You have a mind of your own, and you still have some of those old ways living in you. And check this out: You're unable to handle vengeance, forgiveness and some other emotions, like any other human being."

I didn't get his point and let him know it with a blank stare. He bounced back, "Brother Ken, the spirit of Christ came into your heart when you asked Him to come into your life, but it didn't destroy what the Bible calls the old man or the old sin nature. Each day, and sometimes each moment, you have to choose which one will rule, the old man or the new man."

What he said impressed me, but I didn't like it. "How can I live with myself if I don't avenge my son's death?"

"That's the wrong question. The right question is how can you live with yourself if you *do* avenge your son?"

I gripped the cold bars with white-knuckled hands and turned to look into his eyes. It took a long moment before I said, "I see what you mean. It would put me back into my personal prison."

"Right now, Anthony Jordan is scared to death. He's figuring you're coming for him. I talked to him. He told me his fight with Lee was a fair one, and he's really sorry for Lee's injury."

Hearing about his remorse got to me. I realized that I might have jumped to conclusions and didn't really know the facts. I threw my hands up and surrendered. "I guess it makes sense to find out what actually happened."

"Are you willing to meet with Jordan in the chapel so you can hear his side of the story?"

I took a moment to think about it before I responded. "Why not? It can't do any harm. Sure." I added with a slight grin, "The new man in me made the decision."

Mark laughed and patted me on the back. "You know it."

My eyes locked on his. "Hey, thanks for your help."

The next day, before an evening service, I met with Jordan in the rear of the chapel. As I sat beside him I noticed he was about Lee's age. As he turned and faced me he wept. I recognized his sincerity and reached out to him. "I'm not going to come after you," I offered as I touched his hand.

He used his sleeve to dab his eyes and said, "I can't ask for more."

"I can, but let's leave it at that," I said as my lips tightened. The old man in me still wanted to punch his lights out or get someone to do it for me, but I fought the urge.

Something in his eyes wouldn't let go of me. This young man was real. He was sincere. I sensed that, if he had it to do over, he would have walked away from Lee and saved his life. I felt like a fool and asked God to forgive me. "Hey," I said, "chapel service is about to begin. Let's go up front and sit together."

During the service when the congregation "passed the peace" as the chaplain called it, Anthony and I shook hands and then hugged. I never felt so much compassion, but it reminded me of the many hugs Lee and I had shared. I regretted I would never be able to feel Lee's embrace again. It was a battle, but I was getting through this first test of my faith.

The second test was on the horizon. It came on my day of reckoning, December 20, 1982. I stood before Judge Harry Lee Coe III to receive my sentence. My attorney, Ky Koch, stood beside me. Judge Coe's penetrating stare went through me as he ruled, "Kenneth L. Cooper, I sentence you to serve ninety-nine years in the Florida State Prison System."

The judge couldn't have hit me harder with a baseball bat. I gasped, "Oh, Lord, what is this?"

I turned to Ky in shock. He had assured me I would receive a twelve-year sentence. There had been extensive negotiations with a plea agreement. I frowned at him. Ninety-nine years?

As if his "life and then some" sentence wasn't enough to satisfy Judge Coe's appetite to see me rot behind bars, he added to the pronouncement. "And I retain the court's jurisdiction over you for one-third of the sentence"—I thought I detected a slight smile as he continued—"to guarantee to the public that only *I* can release you from prison."

He appeared to have a satisfied expression. I wasn't really certain. I was expecting twelve years, so maybe it was the shock of his judgment that made me cringe with paranoia. Hatred glared from his eyes. I knew I deserved to die in prison, but it seemed he took great pleasure in handing me a life sentence, and even taking personal control of me for the first thirty-three years.

My shoulders slumped and my arms hung limp at my sides. I wanted to cry to God for help, but nothing came out. I wanted to question Ky, but I couldn't. My mind raced across the various aspects of what he had promised me. There was no way to find out where the breakdown had occurred.

Judge Coe continued, but I couldn't take in every word because my brain wasn't functioning well enough to keep up with all he was saying. But he caught my attention again. "Mr. Cooper, you took hostages when you robbed those banks. That is the reason you will never walk the streets of America again."

A sharp stabbing pain penetrated my forehead. My mind shut down. I was dumbfounded. I could only go over plowed ground again and again, continually asking myself what happened to the plea agreement. My attorney bargained on my behalf, and the district attorney bargained on behalf of the state to come up with the promised twelve-year sentence. It was a "done deal," or so I thought.

I was shaken back to reality when I heard the judge ask, "Mr. Cooper, do you have anything to say?" His brow was pulled tight and he glared at me from the high bench.

I took a deep breath and managed, "Thank you, Your Honor."

What? What was that? I could feel my eyes widen with amazement at my own words. What had I thanked him for? I didn't know. It just seemed to be part of my makeup.

14

As I left the courtroom, the officer escorting me was no gentleman. He jerked shackles and chains on my ankles and slapped cuffs on my wrists behind my back to ready me for the long walk back down a dark tunnel connecting the courthouse to the jail. As I shuffled along in front of him, I considered the sentence I had just received. That's when the words of Proverbs 16:18 surfaced. My mother had burned them into my soul: "Pride goes before destruction and a haughty spirit before a fall."

I was shaken and stumbled against the tunnel wall. The officer jabbed his riot stick into my side like I was an animal, forcing me to continue my baby-step hobble.

Although the guard was there with me, I felt alone and at rock bottom in the clammy passageway. None of my family came to the sentencing. I didn't expect them to, but it really hurt when not one showed up to support me, not even my mother.

"I'm destroyed!" I muttered. "I must be so full of pride that everyone has given up on me."

The guard snarled over my shoulder, "What did you say, convict?"

I glanced back. His mouth was swollen with a chaw in his jaw and he slurred his words.

"Nothing, sir!" I said. "Nothing at all!"

"You said something."

I sighed and tried to get my thoughts together.

He ridiculed me. "Hangin' Harry socked it to you, didn't he?"

Disdain punctuated his judgment and burned into my soul, just as the recall of my mother's biblical quotation did. It seemed I was now hypersensitive to his chiding. His words were like wasps stinging me.

Even though he delighted in my agony, I needed to get rid of my frustration. "Yeah. You're right," I answered. "I feel sick. I can't believe it. He gave me ninety-nine years." I shook my head. "We had a twelve-year plea agreement with the DA and Judge Coe reneged on it. It was a done deal."

The guard snickered. "C'mon, he hates your guts! He ain't gonna make no deal with you."

I agreed. "Uh-huh. I could see the hatred in his eyes when he glared down at me." As we moved along the tunnel I nearly whispered, "He wants me to die in prison."

"You're lucky he didn't fry you for taking those women hostages." The officer shoved me from the back, and I stumbled again. "*I* would have," he said.

I was silent. My reflex was to shrug, but I couldn't. With my hands cuffed behind my back and my mind overwhelmed with the distress of the moment, the gruesome thought that I would die in prison took hold of me, and for the first time in my life, morbid fear shook my entire being.

As we left the tunnel and approached the cell block, my

tormenter seemed happier than ever with my agony. "You're gonna like this holding cell."

The venom in his voice made me cringe like a child caged with a deadly snake. One part of me wanted to die right there.

"I'm locking your rotten carcass up with our craziest cons." He was laughing at my horror. "Maybe you can take one of *these* animals hostage." He spit tobacco juice against the wall.

The guard's words echoed off the raw concrete block as he pushed me into the holding cell. I had heard about the Lion's Den. It was temporary living quarters for lifers awaiting transfer to prison. The "Den" also was used to punish inmates. It was notorious for horrible living conditions and the sadism permeating every corner of the twelve-man unit. During the five months I served in general population cell blocks, rumors of rapes committed in that dreaded cell overloaded the jail's grapevine. The guards added to the fear of the Lion's Den when they quelled disturbances among the general population. They would sidle up to the bars of a cell block and threaten, "Chopper! Belinski! Norman! You keep arguing over that stupid card game, and I'm gonna send ya to *the Den*!"

After hobbling in and glancing around, I thanked God I would only be there a few days. I wanted to get on the bus for prison rather than deteriorate in that hellhole.

The Den smelled like a butcher shop mopped with a heavy dose of Lysol dumped into a bucket of urine. I gagged on the putrid air and almost passed out. Around the cell, a welcoming committee crowed like birds of prey and stared at my gaunt face. I knew many of them saw me as their next victim, so, with disdain, I frowned at the loudest ones.

They lurked like vultures eyeing roadkill. I stumbled at the thought, but an idea zapped my brain and told me I had to be strong and compose myself or I would be a victim of this rabid pack of animals. Although I could feel the guard shoving my back, I pictured myself standing outside a bank.

Just as before each robbery, I recited my ritual of mental hype, with a religious twist, as I scanned the faces. *I am strong*, I thought.

In my fear I grimaced but continued to pump myself up. *I will not show weakness. God is with me. I'm not afraid.*

Ignoring the vocal convicts I took in the rest of the cell with a quick glance. Men of all sizes and shapes were everywhere. Officials had stuffed twenty-one "lost causes" like me into the cramped cell. Cots were strewn across the floor. It looked like a war zone, but in the corner to my right, I spotted a man standing straight like a general. My gut told me he was the cell boss.

Ignoring the officer's hand on my back, I stared at the self-appointed commander and spouted, "Take me to your leader." He smiled and several men guffawed like hyenas despite the presence of the officer pushing me toward my bunk in the farthest corner. I couldn't believe he guided me to a bed when ten men there before me were sleeping on the floor. As soon as he took the cuffs off and left the cell, the unit's strong-jawed leader, the one I picked out, approached me with an extended hand. "I'm Baltimore; I got eight lifes. What did you get?"

I knew from his bearing, arrogant steel-blue eyes behind his glasses, and a firm handshake, that I had indeed met the cell boss. "Ninety-nine," I said flatly.

"Me, I caught eight hundred years for killing eight people." He said it as though he was giving me a weather report. At the time, I didn't realize this man really was a serial killer. Though he maintained a steely stare as he spoke, I reckoned he was blowing smoke.

He called over his shoulder. "Hey, Buzzo, here's another *ninety-nine.*" He turned back to me and explained, "Buzzo's my right-hand man."

A handsome young man approached. He was a fair-skinned, black man with bulging biceps. He shook my hand ghetto-style and gave me a thumbs-up welcome. Rather than asking me how I was doing, he asked, "Wha'd you do?"

"Banks," I said.

He grunted. "Me, I do houses. They got me on ten counts. They slapped a ninety-nine-year grudge sentence on me 'cause I broke in at night and scared the Crackers. It's a thing. Know what I mean?" I knew *Cracker* is a term sometimes used to make fun of Southern whites.

I nodded as though I agreed, but I'd heard through the grapevine that his last hit was a black cop's house. I resisted scorning his aura of arrogance. His large eyes were empty.

Buzzo smiled. I thanked God he couldn't read my mind.

As though it was orchestrated, I met the cell boss and his main hit man, and we were *friends*. I had been on God's side for a few weeks, so I marveled at what He was doing and the speed at which He was doing it. Of course, I wasn't sure that Baltimore and Buzzo considered me a "stand-up con," so I played it cool.

It wasn't long before Baltimore came over and tapped me on the shoulder. "Play chess?" he asked.

"Some," I said.

"Let's do it. Fifty push-ups."

He beat me, and I got down and did the fifty easily. When I finished, Baltimore congratulated me. "You're better at the exercise than at chess, but you're pretty good. Best challenge I've had in a while." He walked me over to my bunk. "What's your name?"

"Cooper," I said. A smile leaked out as I thought about the strange subculture of this cell.

Buzzo was at his side and Baltimore glanced at him. "Stand-up guy," he affirmed.

Buzzo nodded but looked at me crazy.

I hoped I was okay with the cell boss and his hit man. I didn't know how truly important that was until I experienced the horror of the succeeding days and nights, including Christmas. Baltimore orchestrated a different "game," using men for pleasure. I kept a low profile and lived according to the jailhouse code: *See no evil, speak no evil.*

As a new Christian, I didn't know God's promise of protection, and I feared my new friends would turn on me like a pack of wolves if I interfered with their games. I devised plans to take care of myself, wearing my shoes to bed and sleeping with one eye open, in case they came after me. If anyone crept up in the dim night, I was ready to slam the heel of my brogans into their face and then ask questions.

On the second day, Baltimore introduced me to another hit man they called Tick, a creepy-looking criminal with the dark eyes of a wolf and a nervous *tic*. His full nickname was Tick-Tock Clock, but they shortened it to Tick. Jailhouse nicknames are ingenious, but the instant I met him I felt that, as a clock, he was a few minutes short of an hour.

If I thought Tick was crazy, I didn't know what crazy was. Put two criminal crazies together and it becomes total madness laced with evil. The insanity erupted after lights-out that first night. I lay in the dark for about three minutes before I heard Buzzo and Tick attack an athletic, blond youth who joined us shortly after my arrival in "paradise." As they took turns pounding the new man, who was said to have raped a child, his screams and groans made me cringe. I tried to block out his pathetic cries for help. I couldn't move.

The first round of the sadistic game didn't last long. The young man charged with rape gave up in a few minutes. "No, please don't! Please, please, don't!" His voice grew faint as several men brutalized him.

I wanted to rip those animals to pieces with my bare hands, but I lay horrified, knowing I was incapable of doing anything. Stupefied, I felt like I was the one being raped. Wrapped up in a wool blanket, a cold sweat soaked the pillow and my mind refused to listen anymore.

To keep my sanity, my brain tuned out the madness. Words of my mother sounded in my soul once more. *One of these days, young man, you'll get knocked off your high horse.* I mourned. And the warning of one of the victims I took hostage during a bank robbery flashed across my mind. *You'll pay for this someday! Mark my words, you* will *pay!*

I was paying for taking those helpless women hostage. Waves of sorrow and regret engulfed me, and I cried out to God for forgiveness. I prayed He would heal my victims. The truth that I was no better than these pigs gripped me. During that awful night, bone-deep remorse and sorrow overwhelmed me. After weeping half the night, in my tortured mind I made a vow: "God, I'll never hurt anyone again! With Your help I'll treat everyone with respect and dignity the rest of my life, no matter what."

Four nights in a row, including Christmas Eve, the gruesome gang bang continued in the covering of evil and darkness. The primary targets were those considered weak or "deserving" because of their sex crimes. But I watched with disgust at how the other men were tested. If one showed some courage, put up a valiant battle and was willing to fight until he was so exhausted he could not raise his fists anymore, he escaped. If he refused to defend himself or didn't show the unruly mob the heart they demanded, he was raped. Each night I was in agony and sobbed during the horrific ordeals.

The officers must have known what was happening. They could hear the victims' screams. It offended me that they didn't care. They gave up on us and wanted us locked away. That was public opinion as well—out of sight meant out of mind *for life*. If I snitched on Baltimore and his gang, it would follow me to prison, where there would be hell to pay. This jailhouse mindset kept sufferers from squealing on the rapists. They were warned repeatedly, "You snitch, and you're dead meat." Everyone was brainwashed to believe that they would pay with their lives in prison if not in jail. Many did.

Those nights in the Lion's Den were a wake-up call. Before coming into the place, I thought I was a tough-minded man of the world and acquainted with fear and terror. I had no inkling that men would stoop lower than ravenous animals. At least beasts of prey kill their catch before they eat them. In the Den, the sadists tortured their victims until they lost human dignity. In many cases, it would have been better to die.

The weakest among them gave up hope and stumbled around like dead men living in terror. They had no rights. They were pawns in the hands of the biggest and baddest in the cell. They were trapped and could see no way out. Two of the victims, including the young blond who was sentenced to life for raping a child, tried to commit suicide. Others became gang rapists to please their masters.

Those who could fight were forced to participate in "cock

fights," like the rooster or cock fights I witnessed as a kid in the Appalachian Mountains. Buzzo and Tick served as the bookies who took bets of money, food, cigarettes or coffee as they pitted one combatant against another in a no-holds-barred "fight to the death." Baltimore didn't actively take part in the sex games, but he delighted in the cock fights. I loathed him. He was one sick power monger.

The two men who fought on Christmas Eve were carried out to the medical cell the day after Christmas. Their desperate battle lasted thirty minutes. It seemed like three hours. Their broken bones, black eyes, bumps, bruises and dripping blood told the story of this barbaric game. They almost killed each other. They might have if I hadn't challenged Baltimore to stop the battle so we could play a game of chess in peace.

The day they were carted away, it was announced that none of us would be moved until after the holidays. That was devastating news. If I had known earlier, I probably would have lost my sanity. Though I hadn't been raped during those first five nights, I was stripped of my dignity and considered myself less than a man because I did so little to put a stop to the gruesome brutality.

As I contemplated being trapped there for at least another ten days, a cold shiver brought an instant twinge to the base of my neck. How much longer could I keep my mind from exploding? In the Den, life carried no value. That mindset took its toll. I drifted into depression and escaped into books, especially the Bible and paperback Westerns. Reading novelist Louis L'Amour took me back to an Arizona where six-shooters ruled. Meditating on the Scripture helped me develop a spiritual perspective on power I needed to withstand the mental and emotional onslaught. I memorized 2 Timothy 1:7,

"For God hath not given us the spirit of fear; but of power, and of love, and of a sound mind." I repeated it throughout the days and nights and personalized it by saying, "God has not given *me* a spirit of fear. He has given *me* a spirit of power, and love, and a sound mind."

15

No one else in the cell admitted to being a Christian, so I prayed God would send a strong Christian man to help me stop the madness. God sent a man named Charles the day after Christmas. He didn't seem to be the answer to my prayer. He came to the Tampa jail from a notorious prison at Raiford known as the "Rock." He was transferred in to attend a new hearing of his case and probably was housed with us maniacs because he acted like a crazy man.

Charles displayed several quirks. First, he talked incessantly to invisible beings. He acted as if he were a person of nobility and demanded that we call him by his given name, Charles, rather than by his family name, Johnson. He refused to be called Charlie or Chuck. He slept with his eyes wide open so you could never tell whether he was asleep or awake. He gave virtually all his food to the weak men who were starving because their masters hoarded their food.

Charles told me about prison life at Union Correctional Institution (UCI) and its most horrendous section—the Rock.

It sounded like a war zone in an insane asylum, even worse than the Den.

During one conversation discussing angels, Charles said, "Of course I believe in angels. I see them a lot, and I talk to them all the time." At times he talked to them in front of everyone, and he even called them by name. Baltimore and his henchmen left Charles alone.

I thought he was crazy like a fox, so I was cautious around him. Then, I realized he could be the Christian man I asked God to send. Charles continually read a well-worn Bible. He openly protested sodomy, getting in Baltimore's face. "You're just as guilty of rape as the men you put on these victims!" he snapped.

Charles's confrontation with the cell boss convinced me he was nuts. He knew Baltimore had already killed eight people and had nothing to lose by killing number nine. But after considering it and noticing how Baltimore and Buzzo took his rebuke without retaliation, I decided being bonkers had its advantages. His being crazy didn't preclude his being the Christian God sent to me. *This may be my man*, I thought with a smile.

I joined him as he was reading the Bible and asked him to share his spiritual knowledge with me. From the start, he taught me about angels and how to pray what I soon called the Charles Prayer: "Lord, please send Your angels to work with Your Holy Spirit, that each of us this day will be in the right place at the right time with the right word with the right persons for Your right purposes." Others heard us calling out to God, but we didn't care.

Baltimore ridiculed me. He got me to the side and said, "You know you're sitting at a crazy man's feet like one of Christ's morons." I must have given him a dumb smirk. He shrugged and left me alone.

My brother in Christ taught me about many important spiritual matters, including the role of angels and prayer in a believer's life. He showed me the record in Daniel in the Old Testament and in the first chapter of Hebrews in the New Testament. At my mentor's leading, we asked God to intervene and send angels to stop the rapes.

I was astounded by what happened. Charles said that holy angels came and battled the dark forces of evil. Time after time it seemed the unseen good guys were winning. One rapist clashed with another about who would sodomize the victim first. They fought, and the victim was spared. In another case, an officer happened by at the time of the attack. Within a week, the attacks stopped altogether, and within two weeks, both hit men who instigated the atrocities were transferred to solitary confinement. Baltimore retired as the cell boss and kept to himself.

Charles and I continued to pray his prayer, and by New Year's Day, the Lion's Den had become a lamb's pen. Men who once fought like animals respected each other. On the bunks where carnage occurred, prayers were uttered. Sanity and dignity returned to our lives; there was no more food and blanket theft, and every man slept on his own pillow. To the delight of the jail staff, the floors were mopped in clean water and waxed. The putrid odor evaporated. God worked a miracle through an "insane" convict, and He prepared a wide-eyed middle-aged Christian for arrival at the Rock.

It was late January before an officer came to the holding cell and told me to pack my meager belongings and board the bus for prison. Relief flooded me and washed away the stress dammed up for weeks. Through Charles and others I heard horrible, nerve-wrenching tales about the "Big House," and a few of the abominations committed there daily. Even so, I couldn't imagine it would be worse than the first two weeks in the Lion's Den. A sense of peace came over me as I dropped my personal property into a shoe box.

Within the hour, several of us were herded toward a long gray bus with barred windows. My ankles were shackled and wrists cuffed. I boarded the prison bus and noticed immediately the pitiful look on the faces looking back at me. Everyone was shackled and cuffed, but more than that, their eyes told me they all appeared to be chained to an inner prison. The forlorn emptiness made me think they were serving life sentences not imposed by a judge.

I hobbled down the aisle toward an empty seat next to a huge black man. As I wormed my way down on the torn vinyl, he didn't look at me.

After I settled in, with the shackles digging into my ankles, the bus eased out of the area. A heavy metal screen with a padlocked steel-mesh door secured the driver and his shotgun rider up front. I spotted their weapons beside them, and knew these officers wouldn't hesitate to kill any of us if they felt threatened. That thought made me close my eyes and pray that we would arrive at the Reception and Medical Center at Lake Butler without incident.

It took four hours to make the trip, and we were unloaded in a secure area with guards all around. After being lined up and ushered into a cold, harsh, open area with long wooden benches, one of the officers screamed, "All right! Listen up! I ain't gonna repeat myself. Get it right or pay the price."

He instructed us to strip and put our clothing in a brown paper bag to be sent home or thrown away. "Get 'em off!

Yeah, four-eyes, that means your stinking yellow-stained skivvies! Drop 'em now and turn around and face the wall. Everybody!"

We all obeyed without hesitation.

"Bend over and spread 'em!"

Due to the dehumanization I experienced at the jail in Tampa, the induction and classification process didn't shock me. It embarrassed and humiliated me to be lined up with a hundred other men, stripped naked and have my body cavities probed, but I was determined to hold on to some semblance of dignity no matter what. I did not look upon my nakedness or that of the others.

As guards herded us into a common shower smelling like a mixture of sweat, urine and lye soap, an impression of the Nazi death camps washed over my mind. The insult to my dignity grew stronger as we were debugged and sprayed down like cattle. I raised my eyes toward the ceiling, and, like I did at the Lion's Den, I silently cried out to God for mercy on my wretched soul.

After that ordeal, everything else seemed routine as I was led from one place to another like a dead man. During the orientation process, I was taken to a cubicle where I met my classification officer, a bright-eyed, spirited woman with red hair. She appeared to be about twenty-five and displayed a great deal of pleasure as she studied my file. Without raising her eyes to meet mine, she questioned me. "*Now* how do you feel about taking women hostages?"

I knew there could be no acceptable response because disdain dripped from her lips as she savored the moment. Even so, I let the truth prevail. "I-I've been begging God's forgiveness." Her sense of pleasure took on a morbid tightness around her mouth. My attempt to express myself seemed feeble, even to me, so I said, "Honestly, I am broken and deeply remorseful for—"

She threw a hand up and her face reddened, suddenly grotesque and ugly. She shouted at me from across the desk. "Inmate Cooper, how dare you attempt to con me! Listen, Mr. Armed Bank Robber who took women hostages, I'm sending you to the toughest prison in the system. I am personally going to make sure you are duly punished for your crimes and assure women everywhere that you will not have the opportunity to escape." Her upper lip curled as she slammed my file on the desk. "You are assigned to the Rock. It's what you deserve."

She leaned back with an expression of self-satisfaction. "Just so you'll understand where you're going, Inmate Cooper. You will do hard time there, and you can be sure not one prisoner has escaped from that prison in its sixty-year history. And, mister, you deserve to go there."

I couldn't argue with her assessment. When she got through, it surprised me that I maintained a sense of dignity and calmly said, "Yes, ma'am."

"Do you have any questions?"

"Just one. When will I be going?"

"When we consider you ready," she snarled. "Meantime, you'll be confined in K-Wing. You're considered an escape risk."

K-Wing meant two weeks of solitary confinement. Following processing and orientation and then further preparation through Butler Transit Unit, I was shackled and cuffed. Then, in the darkness of early morning I was driven onto a bus along with thirty other men, each of us bound for our assigned prisons. For me, it was the dreaded Rock at Raiford.

The bus was scheduled to make several stops to let prisoners off or pick one or two up for transfer. Probably out of anxiety and fear, some of the men exchanged war stories on the way, especially those who knew they were headed to the Rock. It was a prison within a prison. They told what they had heard about the horrible old main housing unit at Union Correctional, and about the carnage that occurred there. The more they talked, the more agitated and restless I felt. I ached to shut them up but couldn't, so I did my best to tune them out as we rode.

A big-eyed, worried-looking, youthful convict said, "I hear last week a man was killed there for thirty-seven cents."

Another man chimed in, "Yeah, I hear the place is out of control."

A seasoned con with heavy tattooing added, "The cons run the prison."

His graveled voice dug into my nerves. Even so, I was willing to listen to him.

"Murders happen like the ticktock of a clock." He grinned at the younger man. "Gang rapes come down all the time." I thought of Tick, Buzzo and their victims.

Leaning back against the uncomfortable seat, as cold and hard as the old con's face, I glanced at the man next to me. Our eyes met, but we didn't say a thing. Words were not necessary. He gave me an icy stare and tugged at the shackles on his thick ankles. I felt sorry for him and for myself, but peered beyond his profile through the barred windows to watch the trees pass. I was suddenly hit with a morbid realization—it was my last chance to see the outside world, perhaps forever.

The nervous chatter continued. Our driver heard it all and paid no attention. He sped toward Raiford. It was ten miles to hell.

Once again, as had happened at the jail, a deep-seated yearning to die clouded my vision, so during the trip I relived my life. To my surprise, remembering the good times hurt me more than reliving the bad. Knowing all those good times were gone forever drove me to despair and reminded me of all I had lost. That revelation made me face how far I had fallen.

I sighed deeply and stared out the window at two horses galloping in an open field. Highlights of happy times in Kentucky, which was known for its horses, flashed into my mind, and I recalled my time as the State of Kentucky's director of advertising and tourism promotion. I stood in the Capitol rotunda dressed to the nines, welcoming a band of nattily attired English guests. They flew across the Atlantic to tour the Bluegrass State's horse farms and take in the Kentucky Derby. "Welcome to the Commonwealth of Kentucky, ladies and gentlemen from the Motherland. On behalf of Governor Julian Carroll, his family and staff, I greet you and urge you to not place your bets on Crazy Legs in the seventh race at Churchill Downs on Saturday. Sir Winston would roll over in his grave because you would be sure to lose. . . ."

A sharp turn in the road brought me back from my dream state and into reality. I moaned out loud, "Oh, God, how could I be so crazy? What could have made me act so stupidly? How could those demons take control of my mind and ruin me?"

Before I could regain my bearings, the gray bus rolled through the restricted back gate of Union Correctional Institution where the Rock was located. It was the new home for many of us. Most were expected to die there. But whether or not that was the case, it was an imposing sight in the early light. From our vantage point some quarter mile away, the monstrous main housing unit stood like an old prison fortress rising into the placid morning sky. The Rock imprisoned more than nine hundred men who were sentenced to serve out the remainder of their lives within its confines. It was one of three maximum-security prisons at Union C.I., altogether housing twenty-six hundred inmates. The prison was surrounded by two miles of razor wire with armed marksmen manning guard towers.

I glanced back at the faces of the thirty men on board with me and flinched at the sight of their tight jaws and wary eyes. Even as the officers escorted us off the bus in front of a hospital, I wondered if an early death was my fate, but I wouldn't give in to those morbid thoughts. Taking in the round stucco-finished Spanish design of the medical building, I remembered taking Jennie into Mexico for cancer treatments after the doctors in the United States had given up on her. For some strange reason, that picture perked me up. I set my face to take my medicine like a man rather than withdrawing into my mind to escape from the awful reality before me.

There in that awesome structure we would be checked in and assigned housing. The guard nearest me had flaming red hair, reminding me of my classification officer. Again I heard her declare, "Mr. Bank Robber who took women hostages, you are bound for the Rock."

The abrasive voice of the sergeant in charge startled me as he ordered us to line up in twos on the wide sidewalk leading to a huge stairway into the hospital. I was careful to keep my body rigid and at attention. However, I allowed my eyes to dart around to take in the place. The prison grounds looked like a garden at daybreak as the sun came up. Knee-high daylilies with bright yellow faces graced the walkway. Their radiant beauty surrounded me. A row of huge oak trees between the line of men and the dreaded Rock formed a canopy for a variety of green plants and multicolored flowers. It gave the area the appearance of a well-conceived and manicured city park. I nudged my partner in line. "Hey, this must not be as bad as the rumors say it is," I whispered.

"Yeah," he muttered out of the side of his mouth. "I never could believe that line about all the murders."

I had to agree. "They make it sound like . . ."

About that time I heard a commotion coming from the vicinity of the Rock. Two inmates hurried toward us carrying a loaded stretcher. An officer led the way and another followed as the ominous apparition rapidly approached. The sergeant ordered us to make way, so we cleared a path down the middle of the sidewalk.

When the stretcher came closer, my eyes widened and my heart skipped a beat. I winced at the sight of blood spurting from the chest of a prisoner. The blood spilled over his body and dripped through the canvas, leaving a bloody trail on the sidewalk. He was rushed past us, up the steps into the hospital where he disappeared through the doorway. I knew he had no chance of surviving.

I heard someone in the crowd say, "Welcome to hell."

16

While I was being processed through the prison hospital, the injured man on the stretcher died in an adjoining room. I wondered if I would inherit his bunk when the news of his death came to my classification officer. Someone told me I was assigned to Mrs. Joseph, so my old paranoia played havoc with my mind. She would be the officer who would decide my housing location since the medical personnel found no reason to house me in the hospital. My gunshot wounds were healed, and they gave me a clean bill of health and said I was fit for open population.

Although it seemed things got worse, the good side of me wanted to believe God had not forgotten me and would help me survive. I witnessed His angels overcoming evil in the Lion's Den, but my faith was weak as I entered this dungeon they called prison. Sitting there waiting for Mrs. Joseph to tell me my cell block location, I prayed God would hear my cry and place me where *He* wanted me.

I could barely breathe due to the tension and anxiety, so I sat up straight and inhaled as much oxygen as my lungs would hold. Mrs. Joseph, who appeared to be about forty, didn't seem to notice. Her nose was buried in my open file, obviously intrigued by what she read. When she finally glanced over the edge of the folder and stared at me, the deep furrows on her brow told me her decision would not be good news.

"Inmate Cooper, you are assigned to Cell Block A, cell four."

Although I heard what she said, I had trouble taking in her words, and I could feel the blood drain from my face. All I could do was slump down into my chair. Back at Hillsborough County Jail I had particularly heard of the Rock's A-Wing in the closed custody area wing they called the Dungeon. That was the cell block previously occupied by the man who was killed. Her words were an omen of death.

She peered at me over her glasses. I was sure she expected me to respond to her announcement, but I couldn't speak. I sat there bewildered; it was hard to believe I was headed for the state's version of the Lion's Den, the deadliest cell block in the prison.

Mrs. Joseph's brow smoothed as she stared at me. The file in her hand eased down on her desk, and it appeared she was actually concerned about me. "You look a bit upset, Inmate Cooper."

I tried to speak, but no words formed in my head. I was like a man who could not remember his name and had no idea what to say to this woman who held my life in her hands. Horror must have been written all over my face, and she tried to console me.

As soon as I was outfitted in an ill-fitting blue uniform, eleven other inmates and I were escorted to the Rock's gate, the only portal in and out of the old poured-concrete prison within a prison. It was nothing more than a twenty-four-inch-thick walled concrete and steel structure where men went to die. The stale air loomed over me, and I could smell evil. The place was as gloomy as a concentration camp. I felt out of place, like I didn't belong there. I was different from the slump-shouldered men lined up with me. I couldn't read their minds, but their body language said they felt dead. I admitted to myself that I was scared to death, and my rigid body punctuated my confession. Even so, I wasn't about to give up. As I considered my circumstances, it made sense to give up, but something inside wouldn't let me. I was determined to hang on to any shred of sanity.

The state had sentenced me to die in prison. However, I wasn't going to let the system take my life, and I made up my mind to protect myself from death. I wasn't going out like that man I saw on a stretcher. Sure, I was scared. I felt weak, but I was determined to be Ken Cooper, a living, breathing human being. I was going to do my best to make it.

My determination weakened when I fingered the number label sewed above my shirt pocket, appearing upside-down to me. I glanced down at this strange version of my last name and number and forced a sick smile. I had become just another number. In those few moments, my identity was stripped. I became 087868.

Everything was lost. Separation from everyone I loved was bad enough, and having everything I owned taken from me added to my feeling of worthlessness. Here, I was a number again. It was like being back at the work camps in the coal mining settlements. Those camps were just a number, never named. I looked at the men in front of me lined up to go into the Rock, and I remembered my father lining up like that to head into the coal mine. He owed his soul to the company store, but I owed mine to the state.

A smile inched across my lips as I peered down at the shoe box in my right hand. It was smaller than my father's lunch bucket. That shoe box contained all my possessions after forty-six years of living. I stared at the contents: my Bible; a daily devotional book by Robert Schuller; a few scraps of paper; and a pencil without an eraser.

I took a deep breath and stretched my body in the morning sun, as tall and straight as I could stand. I touched Dr. Schuller's book and remembered it was a gift from James Taylor, president of Cumberland College in Kentucky. The air in my lungs escaped as a long sigh, and I thought about the double life I assumed when I was working with him at the college. Dr. Taylor turned out to be a true friend. When he heard of my tragedy and realized the truth about me, he sent the book to me with his prayers and good wishes. I uttered, "I need your prayers now, Jim."

It was then that the words from Schuller's lesson that morning hit me. I mouthed the words, "I am a son of God; I can live an abundant life even here." My declaration lifted my hope. However, taking in the threatening fortress again, I thought of Auschwitz and considered that I might die behind the dark walls because of the vow I'd made in jail. Back then I told myself I would die rather than become a sex slave. Thinking about what I'd heard concerning rapes every night, and remembering the early days in the Lion's Den, I prayed God would help me live like I was His son.

17

As we waited for what seemed like an hour on the walkway, with the rugged old building looming over us, I fumbled with the Bible and recalled 2 Timothy 1:7, the verse that helped me keep my sanity in county jail. I rehearsed it through clenched teeth and unmoving lips. "For God hath not given us a spirit of fear, but of power; and of love; and of a sound mind." I opened my mouth, licked my dry lips so the words would flow and said out loud, "I have a sound mind. . . . I have a sound mind. . . . I have a sound mind."

Just as those words came out of my mouth, convicts appeared above us, behind huge steel-barred windows. They began shouting obscenities. I tried to shut them out but couldn't as one vulgar threat followed hard after another. I focused above the inmates waiting in line and caught sight of one convict glaring down at me. I felt as if he was trying to hypnotize me while I stared straight into his eyes of death and evil.

Although I was fully clothed, I felt naked and creepy. My eyes dilated, and I stared straight into his eyes of death and evil. With cold fingers I clutched the sleeve of my flimsy jacket.

I swallowed hard and tried to turn away, but his eyes were locked on mine. He didn't turn his head but shrieked to a convict behind another window, "Hey, Psycho, number three there with the fine booty is mine." Psycho disputed the claim, and the two argued over this man as if he were a piece of flesh. I was fifth in the formation and checked to see who was third. My heart skipped a beat and sank into my gut. It was the handsome young man who had talked so much on the bus.

I continued staring at the evil man, as if mesmerized. In the back of my mind I felt sorry for the inmate they lusted for and wanted to help him, but there was nothing I could say or do. Phlegm choked up guilt that stuck in my throat. I couldn't speak. It shamed me that I didn't offer some comfort to the kid, but it disgraced me more that I was thankful to be number five in line, not number three.

The creaky gate finally opened and the officers ushered us into hell. Flesh trafficking continued as a guard led three of us down the catwalk fronting A-Wing. As we passed each cell along the catwalk, I tried to avoid looking at the men bidding for our bodies but couldn't help it. Like the man at the window, their lust-filled eyes were dark and threatening. The uproar rolled like a wave from cell to cell as we passed on the narrow passageway. The insanity of it all infuriated me. These men were transformed into beasts of prey, and the officers did nothing to quiet them. I felt alone, hopeless and unprotected. Faces of my hostages flashed into my tormented mind. I wanted to run away or die, and I couldn't do either. A violent pounding in my head told me my mind would explode, that I'd go crazy.

Finally, we arrived at the fourth cell. For me the horrific parade ended, and I was checked in by the officer. He raised the paper in his hand and read the number on my jacket. He matched it with a number and name on the list he held. "Gimme your name and last four," he said.

I hesitated.

He glared at me. "Get used to it!" he snapped. "Gimme your last name and last four digits of your number!"

I swallowed hard and looked down at my number and muttered, "My name is Kenneth Cooper and my number is . . ."

"Last name! Last name!"

I swallowed and began again. "Ah, Coo-Cooper."

"And . . . ?"

I was stupefied.

"Your last four."

I glanced down at the upside-down numbers again and inverted them. "Seven-eight-six-eight."

The officer rubbed his chin and eyed me closer. "You're gonna learn that number by heart," he said, and then motioned to the barred cell. "This is A-four." His hand swept toward the open barred door. "In here, seven-eight-six-eight." He guided me through the open door and pointed toward the bed on the wall to my immediate left. "You're One-A, top bunk, Cooper." He motioned to it and stepped out of the cell to go on with the other men.

The man on the bottom bunk didn't lift his eyes to look my way as I approached. Something was wrong, very wrong. I perked up as adrenaline surged into my blood. But that body reaction confused me, since the men in this unit were subdued. Even so, I felt something was not right in this quiet cell.

Like a wary dog, my eye darted here and there, then to my

bed. The man on the lower bunk continued to hold his head down, staring at a gray blanket.

Only two of the six men in the cell sat on their cots with their heads up. They were both glaring at me with sardonic smiles. Finally, one of the men said, "Welcome to paradise." Of the two, he appeared to be the more cunning. Yet, they both came across as venomous snakes.

Evidently he was the cell boss. I nodded but didn't say a word as I put my shoe box on the thin pinstripe mattress.

The other man cursed and boasted, "You found a good crib, dude, if you keep the code."

I nodded. He was talking about the "see no evil, speak no evil" convict code I abided by in jail. I held strong eye contact with him as I spoke. "No problem."

"That's my man," the cell boss chuckled.

The other four men in the grungy cell still hadn't raised their heads. They appeared to be totally dominated by the cell boss and his hit man. That gave me the creeps. I feared a repeat of the Lion's Den. As though I wasn't shaken, I spread out the folded sheet and tried to concentrate on getting my bunk made before I did anything else.

As my trembling fingers worked, two loud blasts from a steam whistle filled my head from somewhere beyond the walls, sounding the signal for chow call. The men all jumped up at once and filed out of the cell. I followed them to the dining area and got in line. It was my first day, so I tagged behind the man in front of me and picked up a plastic spoon and a stainless steel tray. I held it out as it was filled with food pushed at me by convicts behind a steam counter.

Hunger escaped me. Dried black-eyed peas, overcooked brown cabbage, a hunk of some kind of grease-laden meat, canned peaches, and a piece of crumbled cornbread repulsed me. But I took the tray, picked up a plastic spoon, a bit of toilet paper for a napkin and followed three cell mates to a circular metal table with four connected steel seats.

Looking directly across the steel table, I studied the man sitting there. His face was pleasant despite deep pockmarks, the kind caused by severe acne. He must have felt my eyes and looked up. When he spoke, his tone was deep, and his dark brown eyes sparkled. "My name's Luke," he said, offering a warm firm hand that felt good in mine. "Dining out with us today?" He gave me the first real smile I'd seen since entering the Rock.

I surprised myself and laughed. Tension drained from my body, and I relaxed. Luke seemed like a normal human being. He even displayed a sense of humor. He used his given name instead of the family name sewn on his uniform. I was intrigued, and had discovered that using the name displayed by the state or using a nickname was the convict way, yet this man belied the norm.

"My name's Ken. The tab's on me." The men snickered. I reached for the salt and pepper in an attempt to eat the awful-looking mess. About the fourth bite I realized I forgot to say grace before I put the first spoonful in my mouth. It bothered me, but I got busy gawking at men all around me sucking up their chow like animals. Since my commitment to live as a Christian, I was careful to always bless the mess set before me. No one at the table said grace, and it seemed like a race was on to see who could eat the fastest. I smiled as I scanned my tray. The food really didn't look good, and it needed God's blessing in order to be eaten.

Luke said, "The goons won't give us long, and we're not supposed to talk, but I'll keep it low while we eat. Those are two bad dudes who run A-four. Rufe, the cell boss, and

Malo are serial killers. They're madmen who'd enjoy killing again, so be careful."

I stopped chewing the awful-tasting stuff in my mouth. This was another Lion's Den. Fear shot a mixture of disgust and anger into my blood and the spoon dropped from my fingers into the black-eyed peas. I wanted to shout out the rage welling up in my throat, but I swallowed hard and didn't say a word.

Luke stared at the spoon in the black-eyed peas. He tilted his face and grinned. "Don't worry; you'll do okay in A-four as long as you let them play God and don't snitch anyone out." He continued. "They're not into the sex stuff, but you gotta watch yourself in the common showers."

I picked up my spoon, wiped the handle with the "napkin" and said, "Explain." My voice carried a higher pitch than usual.

"You've probably been bought by some sex maniac, and he expects to get to know you in the shower tonight." He smiled as if he enjoyed the thought.

I shuddered again. "Is it anyone in our cell?"

"Man, don't ask me a question like that. Remember the code. I can't talk to you about it—I've already said too much."

I hated the situation and didn't care much for Luke either. He was undoubtedly a stoolie of the cell boss, and he hadn't made me feel any better about my chances of survival. Either that, or Luke didn't really know who had bought me. I could see myself in the shower, nude, barefooted, and for all practical purposes helpless against one of the huge sex perverts. They would probably have two or three men against me. As I choked on a chunk of mystery meat, I made a silent vow. They would have to overpower me to take anything they wanted. I wasn't about to give in to threats; I'd die first.

Another man from the cell, a tall gaunt guy sitting across from me, broke into my thoughts.

"I've been here three weeks, and I'm still not gonna shower. There ain't no way."

I gawked at him.

"I'll keep taking my birdbaths, but I'm not taking a shower tonight or any other night. I don't like them anyway."

A mixture of scorn and condescension filtered into my mind. I couldn't stand him and his body odor. I hated myself as much as I hated his putrid stench since I could blame no one but myself for landing in this hellhole with him. His smell wafted into my nostrils. I turned my head, and I knew I had to take a shower. I needed to wash the filth off—and flush the fear out—or I would become like the cowards and depraved animals surrounding me.

An officer came over and ordered us to move on and give our table up to the next four inmates. We left the chow hall. I hadn't finished but tagged along behind my cell mates, who dumped their trays and headed out toward what they called the Rock Yard.

As I stepped outside the building, I felt better, even though the recreation area was surrounded by razor wire with armed guards at each corner. A number of men were lifting weights, others pitched horseshoes, while some played softball or basketball. They were enjoying themselves.

That realization, along with the fresh air and scrap of freedom, loosened me up, and I felt an urge to play some hoops. For a moment I could smell the bluegrass of Kentucky, where basketball is king, but recalling my home state and playing hoops there wasn't enough to make me join them. I was distracted by the scent of sweaty bodies and disturbing images of the shower room, where I would probably face the man who bought me. But face him I would in the common showers like a man. However, just how I would approach it wasn't clear to me.

The only thing I knew for certain was that I needed a well-thought-out plan. I remembered the challenge of planning and pulling off bank robberies. The mental picture amused me until I got serious with myself and muttered, "What are you smiling about, Coop? This is life and death."

A whistle blew, and everyone rushed inside. I hated to leave the fresh air.

Back in the cell, during the first count of the evening, I prayed about my plan to shower, and figured out a strategy. I'd heard there were never enough showerheads for the number of men, so, I'd race to the bathroom the moment count cleared to try to get there ahead of the crowd. In the mix of naked flesh, I'd pick out the biggest, meanest man in the shower and ask if I could share his water. I'd be very careful to not drop my soap.

The moment count cleared, to the surprise of my cell mates, I stripped to my boxer shorts, grabbed my bar of lye soap and towel and left the cell block ahead of everyone. My senses were at high alert. There were no guards in the hallways, and I felt a rush as I took off my boxers. I hung them on a peg on the wall outside the bathroom and eased to the steam-filled doorway. I hesitated there for an instant. Again, no guards were in sight.

The place was wide open with six showerheads and eleven men taking turns soaping up and rinsing off. Just as I pictured it, the biggest, meanest-looking hombre was showering all alone. I felt my muscles relax as I saw no apparent sexual activity. However, when I moved toward my mark, one slimy-looking con about my size eyed me up and down.

"Hey, c'mon over here. We got something for ya," the guy sharing the water with him jeered.

I felt utter contempt rather than fear. They looked like sniveling dogs, so contempt seemed right for them. But I tried not to show it. Instead, I ignored them and the twitch in my left leg as my mind pushed a reluctant body toward the huge man.

Though shaking, I stepped up beside the unsuspecting hulk. "Share your water, homey?"

It surprised me to hear the word *homey* come out of my mouth since it wasn't part of my plan. It wasn't a term I had gotten used to yet, though I knew it was short for *hometown boy*.

He may have been shocked too, but he smiled. "No problem, dog." He eased to the side to turn the water over to me.

The man who'd hit on me a few seconds earlier leered at us. His imagination was getting the best of him. In a weird kind of way I was glad.

The big guy watched me take a little water and lather up. In a moment he said, "You came in from Tampa today. That was my crib a long time ago."

This was unbelievable. I happened to hit a true homeboy. God was watching over me, and I responded with a smile. "Yeah, I came in from there," I said, stepping into the water to rinse.

"I know 'bout you," the big man growled. "I heard the freaks on D-Wing welcome you new guys."

I was still worried, but it appeared he didn't like the sex

merchants. A deep sigh came from my inner being and drained the tension from my neck and back. My experience at the Lion's Den was fresh in my mind, but I was afraid to mention it.

In an attempt to get acquainted, I looked up through the waterfall into his face. "You must be a great rebounder playing hoops. What are you, six-six?"

"Yeah, you guessed it. I get my share off the boards, but I don't like that tackle crap they play on the yard."

It sounded like laughter in his voice as he pictured the rough game the convicts played. It was nothing like the "no-contact" sport of basketball.

His laughter and the easy manner with which we talked eased me off more and made me think I'd connected with another real human being. "I'll team up with you. I'm a gunner from Kentucky. You get the boards, and I'll do the outside shooting." I stepped out of the water. "What do you say?"

"Yeah, sure." He shrugged. "What they call you?"

I grabbed my towel. "Ninety-nine." I toweled off.

"What's that for?"

"Too many years for too many armed bank robberies." I turned away. "I'll see ya 'round." I smiled, "Round, as in b-ball, homey."

He nodded and grinned. "Right."

What I called the joy juices were flowing, I literally skipped back to the cell. I'd pulled it off. When I traipsed back into the cell, my face must have been beaming.

Malo lifted an eyebrow as he appraised me and asked, "How'd ya do in the shower?"

"No problem. I shared water with a homeboy from Tampa. Guy runs six-six."

"Big Lifer?" Malo grunted. "You gotta be one lucky dude. You know it wasn't supposed to go down like that."

I shrugged. "They call me Ken *Lucky* 'cause I'm from Kentucky." I laughed.

Malo wasn't amused.

I checked him out. "How was it supposed to go down?"

"A muscle-bound homo they call Bear bought you."

The news hit me hard, and I died for an instant. Then I managed a smile as I raised an index finger toward heaven. Silently I gave thanks to God for what He had done because this Bear character wasn't in the shower when I had gotten there early. Who but God could have arranged for me to step into the water with a monster from Tampa who accepted me as a homeboy and hated the sex traders?

As I said my prayers my first night in prison, I thanked God for His goodness and asked Him to protect me through the night and to protect me from all my enemies.

18

It turned out that I was personal enemy number one. The second day in prison when I received a call out I had no idea of the battle that lay ahead. On the way to Mrs. Joseph's office, prickly sensations ran all over me. I was going to be assigned a job on my second day in the joint. For most inmates it took a week or two. That would spare me being locked up in a place I called hell.

I could hardly keep from jogging out the Rock gate facing the administration building where Mrs. Joseph worked. Was I ever in for a letdown.

Mrs. Joseph indeed assigned me to a job, but also gave me cage-rattling news. I was so eager to go to work it was hard for me to sit down. From behind her desk, she peered at me over her silver-rimmed glasses. "All able-bodied men have to work. Your file shows you have reading and writing skills that could be useful here at UCI."

"I love to read and write," I said, resisting the urge to sell her on my abilities.

She seemed to be in a hurry or frustrated. "I'm assigning

you to work as a teacher's aide at the school where you will teach men how to do just that. You'll be teaching the basic GED class."

"I'm delighted. I've always thought it would be fun to teach. And going to work will get me out of the Rock, anyway."

Mrs. Joseph smiled. "You're assigned to Mrs. Benton. You'll go down to the education building to work six hours a day in her classroom, beginning July 14 at 9 a.m."

"July 14? Did you say July 14? That's over a month away."

"Yes, I don't like it either, but an order came down that you are confined to your cell except for chow hall and a shower until that day."

"Mrs. Joseph, that's impossible!"

She glared at me over her glasses. "What do you mean by that?"

My hands trembled so I put them between my legs and squeezed them. "I don't mean any disrespect, but if you remember, the other day when I came into prison, I didn't check into solitary confinement because I can't stand to be locked up in close dark places."

Her eyes narrowed.

"I understand my violent crimes and ninety-nine-year sentence branded me as a rabbit, but I promise you I'm not an escape risk. Please don't let them do this to me."

Mrs. Joseph stood up. I knew the conference had ended.

I jumped up too quickly and stuttered when I asked, "Tell me again when I go to work."

"July 14."

"Thank you."

As I sidled out the door I remembered saying the same two words to the judge when he slapped me with a life sentence. *No wonder they call me Mr. Polite.*

I tried to keep my head up but couldn't do it. It seemed to me that my slumping shoulders drew my head down between my shoulder blades. A dark cloud covered me, and I moved like a coal miner with a worn-out body. I had to drag my body back to the Rock.

Returning to the dark cell, I remembered my dad working in the darkness of a coal mine and wondered how he could stand it day after day.

He had taken me down in a mine shaft one time and convinced me that I did not want to work in that kind of darkness. All he had to do to persuade me was turn off the carbide light on his cap. Instantly I was engulfed in total darkness. It terrified me that I could not even see my hand an inch in front of my eyes.

Dad, if you can't come down here from heaven to turn the light on for me like you did in the mine, please send someone to do it.

Agitated, I jumped up and paced back and forth in front of the bars facing the catwalk. A face flashed before me and seemed to dance in between the bars. I slammed my hands onto the bars and grabbed hold. It was the redheaded classification officer who had sent me to the Rock. I gripped the bars. My knuckles turned white as her words echoed in my mind, "Mr. Bank Robber who took hostages, I'm sending you to the Rock. And that is where you deserve to be."

I know this is where I deserve to be, redheaded classification officer, but please, God, don't let her keep me in this dark hole until I suffocate and kick the bucket.

The more I paced, the more paranoid I became.

She did this to me, too! She's got me under her thumb, and she wants to crush me like a bug. God, You know I can't stand this.

Picturing my body under her huge thumb made me laugh an eerie kind of laughter that caused the man who talked to me in the chow hall the previous day to turn from the TV and stare at me.

As if on automatic pilot I slumped down on the bed and turned my back to him.

I missed chow that evening and slept till the wee hours of the morning. That's how my third day began and ended—on my bunk, getting off only when nature's call forced it. A deep depression caused me to withdraw into my own world. I could not bear to open my eyes and face the horrifying claustrophobia. The fear of being closed in that grungy, smelly hellhole for a month handcuffed and shackled me just as surely as if a prison guard had done it. I loathed myself and the men locked up with me, convinced that they were the scum of the earth.

The second, third and fourth days I refused to go to chow, although that was a way out of the cell. No one seemed to notice, and no one seemed to care. That suited me just fine. I was glad that they kept to themselves and did not approach me. All five of them left the cell and stayed out all day except for the eleven and four o'clock count times. The solitude helped me escape into myself.

Afraid the cell mates might turn me in to the shrinks, who would zap me some kind of medicine to lift the gloom, I propped myself up on the bed when they were around and escaped into Louis L'Amour Westerns or wrote poems about everything from clouds to rain to trees to birds and bees, to rivers and oceans. Never in my life had the words come so easily and naturally. In a strange way, it amused me that the creative flow was springing from the despair caused by deprivation. As I visualized the things of earth that I feared

I would never see again, the hues and tints, the light and shadows were crystal clear and more real than in life.

On the fifth day, I came out of my shell enough to consider life around me, but still would not interact with my cell mates. I reached out to Dr. Robert Schuller's *Daily Power Thoughts*. It had changed my life before and was right there in the shoe box that contained my worldly goods, but in my depressed state of mind it had repulsed me. It was about God and spiritual things, and I wanted no part of it.

Picking it up and debating whether to open it, I talked to myself out loud. Grasping the book and holding it up toward the ceiling, I said, "Robert Schuller, you have never been locked up in your life so you don't know a thing about power thoughts that could help this powerless scumbag hostage taker." Placing the book back in the shoe box, I began carrying on deeper conversations within my head. I knew it was insane but I seemed driven to escape, and that was an acceptable way to do it.

By the sixth or seventh evening, days and nights were all the same, and I had no idea of the day of the week much less the date of the month. When my solitude was interrupted by count time, I wasn't able to deal with reality. The officer came by our cell for the final after-lights-out bed check. Every man responded with his department of corrections ID number, punctuated by, "Sir!" When the officer stood beside my bunk and looked at me, in my mind, I focused on the trouble I'd had the first day calling out my number. In a fog, I shouted, "Zero-eight-seven-eight-six-eight, Sir!" The officer scowled, looked down at his record and barked, "Convict Cooper, you are a zero, but there is no zero in your number."

I was dumbfounded.

"Get this straight, Egg Head, your number is Oh-eight-seven-eight-six-eight. Got it Cooper?"

"Yes, sir, Oh-eight-seven-eight-six-eight, Cooper!"

His face turned red. "I should write you up for verbal disrespect and ship you to the Flat Top. You're one of those smart types who thinks he's better than everyone else, but you are one big zero to me."

My flesh crawled. The Flat Top was a sixty-year-old ruin that served as a jail within the prison. "It won't happen again, sir!"

The officer smirked, but went on to the next cell on A-Wing.

I returned to my inner discussion. Perhaps I wasn't any saner than the rest. My being in the Rock put me in contact with all kinds of dangerous, deranged convicts. Fear had been the driving force in my life. Perhaps throughout my life it had kept me sane. Now fear was under control while I was locked down from open population. Maybe I was missing the old adrenaline rush I had always gotten from living on the edge in the outside world.

This thought launched me into a conversation between me and myself about whether I was bonkers or not. Actually, the strange running dialogue was becoming somewhat entertaining. Still, the underlying issue was a serious one. Believing God was somehow behind my lockdown, I felt abandoned by Him and told Him I would not talk to Him until He told me why I was locked up like a caged animal.

Mind You, I'm not talking to You, God, but if I were I'd ask You to at least let me get out of this cage for recreation once a week or so. But You are not listening, so that means my problems are mental, not spiritual.

My bunk partner made a weird noise below me and I came

out of myself. Once my eyes adapted, I focused on Rufe and Malo playing chess with Rufe's red and black chess set. I thought of Baltimore challenging me in the Lion's Den but strained to hear what moves they were whispering back and forth from bed to bed as count time continued. Rufe played the red pieces and Malo the black, meaning Rufe moved first and usually won. That went against my grain.

The officer's voice echoed from somewhere on the cell block as he called out a name and recorded the convict's number. The sound of authority grew faint.

As I stared at Rufe and Malo, I realized what they were doing was typical of them and most inmates like them. They tuned everyone out. To them no one was worth a cup of spit. They only heard each other out of mutual disrespect for everyone else.

But what about you, Coop? How is your life different from theirs? Fear of dying is not the problem. You are already dead.

I don't feel alive at all, but I should. My mind and my body are functioning. Maybe faith in God is enough to live on here, but I doubt it.

I held my hands up, turned them over and studied the length of my lifeline. It showed that I should live to at least ninety-nine years. I grinned.

Perhaps I am afraid of death. Perhaps I am losing my faith and slipping back into my old addictive, self-centered ways.

At that point my mental conversation with myself had apparently gotten too loud. Rufe glared at me from across the cell, so I withdrew into deep thought and near inaudible muttering. My lips barely moved.

I believe fear has kept me from totally cracking up. The

more I force myself to do death-defying things that turn on the adrenaline flow, the better I feel. It may be crazy but it sure makes sense to me.

I stretched my head out enough to catch a glimpse of the guy below me. Though no one seemed to talk to him, I had heard them call him Flip, as in "flipped out."

I'd rather talk to Flipper about my problems than Flip.

I grinned at my childish play on words about the television series named for a dolphin called Flipper, but I worried that I might indeed be flipping out like him.

Maybe Flipper will come and save me; no one else will.

I hated myself. To feel better, I peered up over the edge of the bed toward my bunk partner and regretted that I had never tried to carry on a conversation with him. I grunted a greeting in passing but had no desire to get to know him. I wondered why.

By the seventh day, I smelled like Lurch and that may have been the reason I decided to get up, take a shower after count and go to breakfast.

I followed a cell mate to the eating table. He seemed glad to see me. "Ninety-nine, it has taken a lot of discipline for me to leave you alone. What gives with you, man?'

"I've been depressed, and still am."

"Well, these rubber eggs and lumpy grits are not going to cheer you up."

For the first time in a week I smiled. And with the smile came a desire to eat. When a few bites had been swallowed, I had a burning desire to find out about my bunk mate.

To be polite, I asked, "Er, what was your name again?"

"Luke; my dad is a preacher man, and preacher men name their kids things like that."

"I'm sorry, Luke."

He laughed, as did the strange-looking little man seated with us who was shoveling in food like he was starving. When he opened his mouth, instead of teeth, all I saw was a gaping hole filled with eggs. My stomach lining grabbed and wanted to eject the stuff I'd swallowed, but I managed to keep it down.

"By the way, this is Moe," Luke said, motioning toward our breakfast mate. He was as grungy and unkempt as the room where we stayed. It bothered me that he didn't look up when Luke introduced us. He was fiddling with the grits and eggs on his plate, raking the mess around as if he were looking for bugs or something. I figured they were there but hoped he didn't find any.

Finally, I spoke to him, "Hi, Moe, you can call me Ninety-nine."

"You ain't that old, is you?" he retorted.

I laughed again and washed my mouth out with coffee.

"Hey, guys, what's up with the guy you call Flip?"

Luke answered, "Like you have been doing, Flip rarely talks to anyone."

"Boy, you stuck me with that zinger."

"I didn't mean to, but I don't want you to take the next step."

I reluctantly asked what that was.

"Flip seldom talks to anyone besides the voices only he hears. He told me his advisors speak to him from the Book of Revelation."

I looked at Moe. He was still playing with his food.

"They tell him that God has appointed him to serve as one of His two witnesses preaching Christ's return to earth."

That remark got a rise out of Moe. "Flip is one of a dozen 'preachers' who spout their own versions of the Gospel to an unseen audience. No one pays any attention to the self-appointed prophets."

I was amazed by how well Moe expressed himself and by what he said. Luke chimed in. "Most of the convicts steer clear of the crackpots."

I hope these guys can't read my mind. I might be on the edge of becoming a nut like him.

An officer rescued me. He stopped at our table and told us to move on. Like little boys who had been scolded, we grabbed our trays and scurried back to our assigned areas.

Following that encounter with two of the five human beings in my "house," a need to bare my soul to somebody, anybody, arose in my gut. As far as my cell mates were concerned, the prospects seemed more promising. Luke appeared to be a stand-up son of a preacher man, and Moe, to my amazement, talked like a schoolteacher.

I repented then and there of my arrogance. *Father, please forgive me for my attitude toward my cell mates. But Lord, You'll have to admit that they are quite a mess. Luke, his sidekick, Moe, and Lurch are like pawns in the hands of the cell boss, subjects of King Rufe. I'm sorry I've thought of them as a pathetic bunch that disgust me.*

I thought back through my confession and smiled.

Lord, that wasn't very good, I know, but they really do disgust me. Then, maybe I disgust them, too.

Fumbling with my Robert Schuller devotional booklet, I said, *If I can't talk to them or to myself, I'll have to talk to Schuller. He may not understand my plight, but he's not crazy.*

I placed the book at the foot of the bed and stared at the back cover. Through his daily "power thoughts," Robert Schuller had patched me up during many low moments in jail and on my way into prison.

In that moment I regretted that I had not read his booklet for weeks. When I was into its daily lessons, it seemed as though the little book was written for me. Time after time, the theme for the week and the topic for the day were aimed directly at me and my situation.

What had possessed me? How could I turn my back on Schuller?

I grabbed the book and focused on the back cover, where Jeremiah 29:11 popped off the page: "For I know the thoughts that I think toward you, saith the Lord, thoughts of peace, and not of evil, to give you an expected end."

I looked toward the ceiling and asked God, "*What's with these thoughts of peace? Don't You understand? I've got ninety-nine years. I'm locked down for thirty days, and I'm surrounded by evil with no future and no hope. What's this expected end You're talking about, God?*"

God did not answer me, so I glanced back at the book and talked to it.

Little book, I hope Dr. Schuller won't mind me just calling you "Schuller," but you're all I've got.

I opened the book.

So, why don't you help me now, Schuller? Talk to me.

A glimmer of hope rose inside, and I turned the pages to the lesson for the day. It was the twenty-fourth day of June. I couldn't believe *that* was the date on the page. It was Becky's birthday.

"Schuller," I mumbled, "I've become so disoriented I can't even remember my daughter's birthday." I broke down as I thought about Becky and Jennie. I felt like I was separated from them and in hell forever. I had no visits from the outside, and more than ever I wanted to see Becky.

I refocused on Schuller and strained to read the small print through teary eyes. The day's devotion was entitled "God Cares."

The words were meant for me. God was reminding me that He loved me and had not forsaken me because Jesus gave His life for me. I thought about Jennie. When she got pregnant, she would not allow the doctors to abort the fetus, and she ultimately died sooner due to the pregnancy. Jennie loved Becky enough to give her child life at the cost of her own.

I wept silently and asked God to give me her kind of love—*His* kind of love. In that moment of faith and devotion, the thought occurred to me that I should start the process of love with my neighbors. I needed to stop judging them and love them as I loved myself.

Almost as though Schuller spoke back, an inner voice interrupted, "Do you truly 'love yourself'?"

I ignored it and refocused on my cell mates, certainly the closest people on earth to me. *God wants me to love these guys? I look down on them, and that makes it difficult to see them as my neighbors.*

That question made me wonder: Had God locked me up in A-four for thirty days and withheld His close fellowship from me to force me to look at these pathetic excuses for men in a new way? I was to love them, maybe even give my life for them. I dismissed that radical thought, figuring it might be dangerous to try such an experiment in that deadly place. Besides, I told myself, to love means to relate, and in my cell there was no basis for relationships.

Well, at chow a while ago, it seemed that maybe we could carry on a decent conversation. But Schuller, in my mind we are seven subhuman islands, and even Flipper can't save us.

19

At noon, the day I got out of lockdown, Luke was in the chow line ahead of me. I was dead last, near the only door opening into the dining area, so he spoke to me over his shoulder. "Watch your back. Keep your eyes open for Bear, Ninety-nine. They say he bought his rights to you last month from a creep named Psycho."

"I'm not worried," I said, lying. I remembered Psycho staring me down when I first entered the Rock.

Luke turned his head to the side. "Just take my advice and keep on guard."

"Why? You hear something I don't know?" I whispered.

He didn't turn to look at me but gave a shrug. I heard him say, "He's sneaky. Just watch yourself in the dark hallways around here."

The line was slow moving and my mind drifted to picture the dark places within the prison. There were a number of recesses in the concrete and steel that afforded the opportunity for a man to be jumped. I focused on silent prayer.

Suddenly I sensed that someone was standing behind me in the line, and a gravely voice growled into the back of my neck, "You're mine, fresh fish. I bought ya, and you are mine."

A whimper came out of me so that I sounded like some of my hostages—terrified. Luke and other men spun around. Most of them glared past me. His graveled threat sent shock waves down my spine. The hair on my neck stood up. Luke's eyes reflected fear. Stunned beyond any fear I'd ever experienced, I couldn't move.

When I didn't turn around, the rough voice whispered in my ear. "You can run, Ninety-nine, but you can't hide. Kenneth Leon Cooper's the name, isn't it?" He laughed. "Ya see, I gotcha cold."

My animal impulse was to whirl around and attack, or at least to demand how he knew my full name, but to my shame I still couldn't move. I stood there like a petrified mummy. The fear masking Luke's face didn't help, but then something in his expression softened, and it encouraged me to turn around and confront my assailant.

When I did, I found that Bear was gone, and I was nose to nose with a harmless-looking skinny fellow with a sheepish grin. After jerking a furious glance over my shoulder at Luke, my eyes darted to the grins of others. I had missed my opportunity to confront this Bear man, who now took on the character of a ghost. He was slick, disappearing out the door before I got a look at him. I stood there humiliated and outraged before my angered gaze fell on the silent man's face. He gave me a pitiful shrug.

"Did you see who did that?" I snapped.

"Did what?" His hands were open and his brow wrinkled.

"Came up behind me. I thought I was last in line."

"I'm last," he said.

I threw my hands up at the typical convict response, wheeled around to resume my place in line and seethed. My heart raced when I spoke to Luke through my teeth. "You were right. This dude's out to get me."

He chided, "I warned you."

After staring at the back of his head for a moment or two, I calmed down and muttered, "I sure would like to know what he looks like."

The man behind me chimed in. "Don't worry. You'll get your chance. He's big enough, stands about six-foot-six and over two fifty, so you won't miss him."

The next day I was heading for my cell when a giant of a convict jumped from around a corner and confronted me, "Ninety-nine, what size shoes you wear?"

I recognized the gravel voice; it was Bear. His huge body loomed over me and I took a step back. He was a dark-skinned black man about midtwenties, burly, an intimidating hulk a head taller than me. A frightening, leering sneer stretched a scar from the base of his nose to his right eye.

At that moment a weird thing happened. In his face I saw the faces of my friends he had raped. A loathing hatred flamed up in my belly, fired energy through my trembling body and supercharged it for action. The animal in me was set to fight to the death or flee.

To Bear I must have looked like a terrified rabbit. A roar of derisive laughter erupted from his huge mouth, and in between gasps, he repeated, "What . . . size shoes . . . do you . . . wear, Ninety-nine?"

"They're too small for you, Bear," I managed to say with a squeak.

He was apparently entertained by my answer and laughed all the more.

Somehow his bizarre laughter chased enough of the fear from my body for me to ask, "You *are* Bear, aren't you?"

"That's what they call me." His upper lip softened into a smirk as he glanced down at my shoes. "It don't matter what size they are, I still want them. If they're too small, I'll cut the backs out of them." He grinned, wheeled around and disappeared around the corner.

I swallowed hard and rubbed sweaty palms on my blue-clad thighs. My body was still trembling and my breath coming in short gasps. I stood there in the hallway talking to myself. *What am I going to do when he comes for me? His dark face and hands will be hard to see in the shadowed corridors, and there are so many places where he can attack without warning. He is sure to stalk me and attack. I can't ward off a sex-crazed hulk like Bear, even if he comes for me in broad daylight. Should I get a backup? Who can I trust with my life? And terrified or not, should I even consider going for help?*

I looked at my hands, and gripped them into fists. My body wanted to fight, but my mind told me I had to find another way. Looking for someone who would lend a hand might be the best way. At that moment it flashed into my mind to go to God. *Should I ask Him for help?*

I threw my hands up and said, "I don't think so."

On the way back to my cell, I considered seeking someone to watch my back. To most convicts, to ask for help was a sign of weakness. One way or another, they took advantage of men who couldn't fend for themselves.

That night, on the way to the shower, at the sound of heavy footsteps behind me my heart skipped a beat. Was

Bear about ready to pounce? In the shower I expected him to rise up out of the steam. He didn't show. Still wound up when I went to bed, I couldn't sleep and resolved to get help from some of my friends, whether it made me a target for other predators or not.

Following a basketball game the next day, I told the players on my team about the rapist's threats. They gathered around me and seemed genuine in their concern for me, but their ideas of help set off an alarm in my gut. One of them said, "Ninety-nine, you need a weapon. Next time you think you're gonna be confronted by this slime ball, go to my bunk, reach under the foot and you'll feel the handle of my shank. The point's stuck in between the steel sections. Pull it out and use it first—before he uses his on you." Other men in the little group agreed and encouraged me to take the offer.

A Christian brother named Matt suggested that I ask God to come to my rescue.

I winced. Somehow when I heard his advice I knew he spoke the truth, and the answer to my plight was obvious. I must go to God for help.

I placed a hand on Matt's shoulder and turned to my teammates. "I appreciate your suggestions, but that was my old way. My brother here has reminded me that if I have faith in God to protect me, then I must believe He's big enough to do it His way, whatever that is."

The men looked at me like I was crazy, shook their heads and backed away. Several muttered, "His way," but didn't hang around long enough to ask me what His way was. They said I was daft, and even those who were Christians acted like I was stupid not to defend myself. I wasn't at all sure they weren't right. I had no clear notion of what His way was and no idea how God would handle this kind of problem. I wondered if angels would come to my rescue as they had in the Lion's Den. I hoped God was near enough to read my thoughts and intervene.

One afternoon, a few days into my work experience, I was escorted back to the main housing unit and told at the gate to return to my cell. As I turned a corner and drew close to a shadowed area, Bear lunged out of the darkness.

I froze. A foot-long, double-edged, prison-made sword flashed in a single shaft of light. He gripped it tight and hissed, "I'm gonna take your shoes and rape you. It'll be just this easy." Then, dancing in front of me, he sang, "You're mine any old time I choose, Ninety-nine."

Fear welled up in me but escaped from my mouth as a deep sigh. His brow creased and his hate-filled eyes pulled together.

"One day," he seethed.

I stood like a dead man.

Maybe this is the day.

Instead of focusing on the shank with which he threatened me, my eyes fastened on his demonic, muddy-black glare. And I was hoping *this* was not the day.

He emphasized it would be "one day."

Even so, I was so shaken I still couldn't say a word. He seemed even more terrifying than before, and my mind slipped gears and stalled on a side track. All I could think of was that he was a cold-blooded rapist who had sodomized two of my cell mates.

He must have read my thoughts, because he opened his mouth wide and let out a howl. "You know I'll do it to you—jus' like I did to your cellies. I'll have you when I'm good and ready." The twisted grin pulled up at one corner. "Just you wait and see. I'll get you—one day."

In a split second the big man darted into the dark passageway and was gone. But for days on end, his words slithered around in my head like a demonic snake. *One day. One day, and you're mine. Just you wait and see. I'll get you one day.*

For a full month he played with me, jumping out of the dark at unexpected times. He was like a big black cat tormenting a little gray rabbit until he got hungry enough to make the kill. Each time, mixed emotions of hate and fear rose up in me. There were times our paths openly crossed in the strange dungeon. He toyed with me, clandestinely revealing the handle of the shank, or muttering under his breath, "What size shoes you wear? I'm gonna be wearing them soon."

Sticking to the code, I didn't snitch him out to the officers. Besides, when prison staff got involved in inmate conflicts, it was dangerous for both the inmates and the guards. A crazed convict had killed Sergeant Ben Johnson a few weeks earlier, only forty steps from my cell. At least once every week, some convict killed another. Only five officers per shift were assigned guard duty over nine hundred men. All of those men were sentenced to life and beyond and so had nothing much to lose. This was the end of the line for prisoners in Florida. The exceptions were the criminally insane, who were shipped to Chattahoochee. I was determined not to go there, though at times I wondered if Bear would not drive me crazy.

After most of the encounters with him, I got down on my knees and begged God for help. "Oh, Father God," I prayed, "I don't know what to do. Lead me. Guide me. Help me do things Your way."

Bear continued to torment me, but there was no clear answer or direction from God. When I asked Him to reveal His way of handling the matter, the only instruction I heard was a quiet voice deep within me leading me to read the Bible. I didn't take Bible reading as a practical solution to my problem, but the thought persisted each time I cried out to God, so I read the Bible daily.

One day it occurred to me not to ask God to reveal His way to me but to teach me how to apply His way to my situation. I added that phrase to my prayers and tried to stay alert to see or hear His response.

Twice in one day the Lord gave me His way to apply the Bible to my bizarre situation. While I was in my cell reading Luke 10:17, a phrase caught my attention. I read the passage aloud. "Even devils are subject unto us through thy name." That helped me wonder if my battle was not with Bear but with the demons controlling him.

That evening, in chapel Bible study, Chaplain Larry Shook read from Ephesians 6:12, "For we wrestle not against flesh and blood, but against principalities, against powers, and the rulers of the darkness of this world, against spiritual wickedness in high places." That confirmed what the Bible said in Luke 10:17. I had to confront the demons in Bear in the name of the Lord Jesus.

A lightning bolt hit me. "This is God's way . . . in His name, the name of Jesus Christ." But I didn't know how in the world I could muster the courage to confront Bear's demons even in the name of Jesus Christ.

Chaplain Shook answered my question immediately. He said, "This is not a matter of flesh and blood. It is a spiritual conflict that must be dealt with through the spiritual authority of God."

I didn't know exactly what that meant, but I praised God

all the way back to my house. I sensed God with me and did not listen for footsteps behind me. For the first time in a month, I believed that when the day came He would handle Bear in a spiritual way. But still I prayed that God would be with me that day and give me His words to say.

Finally, on his chosen day, Satan's son came for me. Bear rushed me in a dark corner. Instinctively I knew the time had come. My body stiffened and a jolt of energy shot through me. I backed into a corner and braced myself, ready for the slam of his heavy body, but he stopped at arm's length. To my amazement, instead of trembling, my body was tingling with energy.

He went for his shank. It was a moment out of time. I stared straight into his eerie eyes—they were dark pools of evil—and uttered the weakest words any convict could utter. I said, "Your mother and your grandmother are praying for you."

It wasn't the blast of God's Word that I had asked for, but my predator was shocked. To me the words sounded pathetic, but Bear stood there with his weapon half-drawn appearing confused and helpless. The demons working through him must have felt the power of God in what I had said. Even though they seemed to be the weakest of words, God used them to disarm this possessed man.

It was a couple of seconds before he blurted, "How'd you know that?"

I felt the shift of power. It was not of this world, and I marveled. I stuttered but finally got my mind in gear. "I didn't know it," I admitted. "But God knows everything. He loves you and wants their prayers to be answered, and . . ."

Bear scowled, whirled around and stomped away—*in his own shoes*. That convict's "one day" threat had not come to fruition when he disappeared around the corner. My mouth hung open as I considered how God used my weak words to defeat a strong enemy. As I thought about it, I formed a new perspective about power. When God is in something—anything—then power is inherent. There is no need to shout, scream or blast out words.

This idea was an awesome awakening, giving me an understanding of His way.

A few days later we were in the same hallway when my would-be rapist seemed to forget the previous incident and said, "Hey, Ninety-nine, come on and do push-ups with me and my pal."

I couldn't believe my ears, but the calm, normal look on his face told me there was nothing to fear. He didn't know it, but I was used to doing the rigorous exercise regularly in jail and in my cell. I was trim and strong under my uniform, so I thought about joining them for the workout and the fun of competing with the man who had tormented me for a solid month.

Forgetting Bear's reputation as the "biggest, baddest man in the junkyard," I challenged him. "Let's do sets of twenty-five until you or I drop."

As soon as the words came out of my mouth, my muscles tensed up and I regretted I had spoken without praying first. I pictured myself down on the floor with that sodomist over me. It wasn't like me to put myself in such a vulnerable position without a plan. Then, despite the fear bumps on my arms, I thanked God for being with me. He would protect me and empower me, so I joined in the marathon after telling Jesus I was doing so in His name.

Bear's boy, a handsome white man about twenty-one with about one hundred eighty pounds on an athletic frame, was first, the big man took his turn second and I was third. That was the rotation as we began the workout. I wasn't warmed up but my adrenaline friend had done that for me. Nevertheless, the first set was tough. The second set was easier, but as each man took his turn it got worse. By the time we made it through the twelfth series, it was grueling, and the youth dropped out after about three hundred and fifty. He just stood around and counted after that.

Somewhere above five hundred push-ups, Bear faltered. He got to the middle of seventeen out of the required twenty-five, and his arms quivered. I knew he didn't have the power to lift his weight many more times, but I still had a couple more sets in me. He outweighed me by at least seventy pounds, so he was lifting a much heavier load. He stopped, got up and stuck out his hand. "Look Ninety-nine, I ain't gonna embarrass you by beating you today. We'll let it go. You're all right. Your shoes are too small for me anyway."

We laughed together. I shook their hands and turned to leave. But an urge to reach out to Bear stopped me.

"Bear, I hope you don't mind telling me if the rumor is true about that scar on your face."

The big man snorted, "Yes, I do mind, but I'll tell you. Ten years ago when I first landed in this hell hole, five men jumped me. My face wasn't as tough as the edge of my bunk."

He hesitated and one of his hands trembled.

I attempted to rescue him. "I'll bet they came out worse than you."

A tear formed in his eye. "Eventually they did, but I ain't gonna say any more."

He had said enough for me to know that the rumor that he had been raped as a youth was true. He was doing to others what had been done to him. As I walked away there was no bounce in my step from beating the Bear, but I thanked God for taming my predator His way.

20

Good things and good news continued to come my way. A convict hero of the faith, Chuck Colson, was coming to the prison to hold a seminar. I asked the Lord to prepare me for his coming.

I remembered Colson as the "hatchet man" for President Richard Nixon's administration. The talk around the prison was that he would have killed his own mother if Nixon had asked him to do so. He was a hero to the convicts, and I could relate to this man.

Colson was converted to Christianity during the investigation following the Watergate break-in scandal. Because of his new faith, he had told the truth, implicating himself in the criminal conspiracy to cover up the acts of others. I picked up his books *Born Again* and *Loving God* from the chapel library. Through those books, God gave me the direction I needed to bolster my faith.

Colson wrote that the crucifixion and resurrection of Jesus Christ are historical facts on which we can base our faith. This meant a lot. It chased away the doubt concerning this new way of approaching life. My situation was so extreme that I had a tough time dealing with my daily existence. Doubt created fear that I was delusional for thinking God could be right there to help me.

Colson's writing was based on facts he'd gleaned out of his fall from grace. He stressed that, through faith, he was able to find a balance between the spiritual and mental aspects of human existence. This conviction challenged me to find that balance. I dared not compare myself with such a man, but I found that, to me, my fall was just as great as his and my situation in prison much worse than what he described in his books. His writings intrigued me and gave me the desire to learn more about him and his ministry organization for jail and prison inmates, Prison Fellowship.

Shortly after returning the Colson books to the chapel library, I heard news that one of his Personal Growth Seminar weekends would be conducted in the prison in a matter of weeks. The concepts they taught would help me apply Christian faith to my daily life. The anticipation of the seminar excited me and gave me hope. I knew God was answering my prayers. This was exactly what I needed to know, and I was encouraged to let God handle my adversaries. I signed up to attend.

Colson's seminar disappointed me in that Mr. Colson did not conduct the weekend himself. But I was not disappointed with the Christian leaders he sent in his place. I could relate to them. At least they would not be out of their minds like the crackpots all around me.

The two-day session was in the chapel. It began on a happy Friday morning. Being so spiritually needy, I had looked forward to it for a long time. Filing through the chapel door with an army of men, I felt like a kid skipping into a candy store.

As the little boy in me expected, the seminar supplied the spiritual nutrition I hungered for. The Prison Fellowship teachers helped me apply Scripture in a practical way to my prison life. It was good for me socially as well. I loved mixing with the "normal" upbeat people and was encouraged by relating to them, as well as being challenged by their teaching.

Pat Bloodworth, an attractive young woman who served as my group discussion leader, caught my eye. Having been separated from direct contact with women for what seemed a lifetime, I was pleased that I could relate to her as my sister in Christ, rather than in a romantic way. This was a new experience for me and gave me hope that my old attitudes toward women had died when I was born again in jail. She was effective in drawing out the six of us in the circle, but I couldn't open up and reveal my weaknesses and flaws, especially as they related to the major theme for the seminar, the "Law of Love."

Miss Bloodworth must have snitched me out to Don Weston, coordinator of the weekend. On Saturday, during the last break between sessions, he spoke to me personally. Apparently in a hurry, he got right to the point: "Ken, the law of love will work anywhere, even in the toughest prison setting."

I looked at him like he was crazy.

He ignored my look and went on, "If you want to stay close to God, you must stay close to your neighbor."

I still didn't say anything. Maybe it was God who had snitched me out.

Placing his hand on my shoulder, he said, "You've got

to show the men in your cell block that you care about them."

My back stiffened at his authoritative manner. "Why would I want to do that?" I asked.

Don smiled. "It will help you get your mind off yourself."

Just like that he pierced my façade with the truth.

I stepped back. "I didn't want to hear that."

He seemed encouraged. "Ken, the key to the law of love is to expect nothing in return from your neighbors as you reach out to them in kindness."

Cynicism raised its head again. I laughed at him and retorted, "You're out of your mind. It'll never work. They'll take advantage of me. That's what I expect in return."

Mr. Weston nodded his head as if he understood.

This man does not understand who my "neighbors" are. He is naïve.

The good guy in me wanted to back off, but the bad guy spoke up instead, "I'm not gonna even try to demonstrate love to these cons. They'll think I'm a pervert, or at best, take advantage of me."

Don delivered a shattering, breakthrough blow with a simple question: "What have you got to lose?"

That stopped me cold. I shrugged.

He smiled at me like a father who just got the upper hand. "Listen, Ken, why don't you just give it a try?"

My lips pinched together as I considered testing the law of love. Finally I broke. "Okay, I'll give it a try." I held up a finger. "But no promises."

An hour later, when we said good-bye, he smiled. "I'll be praying for you, Ken, as you try the law of love for yourself."

He turned and left the chapel with Pat. I hated to see them go. They had challenged me in unexpected ways, and

I worried that their going would leave a void in my life that couldn't be filled in prison. But, more than that, without their support I was sure to fail when I tested the law of love in the Rock.

When I stepped into the darkness of the cell block and heard the metal door clang shut behind me, the urge to escape amplified my doubt. Then standing by my bunk, I admitted that it just wasn't in me to hype myself into believing that the law of love would work. It meant that I would have to show love to someone on my wing, if not in my cell. Then I recalled the promise I'd made to Don.

While I stood there contemplating, Rufe came up and asked sarcastically, "What has been bugging you, *zero*-eight-seven-eight-six-eight?" He eyed my number.

I was shocked. His tone was cynical and he was ridiculing me for misstating my number during count, but he had never been within five feet of me, much less spoken to me in a caring way. I wasn't sure how to respond, so I resorted to my tough guy mode.

"Why? Do you think I was bothered by something?" My old way was proven with power mongers. He was merciless with pawns like Lurch and Flip, and I certainly didn't want to show this chess master any weakness.

"You've lost your mind, Ninety-nine. You sleep all the time, and you're talking to yourself. I saw you babbling like an idiot during count the other night."

"You're half right. You called me by my nickname, but I wasn't talking to myself. I was talking to God about you." I was appalled to hear my flippant words to a man reputed to have killed convicts for much less.

The "king" turned as red as his chess pieces. He clenched both hands into fists as if I challenged him to fight.

I just stood there unable to take my words back and for some insane reason, not backing down.

"You'd better not be praying for me," he warned.

Some A-juice just kicked in; my face and neck feel prickly. "The truth is, I am intimidated by you, Rufe, but I'm more intimidated by this cell."

"Well, tell me the truth, then."

Now my arms are tingling. "I lied to you. I really wasn't praying for you. I *was* talking to myself."

"So you *are* going crazy."

My pupils have dilated, hope he doesn't notice. "I don't think so. But I am afraid of falling back into my old double personality."

"You better not do that double-life crap! You do and I'll punch the lights out on one of you guys." He threw a fist past my left ear as if striking an imaginary person and then laughed.

I laughed, too. I grabbed the imaginary head he slugged.

"There it is! You felt that. That proves you'll be on the next busload of crazies headed for Chattahoochee." He turned and marched toward his bunk.

I was confused. Rufe actually displayed *his* style of friendship. He wouldn't have agreed with my assessment, but I saw his confrontation as an act of kindness. That amused me, since Rufe did exactly what Weston had challenged me to do. He was testing the law of love God's way.

Back in the cell block, especially after lights-out, my inner struggle returned, this time in the form of fantastic nightmares. I was caught up in the same agonizing drama each night as I lived out a horror scene with my stepson.

In my dream, I could see Lee falling from the apartment building balcony and splitting his head open on the concrete below. Each time I relived this moment I saw his spirit come out of the crack in his skull and fly toward the gates of hell. I stood there watching in shock, straining to do something, yet feeling utterly helpless. Finally, I would take flight and zoom toward hell to stop him. Before I reached him to save him, I always woke up, terrified.

Guilt pressed me down as I tried to cope with the nightmares. It tormented me that each gruesome saga ended with me being stuck at the gates of hell, not knowing if Lee had been swept into its fire. I couldn't go back to sleep and feared for my sanity as the nightly agonies continued.

I worked on the problem and reasoned that, if I could discover the meaning of the nightmares, I might stop hearing the voices telling me I was losing my mind. In my desperation, I found the courage to seek help. My problems were obviously mental, but I didn't trust the psychiatrists and psychologists who worked at the prison. They sedated their patients with Thorazine, a drug used to treat schizophrenia and manic depressive illnesses. A high dosage of the drug turned their patients into babbling idiots or zombies. I saw many of them carted off to the mental prison, and I was determined not to join their ranks. But I had to get help, and rather than seeking out a staff person, I turned to my peers in A-four.

One evening when count cleared, I walked over to the commode, located right under the TV, and took care of business. Then I turned around and addressed the greater need that had been bugging me for weeks. I held my hands up to get everyone's attention. My fingers showed up as shadows at the bottom of the screen. They all had their eyes glued on the television set above my head, watching *Colombo*, our favorite detective, but with the intrusion they blinked and focused on me. I called out, "I want to pray." I pointed up to the boob tube, hoping Rufe would turn it down. Everyone frowned at me like I had flipped, especially Rufe. Gesturing toward the television was the worst thing I could have done. No one but the cell boss or his designee dared to touch the TV or say it was too loud. Cons had died for less.

Rufe jumped up and rushed toward me. I braced for the worst, but just before he reached me he turned sideways, glided by and turned the volume down in one smooth motion. He wheeled around and announced, "This man wants to pray."

I was stunned, but I managed to thank him. Then with the volume so low no one could hear the program, I asked, "Anyone want to join me in prayer at my bunk?"

They hesitated for a long moment, and then Luke and Moe raised their hands. I smiled. "C'mon," I said. They followed me to my bunk.

Before I prayed, I said, "Thanks for joining me." I took a deep breath and told them about the nightmares and the guilt I felt over Lee's accident and his vegetative state.

Luke asked, "You mean he really did fall off a building? It ain't just a dream or sumthin'?"

I nodded. "It's real. I taught him to defend himself and how to fight. During a fracas on a third-floor balcony, a guy delivered a haymaker that knocked Lee over the railing. It really happened."

I told them I learned through Chuck Colson that all men are created in God's image. "We're three-part beings. We have a body, a mind and a spirit." I gathered strength to bare my soul and said, "Guys, I have those horrible nightmares about Lee's spirit that are about to make me lose my mind."

Luke and Moe glanced at each other, and then at Flip as he sat cross-legged on his bunk.

I ignored their insinuation. "It's obvious to me that even though he's in a vegetative state his mind is in the prison of his body. But is it possible his spirit is free and outside his body? Is it possible his spirit is not in lockup like his mind is?"

"Whoa, that's spooky," Moe said. "Ninety-nine, I'm concerned about you."

Luke agreed. "You haven't been yourself lately."

I didn't know them well enough to really open up and rejected their concerns for me. "Forgive me for not being very friendly. My gut tells me God will give us the answer to this question as we pray together."

Both prayer partners agreed, so I bowed. "Father, You know I blame myself for the prison Lee is locked up in. I was instrumental in his life. When he came to me as a teenager and told me he discovered a relationship with You, I mocked him and scorned his experience. I'm sorry, Lord. Please forgive me for my depravity. Now that I know You and understand all humans are made up of body, mind and spirit, I see the probability of Lee's spirit being free." I hesitated. "If it's true that his spirit is not locked up, please let us know." At that moment a Bible reference lit up in my mind. It was Isaiah 28:18.

I raised my head and smiled at my new friends. "Fellows, our prayer is answered." I jumped over to my bunk and grabbed my Bible. I read, "And your covenant with death shall be disannulled, and your agreement with hell shall not stand; when the overflowing scourge shall pass through, then ye shall be trodden down by it."

"He's free! He's free!" I said, louder than the TV. "His body is beaten down, but his spirit is free and not in hell."

Rufe jerked a look at me and lowered the volume. He then turned both palms up.

I shared the Scripture and explained to him and the rest of the men what God said about Lee's spirit being free. As I read the rest of the passage aloud, even Rufe and Malo agreed that something supernatural had occurred.

Malo added skeptically, "If you didn't fake the whole thing; knowing the reference all along."

They all went back to watching television.

Luke, Moe and I accepted it as a miracle. We openly praised God, and I marked the date in the flyleaf of my Bible. It was July 31.

That night the voice of fear was silenced, and the voice of faith prevailed. The spirit of intimidation in A-four was broken and replaced by a spirit of peace. The law of hate was defeated by the law of love, and I treated everyone as my neighbor. Reaching out to Moe and talking with him, I discovered he was much more than a diminutive fellow with bushy eyebrows and slumping shoulders, who drank more coffee and smoked more rip tobacco than anyone else in the cell block. He loved his mother and his three children and wrote to them every week. Though he couldn't see beyond three feet, he quoted the Scripture like he had written it, and before long, joined with Luke and me in impromptu Bible studies.

We encouraged each other to live the Word of God we were learning and seven isolated "islands" began to form a united continent—a neighborhood.

21

At their request, Rufe, Malo and Flip were moved to other cells. Two Christian men, Lyle and John, along with Kenny, a youth of about twenty-one who said he didn't know God, took their bunks. All three were more than happy to be locked up at night with us in a place of peace.

Kenny's honest statement to the believers in the cell concerning his lack of faith impressed me and motivated me to get to know him. An opportune time came one day on the Rock Yard. I asked him to walk with me so we could get acquainted. As we started out I sized him up. He stood a few inches shorter than me but outweighed me by at least thirty pounds. His quick wit and brilliant blue eyes, which sparkled above his pockmarked face, reminded me of Luke.

Walking briskly around and around the trail following the curves of the fence seemed to open him up. I found that we had more in common than our given names. He was born on September tenth, and my birthday was September thirteenth. He came from a proud family of hardworking country folks like mine.

When I asked him to slow his pace, we laughed about the fact that he took the long strides of a farm boy headed for Saturday night in town.

Though we shared troubling thoughts, Kenny walked with his young head up high rather than moping along like the convicts who had given up hope.

By the third lap, I learned that, like me, he loved his mother and carried a lot of guilt for "breaking her heart and ruining her life."

When those words came out of his mouth, he dropped his head and stared at the dusty trail, "You, know, Mister Ken, I have a life sentence before me."

"You seem to be doing your time okay."

"Yeah, I grew up to be tough, but I've always had a tender spot for my mom."

"My heart goes out to you, Kenny, and to your mom. Does she come to visit?"

"She's going to when she gets things together."

"I'm glad."

"Thanks for reaching out to me, Mr. Ken."

I liked his spirit, and we immediately became friends. He seemed like a spiritual son to me when he accepted Christ into his life.

With the cell totally Christian, God became the Potter King, and each of us, as the clay, joyfully bowed to Him. Except for sporting events, the television was turned off and replaced by worship services and Bible studies. A-four turned into a neighborhood Bible school and a lighthouse for us and the cell block as we sang psalms of praise and hymns of thanksgiving.

By the end of August, darkness had fled from A-Wing and was replaced by light and peace. To our amazement, there were no more rapes in any of the six cells. Most of the fighting stopped, and except for gambling, the Dungeon was a law-abiding community. The officers in charge were as shocked as we were by the incredible revolution of the cell block. Some of them asked us to pray for them and their families.

Though it had been very painful, I thanked God for healing my mental problems His way. I was astounded by the metamorphosis. The worm in bondage was transforming into a butterfly of freedom.

On the first day of September, I was lying on my back in a grassy spot in the Rock Yard, a yellow notepad resting on my stomach. In rapture, I watched the wind puff white clouds across the blue sky. In that heavenly moment I reflected on how an invisible God was changing me His way, primarily through Don and Pat of the Colson gang.

Something at the razor wire fence caught my eye. A gloriously golden monarch butterfly had just cleared the mesh of shiny steel that held me hostage. As the butterfly neared, I grabbed a stub of a pencil out of my shirt pocket and wrote, "When you see a butterfly flutter by, think of me; I'm free." I felt as free as the winged creature. Living the law of love the Colson team taught me had set me free in prison. I put my pencil down, raised my hands and praised God, "Thank You, Heavenly Father, for making me free and shaping me into a more balanced butterfly." I was at peace with God and man and even with myself.

God's presence was so near, tears of joy flooded down my cheeks. I didn't care what others thought. I was truly broken and spilled out as God's nearness overwhelmed me. The inner voices ceased, and I stopped talking to myself and talked with Him and demonstrated kindness to my neighbors.

My peace of mind and spirit lasted for two weeks. But

then, as suddenly as the peace came, it left. All it took was one mystifying nightmare in which I was walking on a dimly lit sidewalk on a foggy night. A cloud of black sea fog rolled toward me, and out of it appeared a terrified woman. As she came closer, I could see her face of horror and her eyes full of pain. Her hands were extended toward me. She desperately needed my help. I tried to rescue her or at least to reach out and touch her to console and comfort. But before I could reach the woman, she faded into nothingness. I searched for her in the dark cloud, but she was gone.

Each night that nightmare returned, and the horror scene repeated. I woke up tormented, adrenaline flowing through my veins, and could not go back to sleep. Once more my life was a wreck, and the lack of sleep and loss of appetite threatened to cause physical and mental breakdown. I considered seeing one of the prison psychiatrists, but then a Thorazine zombie would stumble by. I couldn't bear the thought of becoming like that.

Fearing a mental collapse, I forced myself to bring up my problem in a Bible study around Moe's bunk. Though none of my cell mates could tell me the meaning of the nightmare, Luke immediately responded. "Hey, Ninety-nine, you're getting too far out. You gotta keep your feet on the ground."

I flinched. The nightmares were driving me mad, and I needed help. But my new friends seemed indifferent.

I persisted. "This thing is driving me out of my gourd. Can't you offer a little help?"

Moe cut me off, "Listen, Ninety-nine. We can't decipher your dream." Then he gave Luke a sideways glance. "But maybe we know a man who has that gift."

"Yeah," Luke added.

I felt better. It appeared they were going to steer me to someone who could really help me. "Who?"

"You won't go see him," Moe responded.

"Sure, I will. Just tell me who it is."

"Flip," Moe announced.

It took a moment for me to consider it, and then I chuckled. I thought about Flip and said, "You're right. I'm not about to lower myself . . ." I caught the final words before they escaped. I sensed that even this joke might be God's way.

When they heard my condescending words and tone, their silence and the looks on their faces told me the truth. I thought I was too good to see Flip. That startled me. I should have remembered my time in jail, when God used the man everyone called "Crazy Charles." I felt utterly ashamed. I couldn't take back what I had said, so everyone got a look into my heart. I was sorry and wanted to recant, but it was too late. However, that night I humbled myself. Once more I asked the Potter to grind away my pride and arrogance on His wheel, regardless of the pain.

The next day I found Flip on the yard. No other inmates were near him. However, I interrupted a meeting he was having with some of his unseen friends. At first he acted agitated, but then he relaxed and smiled broadly when I told him what I wanted. It tickled me that he took great care to ask his invisible associates to excuse him, as "a brother in need is calling." Stepping away from his hidden group, he listened to the nightmare with fascination. His eyes were bright and clearer than I had ever seen them. "The fog is your past," he said. "The woman coming toward you stands for the hostages you took when you robbed those banks."

Flip held his chin in his hand for a second then pointed a bony finger toward the sky as though he would make a great pronouncement. Lowering his head he whispered a prophetic utterance, "You will find the answer, but it's going to be up to you to figure it out, Ninety-nine."

Our session was over.

I thanked him.

He returned to his private conference.

I walked away talking to myself. At the moment, he seemed saner than I was. His answers were clearly "right on" and lit my mind like beacons. I knew I'd heard the truth. But I still didn't know what the strange dream meant, and it bugged me.

As I stepped through the gate back into the old fortress, I asked, "How about it, Father?"

God let me stew for two more weeks. Then the Lord stirred the pot through Chaplain Eldon Cornett. I heard him praying during a worship service and it seemed he was giving me guidance. He prayed, "And help us, Lord, to forgive ourselves as You have forgiven us."

I didn't hear what came next. His words struck a chord of truth resounding in my conscience. I hadn't forgiven myself for the horrible pain and injury I had caused those women hostages. I had a deep-seated need to ask their forgiveness, but I couldn't. I knew that my dream was about forgiving myself and that forgiving myself held the solution to my problem. Then I heard the rest of the chaplain's prayer.

"So, Father, since we are powerless to forgive ourselves, empower us with Your love. Enable us to love ourselves as You love us, so we may live in peace with You, with ourselves and with others. Amen."

I scribbled the prayer on a scrap of paper and underlined, *powerless to forgive and love myself.*

The chaplain dismissed the service. "Wow, Father, You are

something else. I am powerless to forgive myself, and it must be tied to my inability to love myself. Help me, Lord. I want less Ken power and more God power. Please help me forgive myself. Help me love myself and I'll be okay."

That was on a Sunday morning. I left the chapel and returned to the "Potter's House." That was the name I gave the Rock during those shaky, painful, formative days. The revelation that forgiveness and love are linked stuck in my brain. All day I choked on this new idea that forgiving myself was somehow linked to loving myself. I prayerfully admitted, "I need Your power with this one. Please help me get well."

Following a miserable meal of hot dogs and beans, I hurried to the yard. Lying in my favorite grassy patch I daydreamed of Sundays and holidays at home with Mother and Dad and wished for the old times. I thought about whether I loved myself back then. If so, when had I stopped loving me?

A cloud carried me to a moment of special love. I remembered my Aunt Mae. She was my favorite aunt, and I was her favorite nephew. From my first memory when I was four years old, she was always on my side. It didn't matter what I did or didn't do, she loved me and stood up for me.

It was Christmas Day, and the Cooper family was gathering around her dinner table. It was heaped to the chandelier with chicken and all the trimmings. It seemed like everyone was there.

Aunt Mae gave me a pair of slippers that Christmas morning. I was very proud of them. As we came to the table to eat, I danced a jig and did a big kick. One slipper went flying and landed smack-dab in a big bowl of chicken and dumplings. That was Aunt Mae's signature dish. Everyone gasped and then roared with laughter. I didn't. I was scared to death, and afraid I would lose my slipper, but Aunt Mae came to my rescue. She grabbed the little "boat" that was about to sink in the dumplings and pulled me to her bosom. She hugged me with a big love hug.

"Don't you fret none, Kenneth, we'll just scoop a little bit of the dumplings off the top and no one will ever know the difference." Her words soothed me, showing me she loved me more than chicken and dumplings, and that was saying a lot.

My thoughts were suddenly interrupted when the prison count-time horn blared. I stared down at my feet as I walked to the cell to be numbered with the rest of the prison population. It had turned into a restful, good day. I spent most of the time with my family beyond the fences.

22

The warm glow accompanying my recall of Aunt Mae's love lingered, and I wanted to love myself like she loved me. But I couldn't, and it even showed in my appearance. In a matter of weeks I lost ten pounds, down to a boney one hundred and sixty-three. Now I was genuinely concerned about both my deteriorating physical and mental health.

Then, during one bleary-eyed evening count, two free people came down the catwalk to rescue me. Incredibly, the taller one, a silver-haired gentleman, was hawking food. He bragged as he patted his stomach and peered into A-four. "Pizza, barbecue chicken and home-baked chocolate chip cookies are just some of the goodies we're gonna feed you guys at the Kairos weekend."

The tall white guy had a black man with him who wore a collar like a priest. I was confused. They were out of place on the catwalk, where no one but guards was allowed during count, and they were talking crazy stuff about pizza, barbecue chicken and home-baked cookies. It made me pinch myself to see if I was delusional or maybe caught up in another cruel nightmare, this one caused by hunger.

The priest announced, “Guys, any of you who want to go to the Kairos weekend next month, run over to the chapel and get signed up.” He looked like he’d finished his spiel, and the two of them were about to move down the catwalk to A-five.

I jumped off my bunk and grabbed the bars. “I’m going to. I wanna go.” My gut told me God had sent them to help me with my problems. They stopped and stared at me. “But tell me how you got in here to talk to us about food?”

The tall guy smiled. “Whoa, now, slow down, young fella.” He poked his hand through the bars to shake mine.

I held tight onto the bars as if I had leprosy. “I’m sorry, sir. I can’t shake your hand. Making contact through the bars is a serious offense. But please, tell me about that weekend. What did you call it?”

“Kairos,” he said. “That’s a Greek word from the Bible. It means God’s special ‘time.’ ”

I nodded and said, “Kind of like a spiritual time? Is that what you mean?”

“Yes, my man, that’s it exactly. You guys will enjoy soul food, but also spiritual food and Christian fellowship.”

My cell mates laughed with me, and within a week, several of the guys in A-four signed up at the chaplain’s office. However, there was limited space, and I was the only one chosen from our cell.

The weekend was held in the prison school auditorium, just down the hall from my GED classroom. But stepping through the doorway into the love, laughter and music of a down-home Christian get-together was just about like flying into heaven. A man from the street named Earl Porter brought in his guitar and with a five-piece inmate band led us in songs of celebration. The atmosphere was jubilant.

Following the singing I was caught up in an atmosphere of chatter and laughter. Hearing the sound of happy voices, seeing and receiving love in action brought back a sense of being well. The aroma of chocolate permeated the air, and my mouth watered as I took in the scene. This was a huge group of volunteers from the street—at least fifty men, including the two men who visited the cell to invite me to this event. I made a beeline for the tall one and introduced myself.

"I'm Ken Cooper from Kentucky. You came by my cell."

I just about freaked out when he said, "I'm Ken Power."

My dazed mind raced back to my prayer asking for less *Ken* power and more *God* power. I felt delusional and wondered what God was up to now.

Ken Power smiled, turned toward another man near us and said, "Here's another Kentuckian. Meet Jim Epley. I'll be right back." He left us smiling at each other.

Mr. Epley was a tall man who looked a lot like one of my uncles. He shook my hand and said, "Howdy."

"Where are you from?" I asked as I watched him closely.

As only a Kentuckian can say "Louisville," he drawled, "Louavul."

I laughed. "Well, Jim, the way you say 'Louavul' makes me feel at home."

"We're two of a kind," he said.

We watched Ken pull a little guy from a circle that formed near a table. They came over. Ken said, "Meet *Big John* Rapier, our leader for the weekend. He's also from Kentucky."

I looked down into the radiant face of the little man and sized him up. He stood about five-two and was skinnier than me. He must have weighed about one hundred pounds. He was around seventy years old, and he smiled broadly.

He thumbed over his shoulder. "They call me Big John, of course. Good to meet another Kentucky Wildcat."

"I am a big University of Kentucky fan. How did you know?"

"You look like a winner to me, and I'm on furlough from the Kentucky Colonels basketball team. I play center."

I laughed my first real belly laugh in years. Another inmate, John Fitzsimmons, who had attended a previous weekend, came by. He sneaked behind Big John, picked him up and raised him to about the height of a basketball goal and passed him over to me like he was a sack of potatoes. I managed to "catch" him and lower the little man to the floor. He loved it. The rest of us did too. This was my new family.

About that time the black man who had come by my cell came over and took me by the arm. "I'm Evangelist Preston Holmes of Abyssinia Baptist Church."

I responded with the prison way of giving my last name only. "Cooper, er, excuse me, I mean, I'm Ken Cooper."

"I've been looking for you. I'll take you to your table family."

Reverend Holmes wore a black suit with a white cleric's collar. He looked as sharp as my persona as the "Gentleman Bank Robber," but his wearing the wraparound collar didn't jive with my image of a Baptist minister. I was perplexed.

The way he dressed and what he called himself didn't matter as he guided me through a maze of tables to my group. The Baptist preacher and I approached another street man at the table, and my escort introduced us. The guy gave me a huge smile and stuck his hand out. "Hi, I'm Charlie Hays. I'm your servant. Welcome to the Table Family of St. Peter."

I didn't respond but marveled over what this *servant* thing was about. I was overwhelmed, feeling like an alien since I had been separated from the love, laughter and brightness of free people since the Prison Fellowship weekend. I caught the aroma of chocolate again. It was too much. My searching eyes stopped at a basket of chocolate chip cookies beckoning from the center of the table. Charlie noticed the hungry look on my face, motioned toward the basket and said, "Dig in!"

He didn't have to say it twice. I became eight years old again and grabbed a fistful of chocolate chip cookies, actually baked in someone's oven at home.

Charlie smiled, knowingly.

Their scrumptious taste took me back to Mammaw Ryan's kitchen in Strunk, Kentucky. "Charlie, the only thing missing is an ice cold glass of sweet cow's milk."

And that was only the beginning. The weekend offered lots of fantastic food, including barbecue chicken. Unbelievably, oysters Rockefeller and other epicurean delights I hadn't tasted for years graced the table.

This was Kairos Thirteen, and it was certainly God's special time for my appetite. The Friday evening meal started with a Caesar salad with a cavalier flare, gourmet grilled grouper, real baked potatoes with butter and sour cream, followed by coconut cake for dessert. The way I stuffed myself reminded me of the time Jimmie Worley and I ate a year's worth of candy in one day. For the first time in a month I slept well, really well, and woke up Saturday morning refreshed and energized.

When I returned to the school, I was surprised by *how* we got together. We were greeted by a double line of our volunteer buddies. Men were lined up on each side of the entrance area. One by one, the street men stepped out of the line toward a candidate, grabbed an inmate, hugged him and led him to his table family.

Seeing the men hugging inmates made my prison ways kick in, and I held back. I hadn't been hugged by a man since Don Weston put his arms around me at the end of the Prison Fellowship weekend. That had been months before. I figured these guys didn't know about serving time, or they didn't understand what they were doing. Maybe they were unaware that nearly half the men in the Rock were involved in homosexual activity.

About that time a man blindsided me and grabbed me in a big hug. I stiffened when he spoke into my ear, "I love you, Ninety-nine."

It reminded me of Bear terrorizing me in the chow line and whispering my name. I pulled back in fear to see who held me. It was a jovial banker man named John. God chose a burly banker to express his love for me.

A banker!

I relaxed and stepped back into his embrace and told him I loved him too. "John, you're easy to love." Then I added a little lightness that only I could fully appreciate. "I've always loved bankers."

His meaty hands pulled me to him, and I could feel his heart beating against mine. God certainly handpicked the man who hugged me. And he didn't know my crimes. He was someone who could help me love myself. I grew intense as I looked into John's jovial expression. I didn't want to tell him, but I knew I had to. "I'm sure you don't know this, John, but I was a serial bank robber."

John didn't appear startled. In fact he smiled. "Ken, that's behind you. I didn't know, but it doesn't matter. I love you unconditionally."

"But I took women hostages. I still have nightmares—"

The buoyant banker put a hand over my mouth and gave me a bankable hug. "I love you, Ninety-nine."

In his strong arms I felt like God was loving me and telling me I was okay. I patted the burly guy on the back as he released me to go to my table family. The day flew by as I continued to enjoy the fellowship and food, as well as what the volunteers called a short course in Christianity. My table discussion was led by Father Paul Canapa, an Episcopal priest. He loved me, too, though I was still standoffish at that point in the weekend.

Throughout the day, in between classes, I spent the break times with Jim Epley since we had Kentucky horses, golf and basketball in common. But following the Saturday night feast of barbecue chicken that topped Kentucky-fried, Jim astonished me as I sat spellbound in the group, listening to the story of his conversion to Christ. He said, "Following a bank robbery in Kentucky, I hid out in a motel and came face to face with death. This cat's nine lives were used up, and I was about to blow my brains out when I noticed a Bible on the table."

I know my mouth must have fallen open when I muttered, "That's what I did." This free man had been a bank robber like me. Now, I knew the Big Cat had something as special for me as my personal healing.

I couldn't hear the rest of his story. I was too deep in thought. Jim was on the lam after robbing a bank. It was so much like me that I thought it might be a concoction someone set up. But I knew that couldn't be the case. I heard him say he gave his life to Christ right there in that motel room. It was a picture of me when I holed up in a motel watching Ben Kinchlow on the tube, only I didn't give my life to Christ back then.

The theme of Jim's talk was forgiveness. I was truly amazed.

God once again put me in the right place at the right time to receive the right word from the right person.

When my Kentucky buddy finished speaking, an officer came and set a bucket of papers on fire. Everyone was shocked and puzzled at what was happening, so Jim explained. "Make a list of all the people who have hurt you and people you need to forgive. List them by name. If you're like me, you'll put your name at the top so you can forgive yourself first. After you've completed your list, I want you to bring it up here and burn it. As you drop the names into the bucket, ask God to help you forgive these people for what they've done to you." He held up an index finger. "Remember, you especially have to forgive yourself."

Feverishly scribbling, I made out my list and put "me" at the top. It also included Anne, Lee, Anthony Jordan, Bear, Baltimore and the rapists of the Lion's Den, Rufe, several girlfriends, Mother, my brothers Jim and Paul, Judge Coe, the lawman who shot me, the redheaded classification officer, and on and on. I wasn't through with my names when Jim told us to bring them to the front. I crumpled my forgiveness list and carried it toward the flaming caldron as if it was a heavy load.

It was.

When I plunked the names into the fire, the smoke of the burning paper filled my nostrils with the essence of forgiveness. A sweet savor of love filled my soul. I whispered, "Lord, I have truly forgiven everyone on my list." Then I sensed a spiritual nudge and knew I forgave all the people on my list but two—Bear and myself. I returned to my seat and shook my head over this hatred I felt toward him for raping two of my friends and the lack of self-love, maybe even hatred, I held inside for myself.

Plopping into my seat, I was challenged by Jim again. "Many of you must continue to work on forgiving yourself and some of the people on your list."

"Bear and me," I muttered.

Jim looked past me toward the back of the room. "It takes action, so we're giving you a way to do something to help the process."

At his signal, the volunteer gauntlet of the morning came together at the exit.

"As you return to your cells tonight, you will have the usual bag of home-baked cookies, but it is not for you and your friends. This bag of cookies is for an enemy; it's for the inmate on your list you have not forgiven. We want you to take the cookies to him."

I sat up alert, thinking about Bear.

My Kentucky friend continued, "Hand your enemy the bag of cookies and tell him we told you to give them to the one convict in this prison you hate the most or have the hardest time forgiving."

I slipped back into my seat. "I can't do that!" I said.

But I did. Given special permission by the sergeant in charge, I handed the bag of home-baked chocolate chip cookies through the bars to Bear. I said, "The Kairos people told me to give these to the convict I hate the most."

Grabbing the bag in one hand, he steadied himself with the other. "What did you say?"

"They told me to give these cookies to the inmate I find hardest to forgive."

Bear sneered and straightened to his full height. "Ninety-nine, I don't give a damn why you gave them to me." He opened the bag, looked in and a smile lit his face. "I thank you very much," he said gruffly and wheeled toward his cot.

"You're welcome," I said, laughing. I walked away, amazed at God's sense of humor. He tested me through chocolate chip cookies to see if I could love my enemy more than my favorite cookie.

I smiled all the way to my cell. When I settled in my bunk, I felt purged and clean, and I slept as soundly as a baby for the second night in a row. I had no nightmares.

As good as the weekend was, it didn't end my Kairos connection. Jim, John, Ron, Billy, Earl, Father Paul, Ken, Jimmy, Charlie, Preston, Father Bob and Raymond kept coming back monthly, and they gave me many more hugs and home-baked cookies of all types. But only giving up my chocolate chip cookies to Bear rocked me to sleep.

23

In the days following, I continually thanked God for newfound peace of mind and restful sleep. My appetite and good health returned so I could focus on spiritual issues. I repented of a macho self-image that kept me from accepting helping hands of love. I vowed never to return to my old way of thinking. I thanked God for the painful, sleepless crash course. The Kairos weekend had turned out to be a lifesaving experience that reduced my pride to humility and opened my heart to receive love from my Christian family.

Two weeks later, the nightmares had not come back. I apparently needed my new family's love as much as a child needs a mother's nurturing love during its first year of life.

In the coming weeks, I progressed rapidly through the normal spiritual stages of crawling, pulling-up and toddling. I learned that operating solo caused collisions and falls that were easily avoided if I was willing to let other Christians love me and give me guidance. Now, clutching the hands of love in the Kairos family, I greeted the new day with optimism, believing my heavenly Father would someday turn my scars into stars.

After the Kairos weekend, the first person to touch my life in a healing way was an avowed atheist. He showed up on the catwalk before breakfast call. I recognized him as the inmate clerk from the Rock security office. He spoke to me through the bars as he introduced himself: "I'm Garth Gibson."

"I know who you are, and I'm happy to meet you, Garth."

"Cooper, I've been watching you, and the way you carry yourself makes me think you don't belong in this part of the prison. I can move you today."

Having dreamed of just such a moment, I gasped and gripped the bars with both hands. "That's fantastic, but where would I be going?"

His chin jutted and he glanced up. "Security approved your move up to Three-T, into a six-man honor cell—my cell."

"Man this is like an early Christmas present."

I knew his offer was genuine. Except for emergency security matters, Gibson and other powerful convicts like him ran the inner workings of the old prison section of UCI. I was deeply appreciative and would have said yes immediately, but my scars taught me to get God's approval before reaching for a star and making a move. "Garth, I sure don't want to miss this opportunity, but I'd like to pray about it first."

I could see he was annoyed. "Don't wait 'til Christmas." His words were clipped. "I don't know how prayer could have anything to do with it. One thing's sure. You gotta let me know right after morning count." He gave me a slight smile as he softened. "You okay with that?"

"That'll work," I agreed.

As Gibson marched away, I could see that he was perplexed, if not downright frustrated. He'd made it clear that he really wanted me for a cell mate. I was sure it had to do with the fact that I was never in any trouble with the authorities and wormed my way out of problems with other convicts. Then, as he turned a corner I felt there was something else going on. My old emotional wounds opened, and sick thoughts raced back and forth between my ears.

I'd heard Gibson was a child rapist. That raised a flag, making me think maybe he wanted me as his boy. I shook that thought, but it bounced right back at me. I muttered, "I don't think so. Colonel Jackson is an officer of high moral character. He wouldn't allow a rapist to be the Rock clerk, but you never know. Some of these guys are really sickos." I could feel my eyebrows rise as I thought this might be a trick of the devil. Did Satan send him to get me out of A-four now that it's become a Christian cell? That triggered another thought. I questioned whether I was afraid to step out in faith. One thing for sure, I would miss my brothers in this grungy place, especially Moe, Luke and Kenny.

Both Moe and Luke heard Gibson's offer, but they held their tongues until I turned around. Luke smiled at me. "Ninety-nine, this must be a blessing from God."

"You really think so?"

"Yeah, move on up, brother. I'd like to be there myself. It's an honor cell block that Colonel Jackson runs for cons that have shown they can handle a little freedom."

Moe confirmed the move. "Jump at it. You can come and go more."

Luke chimed in again. "You can cook your own meals in a pot, and you're free to go to the canteen for breakfast."

I listened to their advice, but when count time came I prayed, *Lord, You know how many times I've been selfish and self-serving. I don't want to do anything out of the center of Your will. Moving out of this tomb would be fantastic, but I don't want to move away from You.* The officer came by and stood at my bunk to count me. I barked out my number, and as soon as he left I resumed my prayer. *I don't trust my own judgment with all the hell I've been through, so please give me peace to let me know this is Your will. I pray this in Jesus' name, amen.*

Quietness and contentment settled over me. I felt assurance God was answering, so following count, I gave Garth the word to go ahead and move me.

Before I knew what happened, an officer came to escort me to my new house. I threw a bath towel over my shoulder and stacked my Bible and Robert Schuller's devotional book on the same old cigar box. I carried them through a courtyard beyond the catwalk and up two flights of stairs to the third tier. We traipsed past a TV room and an officer's station to the second door on the right. The first thing I noticed was that my new unit faced the courtyard, and it took me two floors above the lower levels of violence. I guessed this was as close to heaven as a man in my position could get.

The transfer took about five minutes, and I traveled less than two hundred feet. It was like moving from a coal camp in a hollow to a log cabin on a mountaintop. I suffered culture shock as I stepped through a screened door into the "cell." There were no bars, not even a regular door; only a screened door.

I entered what appeared to be an old college dorm room rather than a cell. A bright-faced officer was seated on an inmate's bunk strumming a guitar. I couldn't believe what I was seeing and feeling, much less hearing. What a difference from A-Wing, where officers formed goon squads to harass and control the convicts. My mind raced. I felt safe for the first time in months. This was a spacious room, and I would be free to move about in the twelve-room cell block housing seventy-two men. There would be no handcuffs, no shackles and most of all, no shame.

The aroma of succulent chicken and yellow rice cooking in two electric coffeepots teased my nose and grabbed my belly. Suddenly, Garth was there to greet me and show me to my bunk, the lower berth on the wall near the door. "Welcome to Three-T-22, Cooper. I understand they call you Ninety-nine."

I guess I must have looked like a kid who just stepped into the tent of a three-ring circus. "I don't care what you call me. Wow!" I spread my arms and looked at the officer. "I can't believe this room and the fantastic aroma."

"Welcome to Three-T," he said as the officer stood up, patted his belly and left the room smiling.

As I went about placing my stuff on an end table next to the bed, my new cell mates gathered around. They seemed eager to meet me. Folding the bath towel over the bar at the foot of the bed, I smiled at the men, who were dressed in blue uniforms. They looked more like a college basketball team than prisoners. Garth was at least six-six, and the man to my left was about six-four. He introduced himself as Snake. Then coming right at me was a diminutive *point guard* who stood all of five-eight.

"Hi, my name's Henry." He wore a radiant first-team smile as he extended his hand. "You'll like it here. This has been my *house* for twelve years," he bragged.

I shuddered.

The next man I met said his name was Marty. He looked and sounded like Andy Griffith as he shook my hand and said, "Howdy do."

The man called Snake interrupted. "I'm your bunk partner."

Finally a young black man came up to me. "I'm Ezra," he drawled.

It wasn't his size that grabbed me, even though we stood nose to nose at six feet. It wasn't even his strong handshake. It was his bright, brown eyes. They were full of love, and I immediately wanted to hug him. He may have reminded me of Danny, back in county jail.

He put a hand on my shoulder. "I'm glad you're here. You carry a Bible, so let's get together to study."

I knew then what drew me to him and knew God was in the move.

Garth grabbed my elbow. "Let's eat!" He pulled me over to a table under the window where supper was cooking. "This meal is on us tonight, fill up your plate and enjoy."

I could feel my eyes widen. Like a little kid, I said, "This is amazing!"

They all chuckled at my boyish response.

I discovered the men in this honor area were allowed to beg, barter or steal food from the kitchen pantry and fix it in coffeepots in their rooms. We each had a plastic tray and silverware of sorts, without a knife or fork, of course; this was still prison. Here we were free to eat like a family as we sat around on our bunks. The food and fellowship were terrific, and I smiled at Ezra when he opened his eyes after silent grace. I felt almost at home.

The food was absolutely the best Deep-South fixings I had eaten in years. My taste buds went crazy as I savored each and every morsel, while I took particular care to thank my hosts over and over.

"This must be heaven. You guys just don't know." I thought

about my statement and recanted. "Well, I guess you do." Although they laughed, none of them had been confined on A-Wing, so they couldn't really know. I felt like an alien among them.

I relaxed, continuing to eat and get acquainted with the new men. "Hey, guys, you know what surprises me just as much as this food?"

They all looked up.

"It's the screened door for bars." Everyone laughed. At one time each one felt the same and perhaps questioned whether the place was safe.

An hour after eating I settled down on my bunk and stretched out, but I was still revved up. My big eyes could not take in enough. This was a totally different world. It was well lit and as clean and neat as A-four was dark and dirty. There was no TV and no stinking commode under it. The TV rooms were at the far ends of the long, wide hallway. The east-end guys watched regular programming, and the west-end men watched sports. That was perfect for me since my room was a hop, skip and long jump away from sports. The common toilets and showers were in the middle of the cell block. I sure wouldn't miss the deafening noise of the tube and the awful odor of the commode in A-four. "Unbelievable," I muttered. "I'll live with a little dignity here."

Snake may have heard me. He poked his head over the edge of the bed and looked down at me. "Yeah, this setup almost makes you forget where you are." He smiled and added, "By the way, I hear you beat Bear at push-ups. You must be pretty good."

"No, not really, you could take him easy."

Marty yelled over to me. "Watch it, new man. Snake will take your money."

Marty's nasal twang sounded familiar.

I called back across the "holler" separating me from his bunk, "Which of the hills are you from, son, Kentucky or Tennessee?"

"Cumberland County, Tennessee," he announced with pride. He seemed delighted when I mimicked his accent.

"My mom's from Scott County, Tennessee, and I'm from across the line in the Bluegrass State," I said. He propped himself up and stared across the way at me.

Everyone laughed and I went on. "My family had a screened door just like this one." I tilted my head toward the doorway.

Just as we all were about to share front-porch tales and family trees, the lights went out. The whole cell block turned quiet. I nodded off and slept like a long-legged athlete on Kentucky bluegrass. It was my best sleep in a year. Toward the dawning of a new day, I dreamed of a barefoot boy running, while a screened door slammed behind him. I woke up with a grin as my two long fellers sticking out from under the cover greeted me from the foot of the bed. Before daybreak, I slipped on my shoes, stole though the screened door, smiled and eased to the east end of the hall. It was two years since I had seen the sunrise, and I determined to be there before it came up. I made my way to a huge window opening out over the Rock Yard.

The fresh scent of rain greeted me. I gazed across the yard and the fields beyond the fences as the sun burst forth over the horizon. As it rose higher, glistening sunbeams turned the earth into fields of diamonds. Caught up in the moment, I raised my hands toward the sun and greeted God. "Good morning, Lord. I love You. What are You up to today? I want to be a part of it."

Within the hour, Henry invited me to go to breakfast with him at the canteen/restaurant. It was rumored that inmates, as well as guards, could sit down and order steak and eggs restaurant-style. Henry had no idea that I thought it was a joke. Warden Massey and Colonel Jackson rewarded inmates who lived by the rules by allowing them to live in an honor dorm, but I couldn't swallow the image of ordering eggs over easy in a restaurant merely fifty steps from the Rock gate.

When we sat down on the inmate side of the building, at a table with a red and white checked cloth, it was like a dream with living sound. As I stared at the menu on the wall a cheerful inmate dressed in a white chef's uniform asked, "How'd you like them?"

I read from the menu instead of responding to him: "Two eggs with grits and bacon, seventy-nine cents."

The waiter stood by and grinned. I'm sure he could tell this was all new to me. My mouth watered and I scanned the rest of the bill of fare. "With steak, a dollar ninety-nine." I looked back up at the smiling server. I finally said, "I can't believe I can actually order steak."

He laughed along with Henry. "That's okay. I couldn't believe it the first time I dropped in here either." The upbeat man moved the pencil from his pad, then pressed the lead out on the paper. "You want the steak and eggs?"

Henry said, "Go ahead. It's on me."

I couldn't be that extravagant. "No, I'll have two eggs over easy with grits and sausage."

When the waiter left with our orders, I thanked Henry. The morning got even better. Doug Gorham, my main basketball buddy, popped in and pulled up a chair. "I'm surprised to see you in here, Ken—tucky. They let you outta your cage, huh?"

I nodded.

"About time," he said.

"Yeah, isn't this something? I just ordered breakfast and will get it my way. Unreal. I'm having a Happy Meal with friends as if we met at a McDonald's."

The food tasted better than just about anything I'd ever eaten. Sitting there talking with friends and leisurely eating eggs fried in butter, with no guard breathing down my neck and snarling, "Tighten up and move on," gave me a wonderful sense of freedom. I felt whole and healthy. Oh, I was aware of still being in prison, but compared to the Lion's Den in jail and the dungeon of A-Wing, I was delivered from darkness and God was turning my scars into stars.

24

Although I experienced improvement in my immediate surroundings by living with men who cared about others, there were still those at the Rock who were the antithesis of kindness, compassion and gentleness. Such men vented their evil intentions on anyone or anything suiting them—even on the cats that lived among us to control the rat population. Those cats served life sentences right along with us convicts.

My favorite was a huge orange tomcat that was rumored to be fourteen years old. We called him Tigger. He was the patriarch of a clan of about twenty fur balls, including several newly born kittens. The four-legged population did a better job doing their time than we did. From birth to death, they fulfilled their mission with great enthusiasm. They stalked and trapped their prey in the nooks, utility passageways and lofts of the old fortress. Almost everyone appreciated their presence. They not only played havoc with the hated rodents; they also made the hostile environment a little softer.

Marty found a tiny calico ball of fluff. It was one of Tigger's kittens. Apparently, Satan's tormentors abducted the little animal and blinded him with battery acid. The mangled creature was half-dead.

When Marty showed me the kitten, I couldn't hold back the tears. Our cell mates were outraged as well. But after showing him to us, Marty hid the unconscious little fellow in a shoe under his bunk. He lovingly placed the broken kitten on a warm sock stuffed inside his shoe. Marty didn't want prison officials to discover it. They took diseased or handicapped felines out of the prison to be destroyed at the animal control center.

After the lights went out, we huddled in the dark. We couldn't see each other, but we could hear the anger in one another's voices. Two of the guys wanted to take out a contract on the culprits who mangled this innocent kitten. "The Latin Kings are dying to break some legs anyhow," Henry growled. "Julio could get his gang together and whack the sickos." We knew it was true, so we all gave off nervous laughter. The Spanish gang loved the cats and hated the Satan worshipers.

But Snake objected. "Hey, Ninety-nine," he whispered, "you *Christians* should ask God what to do."

I heard the sarcasm drip from his lips but ignored it. "We've already done that, but God hasn't told us how to handle it, yet." I said.

Ezra, one of Tigger's closest allies, said, "Let's talk to Officer Gooding about it. He likes Tigger and the kittens, too." Officer Gooding was in charge of our cell block on the swing shift, and he was the guitar-playing guard I saw when first entering the cell.

"Yeah, that's a good idea," Garth said. "He owes me for free music lessons. Maybe he'll set it up with the other guards to allow us to keep this little guy here while we treat him."

I couldn't believe my ears. Garth was a man handcuffed with a life sentence without parole. Not only was he a hard-hearted child rapist; he bragged about being an atheist. And what he suggested next floored us all. "Ain't Gooding a Christian? That's another reason he'll help us."

Our eyes were getting used to the dark, and we could see each other faintly, but I didn't know if he really meant it or was chiding us. "Yup. Good idea," I said. "But it seems we need the Lord's help." Some of the guys nodded and I said, "Let's pray right now." No one protested as I bowed my head. In the shadows, I could see they all bowed, even Garth. I prayed, "Father, I know You created this little cat, and the authorities allow the creatures to bless us and keep down the rats. So right now, Lord, we ask You to touch this kitten's life by granting us favor with the officers so we can nurse it back to health."

The next morning the kitten stirred in his cozy bed. We gave a collective sigh of relief. He was still alive. The little guy's chances of making it shot up, and the part of the prayer about gaining favor with the guards was answered. Mr. Gooding agreed to let us doctor the little fellow until he could return to the yard with Tigger. He didn't like the fact that the only alternative was to turn him over to the animal control people. We appreciated the depth of the man's compassion. The lifers who'd stayed there for thirty years had never heard of such a thing. News that we were keeping a cat in the cell was the buzz of the cell block.

We no longer hid our new cell mate, and he continued to make Marty's shoe his house. I couldn't believe the tender loving care he received from us six "tough" convicts. He grew stronger every day as we smuggled in bread and milk to tenderly feed him. His first step out of his shoe, however, broke our hearts. His first movements told us he was both blind and suffered from deformed hips. The sadists who mangled him had broken his back. He stumbled over his own feet. He couldn't run and play the way a normal kitten would. It was such a pitiful sight that Snake got down on his knees on the hard concrete floor to gently cup the tiny kitten in his rough hands. He became teary eyed as he lifted the poor, injured kitten off the floor and eased him into Marty's waiting palms.

During the weeks our cell served as a makeshift hospital, the six men and one kitten became family. I knew God placed love in every man's heart as I watched Garth, Ezra, Marty and Snake take turns caring for the handicapped creature. Henry maintained some distance, claiming he didn't like cats.

One day Ezra asked what the kitten's name was going to be. Marty said, "I don't know. I haven't thought about a name for him."

I scrambled off my bunk. "Since he can't see, and stumbles around, why not call him Mister Magoo?" Mister Magoo was a nearsighted television cartoon character.

"Yeah," Ezra said. "That's a good name."

Garth just smiled and Marty nodded. Even Snake and Henry liked the name. So that was what we called the little fellow. From then on, these big guys held Mister Magoo in their strong arms and talked baby talk and sang to him.

Marty teased Henry one evening when he caught him scratching the kitten behind his ears, smoothing his ruffled fur and holding him close. Henry admitted that, like the rest of us, he enjoyed hearing Mister Magoo purr, and holding the fur ball appeared to give it comfort.

"The name sure fits," Officer Gooding said when he found out we had named him Mister Magoo. Mr. Gooding was as hooked on him as we were and allowed us to keep Tigger's offspring, despite his handicaps.

The presence of Mister Magoo changed the cell. We were united in a common cause. I was amazed that a handicapped little cat could bring hope to even one of the men, most of whom were serving life sentences in our cell block. Ezra said he believed God would restore Mister Magoo's sight and went around bragging about what God was going to do. The bulk of the convicts, even those rooting for the kitten's recovery, scorned Ezra. I was numbered among the skeptical, though I didn't ridicule Ezra's belief that God would heal an animal.

One evening when Mr. Gooding came in to count us, he included Mister Magoo. Each of us always sat at attention on our bunk when the counting officer stopped in front of us. He looked each one of us in the eyes and stated our name. In turn, we barked out our DC numbers. Our honorary midget inmate sat at attention at the foot of Ezra's bed that night. Gooding playfully called out, "Magoo!" and poked his finger toward the kitten's face. Magoo jumped back. Ezra's mouth dropped open, and Mr. Gooding was speechless.

Ezra shouted, "He can see. Magoo can see." He almost screamed loud enough for the warden to hear him, "God's healed him!"

Garth grabbed a dangling string from his bunk and waved it in front of Mister Magoo. The cat reached out to swat it.

As though in a fog, Mr. Gooding smiled and moved on to the next cell. He overlooked the euphoria and chaos and went about his business. Despite it being count time, we were all off our bunks sitting on the floor in a circle around Mister Magoo. Each man tested his sight, and the cat swatted at the string again and again. We hoped the warden would come bursting in.

Snake expressed our amazement when he exclaimed, "Wow! Somebody or something really has healed Mister Magoo . . ."

"But I don't think Magoo is completely healed," Garth interrupted. "See, only some of his vision is back. Watch this." Garth took the string and held it off to Mister Magoo's right, and the kitten didn't respond. "He's got tunnel vision." He dangled on the other side. "See?" Garth said, "He can only see straight ahead."

Mister Magoo didn't seem to mind as he frolicked around the cell to amuse us, chasing the twine, a stick, and other toys. But he dragged his back legs. His broken hips were not included in the miracle healing.

He became the mascot of the entire cell block the evening he was healed. After count, when the cell doors were again opened, hardened convicts peeked in to see the miracle cat. It was big news, even among the officers. Tough men whispered to one another like little boys, "Magoo is healed. He can see."

Not long after that, Mr. Gooding told us that Mister Magoo would have to go back to the yard with the rest of the cats. We reminded our officer friend of his crippled hips. He relented and said we could keep the little guy one more week, but then he would have to be taken to the animal control people. Although we were crushed, we appreciated the week's reprieve. It was Friday night. I was scheduled to attend the Kairos reunion in the morning, and I'd ask them to pray for Mister Magoo.

Some of us prayed harder than ever for our little buddy's total healing. And we asked God to parole him to a family on the street. After we prayed, Ezra suggested, "Hey, Ninety-nine, why don't you ask one of the Kairos people to take him in?"

"That's a great idea. I'll do it in the morning if it's all right with you guys."

Garth appointed me Mister Magoo's agent. "Yeah, Ninety-nine, you get him a home."

The next morning I stood up in the prison chapel and said, "There's an unusual opportunity today for a cat lover." The people straightened in their seats as I scanned the audience. "You've probably heard the story about the healing of the little blind kitten, Mister Magoo. His sight was restored. You may also remember, his back was broken by the sadists who blinded him. God restored Magoo's sight but has not healed his back. His life is now in danger."

The large group of volunteers gave out a collective sigh, nodded and leaned forward. I continued, "The prison officials control the cat population by exacting a death sentence for those who are handicapped. They take them out to be destroyed at the animal control center."

The crowd moaned while the Christian inmates prayed. "We Kairos brothers want to see Mister Magoo paroled to a street home. Is there anyone here who will adopt our little miracle cat to save his life?"

A volunteer raised her hand.

"Sandi," I acknowledged.

"I will," she shouted. "I'll adopt him."

All the inmates gave her a rousing round of applause. It was truly a time for shouting.

The prison officials went along with the adoption, and Mister Magoo was on his way the following Wednesday.

That was the day we all cuddled him for the last time,

whispering final loving words. We knew we would miss the little fella terribly, and he would miss us.

A month later, "Miss Sandi" stood up in the prison ministry meeting. "I've got to tell everyone what God has done," she said. Excitement filled her voice. "None of you were aware that when I volunteered to take Mister Magoo, I knew I was allergic to cats." She seemed a bit embarrassed and added, "But I felt like the Lord was urging me to take him anyway." Her embarrassment subsided. "I argued with God but it seemed He wanted me to adopt him, so I just put my hand up, even though I'd have an allergic reaction." Sandi dabbed at her eyes. With radiant face she beamed, "I've had no allergic reaction." She nearly shouted, "I'm not allergic to Mister Magoo! Isn't that wonderful?"

We all roared, shouted, clapped and gave each other high-fives. I noticed a couple of men brush the back of their hands against damp cheeks.

When the pandemonium subsided, she continued, "In fact, the little crippled guy's lighthearted playful ways have changed my home."

Although Mister Magoo was paroled into Miss Sandi's loving care, he surely couldn't forget the six "fathers" who mothered him to health at the Rock.

25

The day following Mister Magoo's parole, Garth transferred Moe and Luke from the dungeon to Three-T, almost directly across the hall from our screened door. I was elated to have them as neighbors, but I missed Mister Magoo terribly and worried about their leaving Kenny behind in the dungeon. At twenty-one, he was a prime target for homosexual rapists who prowled the dark corners. He was strong of body and mind, but without his "road dogs," I feared a group of the cowards might gang up on him.

Garth saved the day again. He assigned one of his "enforcers" to guard Kenny, so the problem was solved, and I could rest easy and enjoy my new neighbors.

Though I once ridiculed Moe and Luke in A-four and called them Rufe's pawns, we'd become good friends. Just about every evening, following first count, we got together to sing and pray as we had on A-Wing.

Someone from the outside sent Moe a guitar, and he played it like a pro. He joined Bob, his roommate, to form a pickin' and grinnin' duo that took me back to my bluegrass and country music roots. It turned out that Moe was a professional musician and had traveled with Roger Miller and his band. He could make a guitar sing, and he composed songs. One day Moe was singing *You Can't Roller Skate in a Buffalo Herd*, an old Miller favorite he'd helped Miller write. I chimed right in, nasal twang and all, belting out, "Oh ya can't roller skate in a buffalo herd, but you can be happy if you've a mind to." We were truly blessed and thanked God daily for delivering us from A-Wing.

Moe and I wrote songs and poems and had "church" all the time with Luke and Ezra. It was a great opportunity for me to learn how to write music and prose, and I benefited from Luke's knowledge of the Bible and Ezra's prayers.

One day Ezra asked God to protect me and strengthen me, as my confidence and trust in Him would soon be "needed for a special work."

I was a bit unnerved by his prayer about a *special work*, but Luke and Moe said, "Amen."

"What was that all about?" I asked Ezra when we opened our eyes.

"I don't know, Coop. The words just popped out as I was praying, but I believe it's about something the Big Boss will tell you to do."

Ezra was closely connected to God, so I didn't dare question him. Instead, I said, "Ezra, I believe your faith was the key to Magoo's healing, so please be praying I will hear from the Lord. I don't have the foggiest notion what He wants me to do."

The next day God placed an idea in my mind as I overheard two lifers, Homer Hardy and Scar Face, talking on the yard. Homer said, "You know, Scar, I've been down so long I've forgotten how old I am."

"I know you've been here for forty years, Hardy, but what's that got to do with your age, old man?"

"My last birthday was my thirty-first on the street, and I ain't had one since."

"Oh, you've had a birthday every year. But like me, you've just lost track of them because we can't hold no birthday parties in here."

As I moved on toward the horseshoe pits where Luke and Moe were pitching iron, I didn't know God was speaking to me, but Scar Face's words wouldn't leave me. "We can't hold no birthday parties in here."

My thoughts were interrupted by Moe. "Thank God, you're here, Ninety-nine. This city slicker from Los Angeles is no competition."

I took the shoes from Luke and said, "You'll eat those words, Moe. Let's play for the glob of jelly on tomorrow morning's tray."

Moe agreed, and the contest was on. As we pitched, Luke stood nearby, and to Moe's delight, he beat me twenty-one to twelve.

"What's up with you, sucker? You worried about that jelly?"

"No. I was just thinking about what Scar Face said a while ago."

"What did he say?"

"I heard him tell Hardy that we can't celebrate our birthdays in here."

Moe looked puzzled and said, "Yeah, Scar and Homer, and some of the old-timers won't have many more."

Luke chimed in, "They won't ever have a party in here because it's forbidden."

I dropped the horseshoe in my right hand as an idea hit

me. I threw up my other hand and said, “Hey, I’ve got a flash! Why don’t we throw a birthday party for everyone? Homer, Scar, you, me, everyone on Three-T. There’s no rule against it.”

Luke piped up. “What are you getting at?”

I smiled at Moe and questioned, “Why can’t we celebrate Jesus’ birthday, and invite everyone on the cell block?”

Moe chuckled, “Wow, you just did it again, Ninety-nine. That’s the craziest thing yet out of your mouth.”

“Maybe not,” I said. “It’s high time we have a party anyway, and if we do it for Jesus, perhaps it would fly.”

He responded, “Yes, sir! I see what you mean! I’ll bet you more than my jelly that Officer Gooding would do it since he’s a Jesus freak.”

That night, following count, the three of us approached our good friend in his office. To our amazement, he had no problem with us throwing a birthday party for Jesus on his shift, if he happened to be working on Christmas Eve. Gooding told us it had to be a covert operation. He would turn his head so we could “smuggle” the party stuff upstairs and store it in his office until the day of the party. He said, “I’m going to say this right up front. You inmates can’t pull it off because you’re going to need a lot more help than I can give you.”

He then stood up. “Remember! To abide by the rules, anything coming through my office has to include every man on the cell block. If you can’t do that, it’s a no go.”

I stuck out my hand. He hesitated and looked at it for a moment, then shook it. “It’s a done deal,” I said. “We appreciate your help and your prayers. We don’t know how we’re going to do it, but we sure are going to try.”

Officer Gooding laughed and “ordered” us out of his office

with one final warning. "Mark what I've told you." He held up a finger. "And don't forget, this meeting never happened."

Moe, Luke and I nodded and thanked him again before retreating to Three-T-22 to seek the help of a higher power. In their cell, Moe led us in prayer. "Dear Father, we know this is an answer to Ezra's prayer about a special work, and we dedicate ourselves to do it as You lead us. We know it will take a Big Cat like You to pull off this job. Amen."

Luke and I snickered at Moe referring to God as a Big Cat. We knew he didn't mean any disrespect. We agreed with him that God would help us. I slipped over to my cell and got on my knees. "Oh, boy, You've really gotten me into a *special work* all right. Now, You're going to have to see this thing through. I don't have what it takes. It's all up to You."

The next day we began working on what we called Project Big Cat. It was July 10 and we little cats were given five months to make it happen. There were several major problems. The biggest obstacle was our lack of money. The three of us were very poor even by prison standards, so it seemed impossible for us to raise enough money to hold a party for the entire cell block of 72.

But we soon learned it was not impossible for God. He moved in several people's hearts to send money into our accounts, and from July 10 until December 1, the three of us scraped and saved ninety dollars to be used for the party.

We met on the softball field after noon chow to discuss our situation. A plan was coming together in our minds. All we needed to do was put it into action. Luke was good with detail, and Moe was as sneaky as a mole. We made a great team, though they ribbed me about being the top cat. I knew who the Top Cat really was, so we started our meeting with prayer. Afterward, Luke asked, "What party stuff are we going to buy with the ninety bucks? There are sixty-nine inmates, not counting us, so we have to provide seventy slices of cake with coffee."

"Seventy?" I questioned.

"Yeah, we have to include Officer Gooding."

"You're right."

Moe nodded but threw Luke a curve. "Every birthday party must have a real birthday cake with candles, not slices," he said.

Luke laughed, "Now there's a monumental obstacle."

Moe held up his hands. "Ninety-nine, how are we going to get a cake up to Three-T that'll give us enough slices?"

He had a right to be skeptical, so I threw up my hands in surrender.

He continued, "Even if we got a super big one baked in the kitchen bakery, how would we get it up to our cell?"

I agreed that we might be stuck. "It's going to have to be a cake big enough to feed seventy massive appetites. I mean big slices. If we serve tiny wedges, they'll laugh at us."

Moe caught the spirit of the event and sang, "Happy Birthday to me. Happy Birthday to me."

"C'mon, Moe, get serious," Luke said.

"I am serious. I want to see this thing come off just as much as you do. I'm looking forward to it, even if it is impossible."

I had to admit the challenge was daunting. I said, "Several smaller cakes will probably work best." I stared at the roll-your-own cigarette Moe held and said, "We'll buy some tailor-mades with the money. All the guys like machine-rolled smokes."

Moe was beside himself. "What's real cigarettes got to do with anything?"

"Everything," I said.

"Roll-your-own are cheaper," Moe protested.

"Moe, you don't get it," Luke said. "We'll buy the store-bought cigarettes and use them as trade-offs for the cakes."

"Let me get this straight," Moe coughed. "We're going to fund a birthday party for Jesus with smokes?"

"That's right," Luke said. "You'll see it can be done because tailor-mades bring more on the black market than anything else."

I supported him. "Absolutely, and Moe, since you're going to quit smoking and pitch those savings into the pot, we'll make it."

Moe didn't stop smoking, but cigarettes were at the center of our plan. Step by step we worked it. We traded tailor-mades for the cakes and bartered with the smokes to obtain the coffee we needed. We kept things hush-hush. That may have been the biggest miracle of all. The three of us made our own Christmas cards out of file folders "gotten" from Garth and other inmate workers with access through office jobs. Each card was personalized with the recipient's name, and we crafted a banner out of sheets of typing paper and ink markers so we could put together signs for the occasion.

Finally, Christmas Eve arrived. Though we didn't feel ready, we let the word out. Beginning just before the regular evening count, whispers spread like butter in a hot skillet. "There's gonna be a 'Happy Birthday, Jesus' party in Three-T twenty-two, right after count. Everybody gets a gift."

Some of the hardened men were skeptical when they heard the news. There were unbelieving stares, sheepish grins and sardonic laughter. It had never happened before, and almost everyone doubted it could. Homer and Scar were numbered with the long-timers who spit out their cynicism. "Ain't never been no birthday party here. You might's well forget it."

Though we were in an honor dorm, two stories above the dungeon, almost every prisoner subscribed to Scar's assessment. "Keep this cruel joke under your cap. Even if the rumor's true, it can't happen. The goon squad will blow out the candles before they're lit."

Following count, Mr. Gooding turned his head as we transferred the party stuff into Luke and Moe's cell. I noticed Mr. Gooding appeared to have a slight grin all through the process, and his face beamed as we thanked him again for helping us.

We three "kings" hurried to put up the banner and signs and decorate the cell. The banner hung over one bed and read: *Happy Birthday Jesus!* We pulled two tables in from the dayroom. Stacks of cigarettes and large slices of cake graced one table, and we offered coffee at the other.

We distributed the Christmas cards and sang carols to the men as they discreetly wandered in under the supervision of our friendly guard. Most of the men were in shock. Some took the gifts with shaking heads. They just couldn't believe it was really happening. Even so, some of the hardest lifers carried the radiant smiles of little boys, and all the men exuded pure joy. Homer and Scar Face were among the happiest and most shocked celebrants.

With a fistful of tailor-mades in one hand and a Christmas card in the other, Scar said to Homer, "Now we can die in peace 'cause we celebrated our very own birthday party."

Homer stood there crying and laughing but recovered quickly to shovel a slice of cake into his toothless mouth. Washing it down with coffee, he spouted, "Scar, this is a party to top all parties."

What a birthday party it was. The love of Christ flowed from one man to another. There were warm handshakes, even some hugs.

Men who hadn't sung for years were singing Christmas carols, truly celebrating the humble birth of our Lord. The love of the Christ child passed from man to man and cell to cell. The peace of the Lord prevailed for days. The men of cell block Three-T discovered the grandest birthday of them all, at their own birthday party, pulled off by the Big Cat.

26

Despite the spirit of joy Magoo left behind, and the buzz the Christmas party caused, Christmas Day was dark for those who didn't receive visitors. That wasn't the case for me, though I didn't expect a visit. About eight that morning, I called my mother to wish her a Merry Christmas. She accepted the charges, and we had a wonderful visit.

Toward the end of our fifteen minutes, she said something that made that Christmas the most memorable, brightest Christmas ever. She sang a song, "Wonderful Peace," that I had once hated. Now as a Christian, I cherished every word as her voice came over the wire, "Peace, peace, wonderful peace coming down from the Father above; Sweep over my spirit forever I pray, in fathomless billows of love."

I said, "Mother, that song means a lot to me. Peace is what I searched for all those years. You just gave me the best Christmas present ever. Peace is the ultimate—"

She interrupted me by laughing, and said, "That's nothing. It will be coming to you in the mail; you'll have your very own copy of the song so you can learn to sing it, too. It was written by a Cooper, you know."

I wondered who that Cooper could be and hummed the first words of the song, "Peace, peace, wonderful peace . . ." all the way back to the cell. As I opened the screened door, an officer called my name for a visit. "Who could be coming to see me today, on Christmas?" I asked myself. I had been getting regular visits from Jim and Susan Stoneham, but I didn't expect them to come on the holiday. I was ecstatic when the officer called my name again. "Cooper, you got a visit."

When I entered the visiting area, the holiday came alive. Susan wore a Santa cap with a white tassel dangling off to one side. Jim wore a Christmas-green jacket and greeted me with a warm embrace. "Merry Christmas!" he said as he backed out of the hug. "It's going to be a bright Christmas. I sense it. Don't you?"

I had to admit, having a visit from this devoted Christian couple brought joy to what would have been a letdown following the party the night before and the call from Mother. During the visit I told them about the birthday party for Jesus, about Mister Magoo being at his new home for the holiday and about the new lifestyle that had evolved from my mission. They were delighted, but I sensed they came for a very special reason and were dying to share this important news. As they sat across from me I could see it in their eyes. They glowed. Susan was especially excited about something. I caught it on Jim's face as well. My gaze went from one to the other. "What's going on with you two?"

Jim began, "We have some good news that will *really* make your face beam."

These people loved me. I was filled with thankfulness and hoped I had truly expressed my feelings to them. "Just seeing you and basking in your love makes my face beam," I told them. "So, whatever news you have is secondary to your love. Every time you come for a visit, I'm reminded of my jail time and my initial encounter with Jesus." I paused and reached out and touched Susan on the arm, "I can't thank you enough for sending Syd Barrett," I said.

She nodded and reminded me, "Abe Brown is to be thanked too, because Syd came to the jail as a part of Abe's prison ministry."

I had to agree. "But you two went the extra mile since you were with me when I was sentenced."

Jim and Susan laughed. "This is perfect," she said.

I frowned. "What's perfect?"

Jim pointed at me. "What you just said. It's a perfect time to give you our good news." He cleared his throat as though making ready for a grand pronouncement. "We're going to get Judge Coe to release his jurisdiction over you."

"How will you do that?" I could feel my brow wrinkle.

"It's really quite simple. We're taking Ky Koch, your old attorney, to meet with Judge Coe in his chambers. Ky has already agreed to write a motion for Coe to release his jurisdiction over you. He won't charge anyone a dime for his services."

I was ecstatic. "Fabulous! That answers all my questions, except *when*."

"We'll do it in the next few weeks," Susan interjected.

The words had no more than escaped her mouth when Moe popped over to our table carrying his guitar. His mother was visiting him that day. It was the first time we were in the visiting park at the same time. Without saying a word he strummed and sang, "Brighten the corner where you are. Brighten the corner where you are . . ."

"That's what Jim and Susan are doing," I said, interrupting the self-appointed troubadour, and then I introduced them.

They hit it off instantly. We had a super visit, and Moe rejoiced with me at the news they brought. But I saw a question in the furrows that formed on his brow when Jim mentioned the release of the judge's jurisdiction. "What's up, Moe?"

"Well, I was thinking what a tremendous miracle it would be to get Judge Harry Lee Coe, the toughest of the tough, to sign a motion like that."

"It will take a miracle, for sure," Jim agreed and Susan nodded.

"But," I said, "let's get to that question I saw on your forehead."

"Okay, Ninety-nine, you read me like a book, but are you sure you want to hear what I'm concerned about?"

"Like I said, what's up, Moe?"

"It's just that you've served so little time on your ninety-nine."

Susan jumped in before I could react, "You don't mean that Ken should not pursue this now?"

"No, not at all. I was thinking like prisoners think. There are lots of cons here, guys who have done thirty or forty years."

"For much less than what I did?"

"I wasn't going to say it, but yeah, they won't think it's fair."

Now, it was Jim's time to intercede. "I see what you mean, Moe, but it's not about what's fair; it's about God's plan for Ken and us."

"That's it," Susan interjected. "Jim and I believe we should take this first step toward Ken's release."

When she said that, I pictured walking out the main gate, a free man. The first emotion was a tingling sensation of joy, but then a cloud of guilt brought me down. I thought about my many victims and how they would feel, so I asked Jim, "Are you sure God wants you to do this?"

"Not only that, Ken, we believe the judge will sign away his hold over you."

He hadn't really answered my question, but to my relief, Moe said, "I believe it, too."

"Well, let's pray in agreement right now," Jim said, as he extended his hands toward Susan and me.

As we held hands in a circle, Jim prayed, "Lord, we ask You today to put it in Judge Coe's heart to sign a motion to release his jurisdiction. And, Lord, if You have to, place Judge Coe in a mental fog so he won't know what he's doing when he signs the motion." It seemed like a strange prayer to me, but we all said amen, though I wondered about asking God to put the judge in a stupor for a scumbag like me.

Following the visit, though, Moe and I practically skipped back to Three-T. We talked about the faith of the Stonehams. Moe said, "The way they pray is awesome. They spoke to God as if there was no question about whether He heard, or whether He'd answer. It was like He was right there listening."

I had to agree. "Their faith and their prayers have confirmed my hope; it's not just us crazies in the Rock who talk with God."

Moe and I were bolstered in our faith, and our prayer lives improved as our trust in God grew. With the night officer's permission, we met to pray in the TV room at 3:30 a.m., three times a week. During each session I repeated Jim's prayer, "Lord, please cause the judge to release his jurisdiction over me without knowing what he's doing." In time, despite unanswered questions about my deserving God's favor, we believed it would turn out that way.

In my growing faith, I anticipated that I would be set free. I remembered what I told the younger men on the basketball court, and my family during the Stonehams' brief visit: "Faith tells me I'll do three to five years."

27

Trusting God with my release date had built a bridge of hope, and the Christmas spirit continued throughout the cell block during the holiday week as we anticipated the annual Frank Constantino New Year's Eve Worship Service in the chapel. It was the most popular event of the year.

Frank always brought his lovely wife, Bunny. I hoped there would be a chance to socialize with them. I went into the restroom to freshen up.

Ezra stepped up to the sink next to me. "I sure do hope we'll have a chance to talk to Frank and Bunny tonight," he said.

"I'm for that."

Ezra nodded. "I wanna talk to Frank. He's my hero."

Much like Chuck Colson, Constantino was popular in prison. He brought inmates hope because he was "one of us." He had not only successfully returned to society and stayed out of prison for ten years, but he was a nationally known prison evangelist. Perhaps more important to inmates like me who had an addiction problem, Frank founded and operated a recovery ministry in Orlando called *Bridges of America.*

I walked back to the room, mopping my face with a towel, and prayed for Jack Murphy, the famous jewel thief, who had recently left the Rock to reside at Frank's place. He was something of a double hero for me. In my old life as a thief, the rogue who stole the Star of India sapphire served as a negative role model. In prison at Union Correctional Institution, he became an even greater influence on the positive side. To get the word on how Jack was doing, I asked God to give me a moment to check with Frank and Bunny, Murphy's friends.

As I pulled my black brogans from under my bunk and gave them a quick spit shine, I thought of a videotaped lecture Jack gave in an inmate-led life skills program called Growth Orientation Laboratory, or GO-Lab. Jack had explained my crazy out-of-control behavior in a way that made me analyze my problem. He helped me understand the taproot of my addiction.

In the lecture, Murphy said, "I'm an adrenaline junky just as hooked on my internal drug as alcoholics and drug addicts are hooked on the illicit drugs they inject into their bodies."

That statement captured my full attention. Then he slammed me with the truth. "I was hyped up on adrenaline when I stole that famous jewel in New York City."

He explained, "I got higher on internal waves during the robbery than I did while surfing the huge breakers off Hawaii." As I took another look at myself, I realized a part of me still yearned for that kind of high, meaning my problem was more serious than I cared to admit.

Without saying a word to anyone, I attended Alcoholics

Anonymous (AA) meetings, Christian-based Overcomers' support groups and personal growth seminars to work on my weakness.

I slipped into prison blues and pulled on my boots. I thanked God that Frank used his influence with the Florida Parole Commission to convince them to release Jack to Bridges of America. I secretly hoped I would go there upon my release, so I could continue my recovery.

On New Year's Eve, when chapel call was finally given, Ezra and I jumped up and joined a double column line of about one hundred inmates bound for the service. Inside All Souls Chapel, I nudged Ezra as we filed into the first two seats on the third row. I was right on the aisle. The place would be packed, but we had good seats up front. Convicts who never attended worship services came to this one because of Frank and Bunny. It was rumored they were bringing in a women's chorus, so this year the number attending would be greater.

When the house was full and the program finally started, we learned that there was no women's chorus. Those who came just to see the women were upset. The program featured excellent inmate musicians, but as good as the inmates were, they couldn't replace the women we'd hoped to see and hear.

When Frank took his place behind the tiny lectern, he appeared larger than life. His dark-gray, pinstripe suit accented by a red and gray paisley tie reminded me of a gentleman bank robber I had once known.

I smiled ruefully as I ran my fingers over the front of my uniform and gawked at his outfit. That bank robber dude couldn't have been me. It seemed that was another man in another life.

When Frank addressed us, I forgot my prison blues. He spoke in a language convicts could relate to as he challenged us to live for Christ during the new year. His bravado, the way he carried himself and his tough-guy accent reminded me of underworld criminals, but his message somehow gave me hope.

His speaking as a messenger of God helped me believe the Lord would someday bridge the gap between successful ex-convicts like him and me. I hung on his every word. His tone was forceful, but the tough love of a brother who had been where I was shone through the earnest expression on his face. Frank drew me out because he didn't preach condemnation. Instead, he challenged me to stop condemning myself and to be real in my Christian profession. He told me I had to walk the walk, not just talk the talk.

He said, "Walk your talk consistently throughout the new year."

He paused and I leaned forward. "You've got to be real, guys. Real with God. Real with yourself. And you can't fool anyone, so you have to be real with everyone around you."

Ezra nudged me and smiled. I relaxed and leaned back into my seat.

Frank added, "That cell where you live is a glass house. You never have any privacy. Hey, everybody knows your business."

I looked across the aisle at Hans, an AA buddy. He usually didn't attend Christian services. Hans nodded and lifted his eyebrows. We both appreciated the fact that Constantino spoke from experience.

The big man held his hands out toward us. "But something is holding many of you back from building your bridge. Could it be that you are still hooked on whatever whacked you?"

Hans checked my reaction to Frank's question and I shrugged. I wondered why he glanced at me at that moment.

"Even if you're building your bridge, will you careen out of control when you hit the streets again?"

I squirmed in my seat, glanced back at Hans and questioned whether I would still be hooked when my release time came. I desperately wanted to be totally free.

Frank stepped from behind the lectern and came to a spot in the aisle ten feet from me. He looked in my direction. "Your behavior—every action you take, whether it's good or bad—begins with a thought. If you entertain that thought, it becomes an action picture in your mind. If you go one step further and decide to act on your thought, the action you pictured follows automatically. If you repeat the same action over and over, it becomes a habit. And finally, if the habit takes control and drives you to keep doing it, it has become an addiction."

Several men in front of me shifted in their seats. I figured he was getting to them just as he was to me. "And our addictions drove us to commit the crimes outfitting us for these miserable blue uniforms."

I smiled and thought, *Frank has an addiction to nice clothing*, but I said, "Amen!" Others voiced their agreement. Jack Murphy's face in the videos came to mind. "You gotta get rid of your stinkin' thinkin' for starters." Murphy hit it on the head, just as Frank was doing. For the first time, I considered my addictive behavior to be uncontrollable in my own strength.

Without a word, Frank turned, strode back to the front of the chapel and gazed up at the wall on the left side of the pulpit. He pointed to a painting of Jesus writing in the sand. Frank held that pose for what seemed like a full minute.

I tilted my head and stared at the painting with him. It was a full-color portrait of a woman standing behind Christ. He was kneeling and writing in the sand with His finger as she watched. Behind her was an angry mob with huge rocks in their hands ready to stone her.

Frank whirled and faced us. "What picture do you have of Christ in your life? You know what I'm talking about. Many of you are living in condemnation. That's not what this picture is about."

I glanced at Ezra. He was frowning. I felt my lips pinch together before I turned back to Frank.

The big man pointed at the mural again. "This painting shows a loving Christ, not a condemning God." He hesitated, letting that thought sink in. After taking one step toward us, he went on. "So why do you continue to condemn yourself for past sins?"

He lowered his gaze and eased down the aisle to stare into several faces and said, "Forget the angry crowd with their stones." He turned to point at it again. "That painting is about the Lord's compassion toward a woman caught in the act of adultery."

Frank asked us to close our eyes. "Jesus is saying the same thing to you tonight that He said to that woman. 'Neither do I condemn you. Go now and leave your life of sin.' "

In the column of men marching back to the Rock, I thanked God for Frank and Bunny's visit. But when we arrived at the ominous structure, I flashed back to the day I was fresh off the bus and standing at that very spot.

Fixing my blurry eyes on the dark sky above the hellhole, I sighed and sucked in my breath. A mournful prayer came out of my spirit as I softly pleaded with God:

Oh, Father in heaven, on behalf of the countless inmates

who lost their minds or their lives here, I join with the others who have prayed for the closing of this hellacious prison. In the name of Jesus Christ I ask You to send your angels to take control and close it down. Destroy this place, Lord, just as You destroyed Sodom. I ask You to move the hearts of the authorities to make it happen soon.

I glanced around to see if anyone was aware of my mumbling. No one was paying any attention to me so I continued. *And, Father, for the sake of new men coming in, please close it during this new year.*

By the time I reached my room I felt like a heavy load was lifted from my shoulders. I knew that God heard my petition, and I was determined to find someone to agree that the Rock would be closed in 1985. The chaplains taught there is strength in numbers, especially when it comes to spiritual warfare. I saw it work when I was living on A-Wing. Now I knew A-Wing was nothing less than a microcosm of the Rock. I understood a supernatural battle must be waged to shut down the demon-infested prison, just as spiritual warfare had changed A-Wing.

Safely back in the cell that night, I searched my Bible, found 2 Corinthians and read several verses. Since Moe hadn't attended the service, he dropped in to find out how it had gone. I figured God was sending him before the clock struck twelve to begin the New Year. I hoped he would agree with me regarding spiritual authority over the closing of the prison in 1985.

"How'd it go, Ninety-nine?" He stopped short and cocked his head. "You have a strange expression."

"Moe, a far-out thought makes me look like this."

"Talk to me."

I lifted an eyebrow and smiled. "I believe God will close the Rock this year."

From his upper bunk, Snake overheard me and reacted with a curse. He propped himself on one elbow and closed his book. "You Christians think you're God or something." Then he waved it off. "Nah, that's not it. You're stark raving mad."

I laughed and Moe asked, "Snake, do you know Flip from A-four?"

Snake grimaced. "Yeah. There's a typical example. I've seen that crazy dude do his thing on the yard. So what? All of you are as crazy as he is."

Moe ignored the slur. "Well, let me tell you, he's believed for several years that this prison would be closed. He told me he prayed for it a thousand times."

"That's my point, goofballs. You guys have joined in with the other crazies preaching the end of the world ever since I can remember. The only difference is you're now preaching the end of the Rock instead of the end of the world."

I stood up and stared at Snake. "I believe God is about to answer Flip's prayer. When He does, I wonder if you'll think we're crazy then."

He checked his watch and sneered. "It's ten o'clock; I predict the Rock will close at the stroke of midnight," he mocked. "Happy New Year!"

I shook my head, sat down on my bunk and turned to Moe with my voice lowered. "Will you agree with me, this prison will be closed during this coming year?"

He grabbed my hand in a tight handshake. "I agree."

"That's fantastic, Moe."

Snake got in one last dig. "Yeah, that's fantastic, Moe." He snarled, "Goofy people," and went back to reading his novel.

Moe waved him off and turned back to me. "Not only

that," he said, "but I'll also praise God for closing the Rock every time I pray. I'll keep it up until He closes it."

During mail call two days later, I received chain-rattling news. A letter from the Stonehams read, "Today Judge Coe signed the motion releasing his jurisdiction over you."

I threw the letter into the air and jumped up to catch it. I felt as light as a marionette on strings. I shouted, "The judge released his jurisdiction over me. God answered our prayer! The judge released his hold on me!"

Garth and Marty came off their bunks and rushed me. Snake leaned up on one elbow but remained silent this time. I picked up the long-awaited letter, held it in front of my face and waved it before their eyes. "Here it is in black and white. Judge Coe released his jurisdiction. He has no hold on me. I'm as good as free."

Snake tore the paper out of my hand. He scanned it quickly then dropped it.

I grabbed it on its way to the floor and waved it again.

He shook his head and muttered something about dumb luck, but I knew luck had nothing to do with it. God had answered our prayers.

The others were in shock.

Garth finally reacted. "You know what this means, Ninety-nine?"

I held up three fingers.

"That's right, though your ninety-nine-year sentence is still in effect, you only have a three-year minimum mandatory you must do for using a gun to commit a felony. After you finish those three, since you're a first-time offender, you could be ripe for parole on the bank robbery conviction."

I clapped my hands and jumped around some more. "I can't believe it happened. I thought it would, and now it has, but I still can't believe it." I caught myself. "I know it doesn't make sense, but . . . wow!" I shouted.

My atheist friend, Garth, was scratching his head. "How did you get the hanging judge to release his hold over you?"

I held up a hand and said, "I'll tell you guys in a minute. But Moe, will you please go get Ezra? I gotta tell him too."

In a minute or two Moe and Ezra burst through the door. Ezra shouted, "God heard our prayer. You'll be out in three to five like you've been saying."

"What are you guys talking about?" Marty asked.

"For several months now we've been praying that God would make the judge release his hold on Ken," Moe said.

Garth was skeptical and asked, "What did you pray?"

"We prayed God would put the judge into a stupor when a motion to release jurisdiction was put in front of him by an attorney."

Garth squinted. "I don't get ya."

I said, "Look. Judge Coe signed the motion to release his thirty-three-year hold on me without knowing what he was signing. That's exactly what friends of mine, Jim and Susan, prayed in the visiting park. Moe and I have been praying it ever since."

Garth looked puzzled. "I'll just say I'm glad for you. Just when is Coop gonna fly the coop?"

A smile creased my cheeks. "I'll be free in two or three more," I declared. "The handwriting is on the wall. I can hardly wait to tell the jitterbugs on the basketball court. Those young guys will flip out when they hear about God answering our prayers."

Snake listened but held his tongue. When I glanced at him

I could see he was wrestling with this good news and the power of prayer.

"What is wrong with you, Snake? You always speak your mind."

"Ninety-nine, you seem real in your faith, but does God do good things to some people because of their faith?"

"You mean He helps some people but doesn't help others?"

"Yep."

"It seems that way, pal. I don't deserve this break for sure, but it must be true that God did it."

"One other thing, preacher man, don't count your chickens in here before they're hatched outside the gate."

"I'm not, Snake. Garth says I could be on my way out soon, but with all I did, it just doesn't seem possible."

"What you mean, Christian, is it doesn't seem right."

"That's for sure, there are a hundred men in here who should be headed to the gate before me."

"Who knows, Ninety-nine; you may be His favorite."

"I hope not; but I'm not going to turn my back on His blessings."

Apparently through talking, Snake grunted and turned over.

I told him good night, picked up a stub of a pencil and scribbled a note to Mother about the fantastic news.

28

The next day, more chain-rattling news came. During count an officer placed a stack of envelopes on my bunk and muttered, "Cooper, you get more mail than the warden."

I tore open the first piece of mail. It was from Raymond Duncan of Time for Christ Prison Ministry and carried a message that intrigued and thrilled me beyond words. He wrote, "Now that the judge's jurisdiction has been removed, we will establish a plan to achieve your timely release."

In a subliminal flash, I saw the chains of bondage fall from my wrists and ankles. Caught up in the moment, I let go of the letter and watched it float to the floor. As it descended and made a soft landing, I relived its message: "your timely release." I played it again: "your timely release."

I glanced around at the other men in my cell. In prison everything moves in slow motion and rapid-roll activity of any kind is like a pothole in the road. So this "plan for my timely release" gave me a jolt. The hair on my arms became electric. Sure, I spouted that I would be released in three to five years, but it still shocked me that high-powered people like Raymond were committed to making it happen.

With trembling hands, I picked up the letter and continued reading, "As you know, the first step is an interview with a psychiatrist. Dr. Ronald Menard should be coming in to do a mental health evaluation. I am confident it will confirm that you are no longer a threat to society."

I almost dropped the paper again. Raymond's optimistic words written with such clarity and confidence sent shivers up my spine. The letter continued, "Please be praying for that interview. Also, ask the Lord to bring someone forward from the Kairos ministry group who knows you well enough to speak on your behalf at a parole hearing."

Parole hearing?

I read and reread the words. It wasn't so much that I couldn't believe them, it was that the message of good news was simply *too* good. Exhilaration pumped me up until I thought I'd burst if I didn't share this fantastic news. However, it was count time and we were ordered to remain quiet.

My head pounded with pain. Diverse emotions of elation, fear and disbelief churned in my mind. There was the desire to accept this positive turn of events, yet caution told me to prepare myself for negative responses from the doctor, the parole commission and those around me. I thought about my mixed reaction to the letter and a scene from two years earlier came into focus: I stood before a judge who was supposed to give me a twelve-year sentence but instead, slapped me with 99 years. I felt betrayed, but decided I had to live with it, so I settled in for a long, dry solo run.

That I now had several respected street people working on my release seemed unreal. In those two years I'd adapted to convict thinking. I was wary of positives that came along, considering that there was probably going to be a hitch. I held the letter at arm's length and mused, "If it's based on feeling worthy, I'm not emotionally prepared to relate to the real world."

As count time continued and I still couldn't tell the guys that a release plan was underway, my mind offered up other issues. I didn't want to admit it, but like most prisoners serving a life sentence, I daydreamed of my release rather than putting together a step-by-step plan to accomplish it. I dreamed of a hero on a great white stallion galloping into the Rock to rescue me. When despair hovers like a dark cloud, there is something about the human psyche that conjures up a blue-sky kind of hope. So this new twist of reality tightened a knot of worry in my gut.

Although I'd seen God work miracles, I was still very new to this relationship with Him, and I walked in fear. It seemed I wavered from faith to fear and back again. All I knew was that I had to talk to some of the brothers who had faced release. Undoubtedly, many of the cons would be confounded by my good fortune and some strapped with envy and perhaps with anger.

My right hand twitched. A surge of fear tore through me, and I shuddered as scenes of the early days in the Rock played across my mind. Countless unknowns lay ahead, and I needed a lot of wise advice and prayer.

By the time Officer Gooding approached my bed to count me, I settled down to thinking about employment opportunities for an ex-felon like me. In that moment, I came up with all kinds of ways to help God plan for someone who would give me a job, put me into permanent housing and take responsibility for me by signing on the dotted line.

As Gooding counted Snake, I thought about the fact

that I had been asked to serve as master of ceremonies for a Kairos Prison Ministry meeting the next morning. In the middle of all this excitement and worry, I was preparing to address a large group of convicts and volunteers at the chapel. I would be responsible for the smooth management of the program and didn't feel up to it. Like all inmates, I had been pushed out of sight by authorities, so this opportunity to be up front in prison for the first time was disconcerting.

My thoughts were a jumble of emotional upheavals. On one hand, I was too involved in things happening in my life and feared that I'd mess this up for lack of dedication. On the other hand, I was apprehensive, feeling I might revert to my ego-puffing self-centeredness. To keep myself in the right mindset, I decided to take action.

Count cleared. I did not share the fantastic good news with the guys. To give myself time to think about possible negative reactions and to humble myself, I asked the sergeant's permission to scrub the cell block toilets. I got down on my knees and scoured the stinking commodes, muttering, "I'm already a nervous wreck. Now I've got to worry about whether I can do this emcee job right." I went on, "Well, Ken, I hope you're happy."

I thought about Raymond's letter and his promise to ask a Kairos volunteer to speak for me at my parole hearing. The person he selected had to know me well and could be there the next morning.

That night sleep wouldn't come as I prayed and hoped the mystery volunteer would be there. On the way to the chapel, the thought hit me; I had to put first things first. That would be my appointment to see the shrink. This public speaking thing would take care of itself.

Before prison I worked in many areas that allowed me to stand before crowds and speak. I thoroughly enjoyed serving as master of ceremonies. I liked the challenge of saying things well with a few words, introducing the key speakers, keeping the program moving and finishing right on time.

On that Saturday morning, the chapel was packed with inmates and volunteers. I wanted to grab everyone's attention right away, so when I stood up to greet the audience I quoted Ben Franklin: "If you would not be soon forgotten, when you are dead and rotten, either write things worth the reading, or do things worth the writing." I paused to let those prudent words sink in before addressing the volunteers. "You have chosen to minister to the *least* brothers of Christ. Therefore, we are letters written on your hearts, hearts that cause you to do things worth the writing."

The audience beamed. The tension choking my vocal chords subsided so I introduced singers and speakers with gusto and kept the program flowing. Things appeared to go well, and we finished right on time. Yet at the end I wasn't pleased. For some reason I seemed out of sync. I had taken the platform without a lot of practice. It was the first time in three years I had served as emcee.

I felt relieved. The program was over so we gathered for lunch with the free people. I was eager to talk to Raymond, to see when he expected Dr. Menard to visit me. As I scanned the crowd, I couldn't find him, but I noticed an imposing man. It was his first visit, and his height and white hair made him stand out. He seemed to be making a beeline for me, and he had his hand out as he approached.

"I'm James Whyte," he said as we met and shook hands.

His name didn't mean a thing to me. He spoke with a distinctive voice that forced me to listen closely as his words came out as rapid-fire questions. His first question was "How did you prepare for serving as emcee?"

I didn't like his aggressive style and wished he would say something complimentary about the job I'd done. Instead he was asking an unconventional question; even so, I didn't hesitate and chuckled. "I voluntarily scrubbed the commodes in my cell block." I was telling the truth, even though it must have sounded absurd. I knew he heard me, but he didn't respond to my odd answer.

Instead, Mr. Whyte fired another question: "How did you happen to quote Ben Franklin?" Then he added, "That impressed me."

That was my cue to steal control by asking him a question. "Why does a quote from Franklin impress you?"

"He's America's first newspaper publisher."

That statement and his obvious interest in me and my statements still didn't give me a clue as to who this man was. It hadn't entered my mind that he could be the volunteer to speak to the parole commission for me. I guess I displayed a blank stare.

His eyes pierced mine. "I'm in the newspaper business. I work for the *Florida Times-Union* in Jacksonville."

I grinned. "Oh, now I get it. Like Franklin, you're in the newspaper business."

He got control again. "You still didn't tell me why you quoted old Ben."

"I want to be remembered for what I've written, not for what I've done." The twinkle in his eyes told me he appreciated my logic and humor.

His brow rose. "Well now, we can't get into that. Besides

you'll surely have ample opportunity in the future to make Mr. Franklin proud by doing things worth the writing."

Even his reference to my doing well in the future didn't register. Although we talked for quite a while, his final question nearly floored me. He looked straight into my eyes and asked, "Will you answer my letters quickly if I write you?"

My mind whirled, and I wondered what was going on. He wasn't a regular with the monthly Kairos team. I questioned why this distinguished businessman would want to write to me. Even at that point, it had not hit me that he was sent by Raymond to evaluate me according to a master plan for my release. I finally muttered, "Sure, I'll write back when you write to me."

He smiled and slapped me on the shoulder. "Good. Since I work at the *Florida Times-Union*, I'll write you from my office."

After the event ended and all the volunteers were gone, a big-eyed inmate asked, "Do you know who that was you were talking to?"

I shrugged. "Said his name was James Whyte, spelled with a *y*," I responded.

"You don't know who he is?"

Again I shrugged. "Should I?"

"He's the president and general manager of the *Times-Union*."

I felt my mouth drop open. "He said he worked at the newspaper. It's a good thing I didn't find out then who he really is or why he attended this meeting. I'd have passed out."

My friend laughed. "He's a mover and a shaker," he said, and then drifted over to some other guys. That's when I got the idea he might be the man Raymond had sent to meet me.

Maybe he was the hero on a white stallion sent to rescue me, and I didn't recognize him.

I was embarrassed but hope flooded my mind in anticipation of Mr. Whyte's first letter. Even so, I recalled my coolness *faux pas* when I met him. Fear that he had been turned off tried to push itself forward.

When that letter arrived, I answered promptly as promised, and he responded with at least one letter every week. Through our correspondence, Jim and I became well acquainted. We even compared typing speeds. He typed as fast as he could think, while my speed was about seventeen words a minute, slightly slower than I think. I never mentioned his representing me before the parole commission. Neither did he. But, after a few letters, there was no doubt in my mind that he would do it when the time came.

Relating to him lifted me out of the timeless despair of lockup, and I stopped worrying about the unknowns of my release. Jim traveled throughout the world, and his letters, along with an occasional picture, took me with him. Through his words, Jim carried me into his days, including his home life, work and recreation.

What a tremendous encouragement he was as he lived up to the challenge of Ben Franklin to write things worth the reading. I tried to do the same. In his birthday card of February 18, 1985, I wrote, "You will surely not be soon forgotten when you are dead and rotten because you have inspired me to write things worth the reading and to do things worth the writing."

29

One Saturday morning in May, while writing a letter to Jim Whyte, I was called in and told, "Get ready for a visit." Jim's face flashed across my mind. I asked who was coming to see me but didn't get an answer, just a scowl. I hurried back to my cell block, put the writing pad away and cleaned up. Brushing my teeth for the second time that day, I wondered who could be making a surprise visit.

Most visitors come early in the morning and spend the day, so the park was crowded by the time my visitors got there. I didn't see any of my close friends in the park. Those of us confined to that part of the prison seldom received visits.

When I saw my sweet little mother coming through the outer gate, she seemed to carry an angelic aura. A great distance separated us as I waited for her. It was hard to believe it really was my mother. We hadn't seen each other for years. She had prayed for my conversion, and I hoped she would be able to see the change in me. But as I waited, I wondered if I had become the black sheep of the family who had *not* been forgiven.

A glow of light and a rainbow of spring flowers along the walkway framed her image as she came toward me. I knew there were other people moving with her, but my focus was on her. The others were a blur.

As she grew nearer, the radiance of her face gave me hope that she forgave me and that we would have a peaceful visit. If the time and circumstances were right, I was determined to beg forgiveness for all the pain and injury I'd caused her and the family. I would finally know how she was doing following the stroke. As she came through the inner gate, she walked normally but seemed smaller than I remembered, even though her presence filled the park for me.

Finally, the long-awaited moment came. Mother stood before me. I wanted to fall at her feet weeping. She must have sensed my brokenness and shook her head. She smiled brightly and opened her arms. I melted into her embrace. The softness and warmth of her body dissolved my fear of rejection. She loved me with all her heart. I stepped back and lifted her chin to gaze down into her face. I watched the back of her hand brush away a tear. She was tiny, vulnerable and precious. I had forgotten that she was only five feet tall. She had aged. Deep worry lines on her forehead made her look older. Concern over her stroke sent a surge of guilt through me, but the joy I felt just seeing her chased the guilt away as quickly as it came.

In that surreal moment, I realized that my oldest brother, Jim, and younger brother, Gene, and their wives stood behind her. They stepped forward and faced me. I didn't know what to expect, but I knew they wouldn't hug me. Mountain men don't embrace. Prison Fellowship and Kairos taught me that they should, but I waited for them to make the first move. Jim approached me first and gave me a warm handshake with a poke on the arm. Gene followed suit. They seemed really glad to see me, but I wasn't sure. The problem with brother Paul was fresh in my mind.

I felt better and relaxed a little when Jim and Gene stepped aside and Dottie and Martha hugged me like sisters and told me how good I looked. The visiting park was suddenly filled with love, family and scintillating excitement.

I took my mother's hands in mine. "Mother," I began, and then looked up to the others, "and you guys, too, there's no way you can understand how much this means to me. To see you, to touch you, to be held by you." I nearly broke down. I swallowed hard before taking another deep breath. When I peered back into her eyes I was able to express my joy. "Mother, this is like going to heaven."

She grabbed me again and pulled me close. "Ken, it makes me feel so much better to see that you are okay. You look really good."

Her voice was frail, but I was relieved that she did not slur her words. I sensed her sincerity and wanted to say something that would please her and ease the tension. I said, "Mother, you'll never know how much it meant to me . . . on the phone when you sang, 'Wonderful Peace.' "

That was the only encouragement she needed. Right there at the gate in front of the guard and other visitors, she let go with

> Peace! Peace! wonderful peace,
> Coming down from the Father above;
> Sweep over my spirit forever, I pray,
> In fathomless billows of love.

To her delight, I sang right along with her. But becoming self-conscious, I looked around to see who was staring at us. A glow brightened every face. That gave me heart, and I said, "Like I've said in letters, Mother, this place has not been easy, but everything's turned around for the good now that I have peace of mind."

She nodded her head, but didn't respond. Then, she glanced at Jim and Gene.

They looked away.

A lump formed in my throat. I wanted to scream out something about the hell I'd been through, but I was afraid it might fall on deaf ears. Instead, I said, "Hey, we're blocking the entrance. Let's go over to one of the picnic tables."

I pointed. "There's one under an oak tree. We can relax and talk."

I led them over to the table, and we sat and visited. The breeze embraced us. The day was perfect. But then I realized Mother did not understand the prison rules. Out of her purse, she took a yellow sheet of paper that appeared to be a page torn out of a songbook. She started to hand it to me.

I looked at the officer watching us and admonished her. "Mother, you can't give me anything out of your purse."

She looked confused.

"It's against the rules, and they will make us leave the park," I blurted.

Extending the sheet of paper toward me she said, "It's another song about peace, this one by Fanny Crosby."

"I'm sorry, Mother; I can't take it now, but please mail it to me as soon as you can."

Tears formed in her eyes as she returned the song to her pocketbook.

"Mother, please don't cry, and do send it to me right away. I can hardly wait to sing another new song."

Mother's face brightened. She laughed and said, "I'm glad

you want to abide by the rules now. I'll mail my song to you as soon as I get back home."

Feeling better, I embraced Mother. Jim and Dottie beamed, and Martha snuggled up to Gene. She pointed to the old prison beyond the park fence. "Is that where you live?" Her voice squeaked with disbelief, if not fear.

"Yeah, that's the infamous Rock." I chuckled nervously. "But I wouldn't call it living. It's a whole lot better now, but it was rough going at first."

Gene jumped into the conversation with a change in the subject. "Forgive me for not answering your letters, Ken." He seemed antsy. "You're now the clerk in the security office. Is that right?"

"Yeah, security has made me secure here." I smiled, but no one laughed. Their silence told me I shouldn't joke about prison, especially in our mother's presence. I fidgeted on the hard park bench and grabbed the opportunity to be serious. "Honestly, God has blessed me to have a really good job and the days go by quickly, as I await my transfer to another place."

Jim coughed, glanced at Mother and changed the subject. "We were here in Florida visiting Paul. He's just down the road at Ocala, so this was an easy stop for us."

That comment cut deep. He made it apparent they did not intend to stay very long, just a quick stop, and that they had come to see Paul, not me. That's why they didn't let me know they were coming. I remembered Jim's warning before the last bank robbery. To shake the thought, I turned to my mother. "You looked like an angel coming through the gate. I'm so glad to see you. Thanks for coming, Mother. I really didn't expect it." I grimaced. Again I blurted out the wrong words.

Everyone felt the tension until Dottie tried to lighten the atmosphere. "Ken, did you really rob all those banks?"

I grabbed at the opportunity. "Yes, and I'm sorry for all the pain and trouble I've caused." I had a lump in my throat and couldn't finish.

Jim glanced at Dottie and interrupted my thought. "We can't stay very long."

Mother interjected, "We want to pray with you while we're here."

"I'd like that very much," I said, but my peace of mind vanished. An old "I'm not OK" feeling rose up, and I silently hoped they wouldn't pray for my salvation. The presumptuous, judgmental attitude of many people coming into prison to "save us incorrigible convicts bound for hell" left me cold. I didn't consider myself in that number since committing my life to Christ two years earlier. I wanted to tell them, but it seemed the timing was wrong.

Jim cleared his throat and suggested we pray.

I bowed my head with them and closed my eyes. He didn't pray for my salvation. I was thankful and glad when we said, "Amen."

They stayed a few more minutes. As they prepared to leave, I leaned over to kiss Mother on the cheek. Words of love stuck in my throat. I couldn't speak. I turned and looked into the face of my big brother, hoping Jim would rescue me. In a way he did.

"It sure has been a good visit," he said.

They were leaving. It seemed too soon. I wanted to tell them about the plans for my release, but I nodded to Jim. I still couldn't speak, so I just shook his hand. After swallowing hard I poked Gene in the chest and said, "I love you, little brother."

"Ken," he said, "I love you, too." He patted me on the shoulder, but he turned his face from me so the tears wouldn't surface.

Martha and Dottie cried.

Mother cried.

I wept.

Jim and Gene stood like statues attempting to maintain their composure.

They couldn't face me. I realized that the lot of them thought I was going to die in prison, so I straightened up and said, "Good grief! This isn't my funeral. Faith tells me I'll do three to five years and see you all again outside." I checked their faces, but they didn't comprehend what I was saying. "Some friends are helping me with that," I added.

There was dead silence. To ease the electricity, I tried humor with my Kentucky twang. "Until then, y'all come back! Hear?"

They laughed and agreed they would come back to see me. As they turned away and retraced their steps toward the outside gate, I watched them grow small. They waved just before passing through the portal. I waved back. My thoughts were with them, and I wondered if I'd ever see them again, especially my dear mother. This had to be just as hard on her as it was on me. She knew I was shackled with a life sentence, and that the state expected me to die in prison.

I was frozen there even after I could no longer see them. A slight smile wormed its way across my lips as I muttered, "God, Jim Whyte and Raymond Duncan will see that I do three to five." I shrugged. "But my family isn't ready to talk about my freedom. They didn't take it in and probably have not forgiven me. I'll understand if they never come back." I finally turned my head. "But I sure hope they will."

As I ambled toward the shakedown room, I considered the visit. Poor Mother was so nervous and uptight that we really couldn't tear down any barriers in such a short time. I knew it would take several hours to find a common ground of understanding because her view of reality differed so much from mine. I yearned to lay the foundation for discussing my true feelings, my guilt and shame, but the opportunity never came. Our brief visit disturbed me. I didn't even have a chance to ask her to forgive me—not the way I wanted to.

Before turning in that night, I shared my difficult experience with Moe, Luke and Ezra. They were eager to hear, but none of them carried a life sentence. Their world was different from mine, though we existed in the same place. They couldn't relate to the horrendous fear my family had that I would die in prison. Because of my friends' lack of understanding, I didn't share the trauma we suffered and sad good-bye during the short visit.

I summed it up. "It went horribly, though it could have been much worse."

"What's worse than horrible?" Moe asked.

"They were not judgmental, but they could have hanged me from one of the oak trees in the visiting park," I observed, not wanting to open up. "Guys, I really don't want to talk about it right now so just pray for me and my family."

Ezra led us in prayer, but it did not bring me peace. I went to bed before lights-out.

The next day Sergeant Fisher was sitting at his desk. "Sarge, I had my first visit from my mother and the family yesterday."

He didn't say anything for a moment, then swiveled in his chair and asked, "How'd it go?"

"Not very well, sir. I crashed after they left. It left me a mess."

"You know, Cooper, the guys who have it hardest are those who get a visit from their family every week."

His philosophizing numbed me. I couldn't believe he was lecturing on inmates in general and ignoring my need to tell him that the visit with my family had stolen my peace and sense of reality. But I said, "I don't think they'll come back anymore, but what do you mean, sir?"

"I mean it's really difficult for a man to establish any kind of life inside the fence if his family, especially his wife or lady, visits him every weekend. It tears him between this world and that one."

I decided to humor him. "Yes, I've noticed. A guy who gets regular visits seems really torn in two. Half of him is in here, and the other half is out there somewhere in limbo."

"I hope your family stayed long enough for you to patch things up some."

I decided he was not ready to really hear me, so I resorted to humor. "Well, not really, that would take more time than I've got."

"That's a bad joke, Ninety-nine."

I said, "Yes, sir . . . as in life." We laughed, and I was relieved when the phone rang. Moe was on the line.

He didn't identify himself as he said, "This is a collect phone call from an inmate in a state prison. If you will accept the charges . . ."

"Moe! Are you crazy? You could get locked up in solitary confinement for this! Where are you? What phone are you using?" I looked at Sergeant Fisher with upraised eyebrows, wishing he were not there. He eased over to the refrigerator and leaned against it. I spoke over the mouthpiece. "This is my friend Moe. He's calling to . . ."

Fisher held up a hand. "Tell him we don't want to know

why he's calling or where he's calling from, but I'll transfer his butt back to A-Wing if he doesn't hang up right now."

Moe heard the sergeant's warning. "Okay, but tell him he'll have to lock up Garth too. I'm calling from the colonel's office. We just wanted to cheer you up, Ninety-nine."

"Well, you've done it, and I appreciate it more than I can say right now, so good-bye." I hung up and looked at my boss.

Sergeant Fisher laughed. "Don't tell him, but I think that was a good thing he did. But he better never do it again, good friend or not."

"I'm sorry, Sarge, but I can guarantee nothing when it comes to Moe except that he will pull a prank or sing a song at the drop of a hat."

"It better not be my hat or my phone," Fisher said.

My boss loved his job and his hat, which looked like the ones the Royal Canadian Mounted Police wear. I enjoyed working for him.

30

My job was rewarding and became less stressful when Colonel Jackson and Sergeant Fisher instituted a get-tough policy against troublemakers.

Due to the stabbing deaths of an officer and many inmates, a security force took control of the prison and locked the problem prisoners in solitary confinement. That included Bear, Evil, Psycho and others.

A new batch of inmates arrived at the Rock, and the cons gathered near the entry point to eyeball the men coming in. Some of the convicts were there out of curiosity, and a handful looked for new arrivals that might need help as they entered the system.

I was among the group that checked to see if anyone needed help. I spotted one particular man stepping off that bus. I focused on his innocent baby face. He looked more like a choirboy than a criminal. His beautiful blond wavy hair would make him a trophy for one of the psychos not yet in lockup.

I had the opportunity to rescue the poor wretch before he was attacked. Through Garth, our little group had rescued several men, and now I was compelled to see to it that this man didn't face the agony of A-Wing. He would be a sure target and like many others could go crazy and be carried off to Chattahoochee.

Back in the office, I looked on the roster of new entries and found George Thompson's picture and description. I approached Sergeant Fisher. "Sarge, we got a new man on this busload who's gonna give Security a problem." Using that particular approach got his attention. The one thing that Fisher didn't want was security problems. They had enough to handle without adding to it.

His eyes narrowed as he stared into my face. He knew I didn't play games and that if I spotted something, it was serious. "And just how's that, Cooper?"

"Well," I began, as I watched his inquisitive stare, "this man, Thompson, is gonna be the target of every misfit in the joint." I let that sink in, and then added, "He'll be nothing but trouble on A-Wing."

Sergeant Fisher's mouth tightened as he thought. He pulled at his chin, and his heavy brow rose as he made a determination. "Move him to another wing, Coop. Find a vacant bed, take care of it and I'll sign the paperwork later."

I processed the order, and within hours, Security moved Thompson directly to Three-T, a few cells from where I bunked.

Thompson came down the hall to my room. He stuck his head in and called, "Cooper?" I looked up, and he said, "Thanks. I really appreciate what you did."

I smiled. "My pleasure. How you doing?"

"Ah, good. This part of the prison is great compared to

below." He hesitated, then added, "Uh, listen, I'd really like to share my testimony with you sometime. Is that okay?"

His gracious attitude and that word *testimony* confirmed what I felt in my gut. I smiled. "We'll find each other," I assured him. "We'll take a walk, and talk."

A couple of days later, I spotted him and we walked the yard. Like thousands of men before us, we each shared our past and hopes for the future as we leisurely circled the inside of the razor wire perimeter. With each step we took on the mile circle, we got to know each other. Sauntering along in the warm afternoon with the sun beating down on us, I could feel perspiration soaking my underarms and trickling down my sides. Dreaded "Potter's Field," the burial ground for many a lifer, came into view as we passed the southwest corner of the loop. I secretly feared joining them but didn't want Thompson to know it.

My hand went out to bring his attention to the well-worn path before us. It was a trench about two yards wide and two feet deep, carved out by thousands of prisoners over sixty years. "Why aren't you afraid you'll be buried in prison just like the many lifers who've trudged this path before you?" I gestured toward the graveyard. "How can you radiate peace and joy all the time when you just started your sentence—a life sentence at that."

When he responded it was as though he didn't see the graveyard. "Most of the time I have peace of mind, living one day at a time. I live today, not yesterday or tomorrow. In this moment, and only in this moment, can we know the promises of God. I have His personal promise."

"Personal promise? Like some special promise just for you?"

He smiled. "That's the testimony I want to share with you when you have time to hear it."

"I've got the time now. Are you saying you believe God's gonna rescue you from this hell?"

His smile broadened, so I dug a little deeper. "Look at this trench. Men like us with life sentences carved it out."

"That's right," Thompson said. "And those men expected to die in prison."

"Don't you?"

"No more than you do. I've heard that you say, 'Faith tells me I'll do three to five.' "

"You're right, and most of the time I believe it."

"I've been talking to Homer, Scar and some of the guys who have been here over forty years."

"What did you learn?"

"They say you can tell by how a man carries himself."

"Yeah, I know what you mean. Most of the lifers mope around and around this giant circle. They have lost hope. For years they clung to hope that there would be some judicial change in the law, or some new evidence would surface to free them."

He eyed me but dropped his eyes and looked down at the trail beneath our feet.

"That's what made this trail," I said. "Whether it was true hope or false hope, this path was dug out by hope. Otherwise those with life to do would simply stop walking and let their time bury them."

He nodded.

"Do you know some of us call this path the Trail of Years?"

"Yeah, I've already heard."

I could feel my eyebrows shoot up. I figured this guy was

just naïve, and I was about to say so, but he lifted a hand to stop me.

"Ken, let me tell you about God's personal promise that gave me this peace of mind. *That's* what has real meaning." His face lit up. "I was languishing in Polk County Jail." The light in his eyes dimmed as he took himself back to that place and time. "Though I was innocent, the judge sentenced me to life for murdering my wife."

Hearing him use my given name added to my emotional gymnastics. "Whoa!" I blurted. "That's a heavy load to carry! If you're really innocent, it must be even tougher for you to live at peace with God and yourself." As soon as I said *If you're really innocent* I wanted to retract it. I tried to cover it with, "Your wife? That must be—"

He cut me off. "Oh, I'm innocent all right. There's a man at Florida State Prison who admits he killed her, but nobody believes him." We continued our walk along the trail, and he added, "But the real killer admitting it isn't what gives me this peace."

My eyes squinted, but not from the Florida sun. An onslaught of questions clouded my vision and blocked the smell of evening chow being prepared.

"Tell me more," I prodded.

George sighed. "As I said, I wasn't doing well at all with my sentence while I was in jail. In fact, I couldn't sleep. One early morning, about three-thirty, I was crying out to God about my horrible situation. In order to gain some comfort, I picked up my Bible and inched as close as I could to the lighted catwalk. I read, but no comfort came to ease the pain.

"A guy appeared behind me and asked, 'What are you reading?'

"I turned to see a guard. He was an ordinary-looking

black man, probably in his forties. His name tag said he was Officer Brown. I told him I was trying to read the Bible, but I wasn't doing very well in my state of mind. I said I wasn't getting much out of it.

"He asked, 'Why?'

"I told him I'd been sentenced to life for murdering my wife but I was innocent, yet still on my way to prison. He didn't question my innocence like others have. Instead, he just said, 'Let's see what God has to say to you from His Word.'

"I handed my Bible to the officer. He started with the first psalm and told me I was the man planted by the rivers of living water, and I would flourish in prison. Then he read promises from other psalms and more passages from both the Old and New Testaments. About an hour later he finished with my favorite chapter, Romans 8. It promises that God is on our side, and we are more than conquerors through Christ. As he read, I took every word to heart, and great peace swept over me."

George stopped on the trail and sighed as he peered into my eyes. "Ken," he said, "when Officer Brown read God's Word to me, it was as if it had been written for me personally. I mean, all the promises were mine. I knew deep inside that God's perfect will was being done in my life, even though I was headed to prison with a life sentence." Thompson must have noted my dismay. He quickly injected, "Stay with me. It gets better."

I had to chuckle. "How can it get any better than this? Even though you're an innocent man, you *really are* at peace." George was lifting me to new heights.

He turned his head for a moment. His upper lip quivered.

When he got control, he continued. "The next day something really fantastic happened that changed my life forever."

He was elated, yet very serious. Again he stopped walking and turned to face me.

I stopped on the Trail of Years and felt the sun's heat on my back. The light in George's tear-filled eyes sparkled.

"I went by the control room to thank a Christian officer who knew my case and was praying for me. I told her how the guard came by that night. Then I thanked her for her prayers and for sending Officer Brown to me. Ken, she was startled and said, 'That's impossible.'

"I asked her why, and she said, 'Thompson, we haven't had an Officer Brown working here for years.'

"It hit me like a thunderbolt, and I wept right there. She was crying, too. It took a minute for me to regain my composure. I experienced a miracle. There was no doubt about that. Both of us were thinking the same thing: God sent an angel to comfort me and to demonstrate His power to fulfill His personal promises to me."

Suddenly, the count-time horn blaring across the yard jarred us out of our euphoria. We had only a few minutes to be inside for late-afternoon count. Even so, George and I laughed. We were lost in that moment of time that changed his life from distress to peace. And for a few sweet moments we escaped from the underworld and lived on a higher plain.

31

Not long after that I discovered that some officers were stealing meat from the compound walk-in freezer and storing it in the refrigerator in the security office where I worked. I didn't say a word to anyone until Sergeant Fisher came in one morning. I was up to here with what the brown suits were doing. "Sarge, there's a serious problem I need to talk to you about."

His brow pulled together. "What's going on, Cooper?"

I walked over and opened the refrigerator door and bent to look inside. "The officers continue to store meat, a lot of days fifty or sixty pounds of it, in our refrigerator."

Fisher glared at me. "Close it!"

His tone told me I was in trouble. I stood up, closed the refrigerator and faced him. "I'm sorry you brought it up." His jaw tightened, and his fists clenched. "Really sorry." He was agitated.

I thought about the thin line I walked. The realization that I'd just overstepped my bounds hit me hard. His glare sent me a message that carried the crack of a whip with it.

Immediately a wall was laid between us, brick by brick, and our working relationship vanished. The room felt cold.

He turned and extended his hands with open palms as if to take the harshness out of the moment. "There's nothing we can do about it. They steal the meat out of the big prison freezer and store it here in the refrigerator for a day before they take it home."

"Okay, sir, I-I j-just thought . . ."

He snapped, "You're not paid to think, Cooper!" The conversation was over.

"Thank you, sir. It really is none of my business."

His face contorted. "You got *that* right!"

I had made a terrible mistake and knew I would pay for it sooner or later. My gut told me it would be sooner, and my days as Rock clerk were numbered.

That night I humbled myself and talked to Garth about it. He was flabbergasted. "Ninety-nine, don't you know the guards live by the same code we do: 'See no evil—speak no evil'?"

"Yeah, I know, but they're stealing meat we should be eating in the chow hall."

"Man, you ain't the po-leece, and who are you to look after inmate welfare? You broke the code and put Fisher in a terrible spot."

"Yes, I know. But I thought he'd put a stop to it."

"Ninety-nine, you're an idiot of an egghead thief. Of all people, I thought you were smart enough to know."

"Know what?"

"Life gives you only what you grab." My cynical friend grabbed me by the arm to emphasize his point.

"My days of grabbing are over, Garth; I just want to—"

Garth interrupted me. "You have no personal integrity. You're living a dream."

"What's my honesty got to do with it?"

"You're looking through rose-colored glasses, so you can't see the truth."

"We're all out of touch with reality in this unreal world," I lamented.

"What I mean is, you're using Christianity as a crutch and not facing reality."

"You're putting me on."

He threw his hands into the air. "Haven't you talked to the outside guys who work at the officers' homes? Here's the reality; the guards are grabbers and takers, just like us!"

I walked away thinking I didn't know anything at all. I thought I was aware of my own shortcomings and surroundings and had a handle on what was going on around me. But Garth's perspective on reality hit me hard. I was out in left field, believing the "good guys" were really good, no matter what color uniform they wore.

Sleep was fitful. Questions about integrity and reality floated through my mind, and I woke up early to make sense of my jumbled thoughts. Grabbing the dictionary, I looked up the definition of the two words and condensed them into one new word. I wrote, "If integrity is 'strict personal honesty,' and reality is 'something that is real or true,' here and now I resolve to make *integreality* my approach to life." I smiled about forming one word from two, called myself a hopeless hillbilly egghead and somehow felt better.

Two days later, on Fisher's day off, Sergeant Jones, the officer in charge of the Main Gate, came into the security office. "Pack your stuff!" he barked. "You've been transferred to my unit."

Even though I knew in my gut it was coming, it hit me like a bolt of lightning. I sat at my desk a moment.

Jones smiled. "Didn't you hear me, Cooper? You've been promoted again. This time your assignment is Rock Gate, man." Sarcasm dripped from his lips.

I didn't show him any emotion and gathered my writings, including my recent work on integreality, and put them in a folder.

He glared at me. "What're you doing?"

I continued to fill the folder. "These are my writings, my only possessions, sir."

"Wrong, Cooper! Those writings belong to me now." He snatched the folder out of my hand and threw it into the wastebasket. "You'll end up in the Flat Top and do a month of solitary if you set foot in this office again."

My heart jumped into my throat. Sergeant Jones was certainly testing my integreality. The Flat Top was a torture box, and I didn't want any part of it. I hated to lose my writings, but I bowed to the truth of the moment. "Yes, sir, I understand."

Meanness etched his words. "I don't care about your understanding, convict. You're out of here and you'd better thank Sergeant Fisher you haven't been locked up for all the stealing you've been doing."

My blood pressure shot up, and it was all I could do to keep from attacking my false accuser. He wasn't speaking truth or facts, but Rock reality conditioned me to swallow my pride and say, "Yes, sir."

He pointed to the door. "Report to the main gate."

Empty-handed and full of hate for the stoolie sergeant, I shuffled down the corridor toward my new work area. An officer was stationed halfway there to intercept, and as it turned out, to harass me. He bellowed as I approached him, "Cooper! Stop right where you are!"

I stopped in the narrow hallway and stared at him. A smirk masked his face. He was savoring the assignment.

He barked, "Assume the position! Up against the wall and spread 'em, convict!"

Like an animal conditioned to respond to his command, I turned immediately, faced the wall and leaned on it with both palms pressing on the cool surface high above my head. Then I spread my legs, totally at his mercy. I hated the feeling.

As he ran his fingers over my crotch and rear end, he leaned forward and whispered in my ear. "You'd be in the Flat Top for a year if I had my way, *hostage taker*."

I was dying in my silence, and it killed me to submit to him. I felt him smack me on the right rear cheek and pegged him as a sexual pervert like Bear and Psycho.

"Aha!" he blurted. "Just as I suspected! There's dope on your person." He spat the words as he patted that pocket. I felt him slip something into it. He spoke through clenched teeth. "Cooper, I wanna remind you of what we can do to you."

My body stiffened.

He nearly whispered, "Yeah, it's a plant. You know it, and I know it, but it don't matter, 'cause we gotcha."

I remained silent.

"One word from you about the meat and you're *dead meat*. You got it?"

"Yes, sir."

Through the cloth, he patted the stuff in my pocket. "Listen to me, Big Timer, you keep this *dope* as a friendly reminder: You belong to us. Now, get yourself down to the gate."

I heard him step back, and by the time I turned, he disappeared around the corner, but I could still hear him roaring with laughter.

Rage seethed in my soul, but my gut told me I had to control it. I took several deep breaths to keep from exploding, then walked toward the gate. My hand slipped into my pocket, and I pulled out the tiny package. Holding it up in the dim light, I saw that it was a packet of sugar from McDonald's. I laughed harder than the guard who set me up. It was a way to release my anger without creating more problems for myself.

Laughing seemed to help my state of mind, so I moved on. Halfway to the gate, my brain clanked into gear and it hit me: I hadn't taken my problem to God. *Oh, Lord, help me. I need You. I can't handle this confusion.*

That brought a sense of peace. Then I voiced a Scripture I hadn't quoted for months. "The Lord has not given me a spirit of fear, but of power. . . ."

I placed my hands against the wall above my head and pushed as if I could move it. *Lord, this is going to have to be by Your power. I've now lost what little power I had. And Father, I thank You for helping me live with integrity in this unreal world, and turning this mess into something good.*

It *was* a mess. I soon found out the officers coming through the gate spewed tobacco juice like sprinkler heads. My new job required me to continually clean up the spittle. The sergeant who threw me out of my office, and the correctional officer who assaulted me in the hallway, were among the worst offenders as they hung out at the gate. They purposely spat the brown juice in my direction, making certain Mr. Power Broker was aware of his humble state. I was cast out of my tower of power and relegated to the lowest, most demeaning job they could find. In five minutes, I had been thrown from the top rung of the pecking order to the very bottom.

Six hours a day I stood by the gate with my mop and bucket and cleaned up the officers' filth as they came into the prison. Though my manhood was threatened and my dignity thrown to the dogs, after a few days, I decided to take affirmative action. I determined to fight the humiliating treatment with an honest, positive approach. So, as each officer popped through the gate and spat his share of the brown juice, I greeted him like he was an angel sent by God. Beaming from ear to ear, I mopped up his spit and chirped, "Good morning, sir. It's a great day the Lord has made."

Their days didn't seem to get any better when they heard me, but mine took on a glow. The more I said, "It's a great day the Lord has made," the better the days became. Sergeant Jones had never heard of such a thing.

Unsure of what to do about it, he took the matter to his boss, Lieutenant Foster. I heard about it from Hinson, a buddy of mine who worked as an inmate clerk there. Hinson overheard their discussion and shared an exaggerated, blow-by-blow account with me.

He said that when the lieutenant asked what he wanted, Sergeant Jones said, "Sir, we're having a real problem with our new gate man."

"How can you have a problem with a gate man, Sergeant Jones? That makes absolutely no sense. He's right there under your supervision."

"Sir, this is an unusual problem. No convict is supposed to be happy at this job. This Cooper guy is happy!"

"This guy's happy? That's the problem you've brought to me today? You think this convict being happy is a problem?"

"Well, sir, every time I turn my back he whistles on the

job. I know it's him. No inmate is supposed to show that kind of disrespect."

"Whistling? What kind of whistling?"

"Like, songs."

"Songs?"

"Happy little ditties."

"And this is the major problem you want me to get involved in?"

"Believe me, sir, it's more serious than it looks. He smiles at everyone who comes through the gate. And he even says good morning to the officers."

When Hinson related the conversation to me, I roared. Without even trying, I managed to make Sergeant Jones look like an idiot by putting a happy form of *integreality* into practice.

A few days later, Jones was removed from his post, and the lieutenant sent word he wanted to meet me. I didn't know what he wanted, but something in me leaped for joy. Hinson introduced me to his boss. The lieutenant said, "Cooper, I'm glad to meet you. I hear you have a really good attitude."

"Thank you, sir. I try to."

"Are you happy?" He waved off my answer. "Obviously you're happy at your current post." He had a twinkle in his eye.

I looked at Hinson, who winked to let me know his boss was referring to Sergeant Jones's complaint. "Yes, sir, I am happy, but it seems to make some people unhappy." I laughed with him and Hinson.

"I like your spirit, Cooper. We need a positive person at the gate. Keep up the good work." A wry smile made his face glow, and he held up a finger. "If you decide you want a different job, just let me know."

Within days, Sergeant Baker replaced Jones on the gate.

Baker was different right from the start. A few days after he took command of the gate, he said, "Cooper, I have plenty of guys who can handle this gate job. How would you like to spend your time during the day?"

I was perplexed. "What do you mean, sir?"

"I didn't want to put it this way, but you can work as few as two hours a day if you've got something else you want to do with your time."

"Thank you, sir. I'd like to spend more time studying religion, philosophy, the psychology of addiction . . ."

He held up his hands. "Say no more. You just let me know what two hours a day you decide on and that'll be your work schedule."

I was amazed at God's grace and the favor He granted me through those in authority. I basked in His blessings and continued to share His light with everyone who darkened the Rock gate. This time He truly awarded me the best job in the place. My perception of reality changed. I enjoyed my days immensely. It was as if God had set me free. I worked two hours a day, from 7 to 9 a.m.—banker's hours—but lived in abject poverty. The poorer I became, the richer I was. My days were my own. The state provided me with shelter, clothing, "three hots and a cot."

I studied, wrote to my heart's content and moved around the entire compound as I pleased.

Sergeant Baker gave me a special walking pass and treated me like some of the older lifers who had served forty to fifty years there. We were granted the privilege of free movement throughout the vast prison.

32

On June 15, 1985, the Florida Department of Corrections closed the Rock. United States Federal Judge Susan Black ordered the housing unit condemned, and all inmates removed immediately. Within a week, five hundred of us were hauled to prisons throughout Florida.

Prison officials did not tell us when we were leaving or where we were going. None of us cared. We were delighted to leave that old House of Horrors. However, we had made friends, and we would lose those relationships. Just like me, Moe, Ezra and Luke were transferees. I knew I would miss my three buddies if we didn't wind up at the same prison.

Such friendships and feelings for one another meant nothing to most of the prison officials. They were doing their job, working with misfits and malcontents, and that was that. Yet, I grieved that we would be treated like a herd of cattle, shoved onto prison buses with barred windows and armed guards, without any idea of what we faced. As I lay on my bunk the night the news came, I wondered if Dr. Menard would label my emotions as symptoms of separation anxiety.

Remembering the prayer Flip and I had prayed, I smiled and drifted off to sleep.

Closing the Rock was the big break that would free me to be transferred from that close custody prison for hardcore, maladjusted and dangerous criminals to a maximum security prison. I would be housed with inmates who committed equally serious offenses but who had proved they could abide by the law in general population.

I woke up in a couple of hours and couldn't go back to sleep. The intoxicating effect of the news flew around in my brain like mockingbirds imbibing at a moonshine still. The birds were singing, "Hi-Ho, the Rock is closed. Hi-Ho, the Rock is closed."

When I finally relaxed, peace settled over me. I dreamed about taking a freedom ride on a sandy beach in an MGB sports car with a beautiful blonde, her hair flying in the breeze. It didn't dampen my optimistic spirit when I awoke to find myself riding on a hard prison bunk, still at the Rock with no idea whatsoever if and when I would be released. But on Tuesday, June 21, 1985, when I shuffled toward the long gray bus for the ride to another institution, I felt like flying. My legs were shackled and my wrists cuffed, but I was free in spirit. One thing disturbed me. I left Kenny, Garth, Henry and Marty behind in other housing areas in the vast prison, and I was sorry I didn't have an opportunity to say good-bye to my cell mates. As I left, I stopped and looked back. My eyes were misty.

A guard came up behind me and whispered, "You wanna go back?"

I shook my head and turned toward the bus. As I waddled up the steps to board the jail-on-wheels, I realized it looked and smelled just like the "charter coach" I had arrived on two years earlier. I flinched, and my stomach acids boiled. My mind knew I was leaving that horrible place behind, but my body couldn't believe it. The thought grabbed at my gut that they might get a few miles down the road and then suddenly turn around and take me back. I swallowed the bile that seemed to choke me.

I was relieved to see five men I knew board after me. Of course, we had no idea where we were going. The officers up front were separated from us by steel mesh. They knew where we were going but did not let us know.

Through the bars on the windows, however, I could see we were traveling northwest on State Road 16, which dissected the prison complex. It came to a dead end at State Road 121. There the bus turned south toward the Reception Medical Center at Lake Butler where my prison stint had started. I cringed when it hit me that the guards might be taking me back there to begin my time over again.

I shook that crazy thought off and concentrated on the ride. Despite being on a smelly jolt wagon headed for nowhere, it was great to just be on the road again. I was relieved when we motored past the turnoff to RMC and took a right turn on a pine-forest road heading north out of the timber and cattle town called Lake Butler.

As the bus jostled us over potholes, the shackles on my ankles tore at my flesh. I felt dehumanized, and the early days in the old dungeon played on the screen of trees flashing by as we whizzed through the woods.

One of the officers yelled, "There goes a bear!"

Immediately a mental image of the "bear" who stalked me at the Rock passed across my mind. However, I came out of my purple haze when he yelled it again, "There goes a bear!"

I peered out and saw a round black beauty lumber across

the road and into the green undergrowth bordering the highway. I said out loud, "That's a picture of me. I'm headed for my freedom." At that moment I claimed release from bondage as I watched the creature disappear. Seeing the bear and thinking about freedom made me feel better. Before I knew it, we arrived at Baker Correctional Institution, a maximum security prison located at the edge of the Osceola Forest on US 90, about forty miles west of Jacksonville and twenty miles northwest of Union Correctional at Raiford.

As they herded us off the bus it seemed I had taken an airplane to a distant land, but the "airline stewards" were the guards who drove the bus. They grunted and cursed me back to earth.

However, my first impression of Baker was that it was quite different from the other prisons, despite the security fences and guard towers manned with tobacco-spitting guards looking down on us. As I stepped off the bus, positive vibrations greeted me, and I wondered if the thirty men who shuffled along with me also felt the good vibes. My antennae helped me know in a hurry that I was not hallucinating. This would be a different reality.

There were several very real causes for the sensation. The first thing I noticed was that the prison staff treated us differently. The cuffs and shackles were removed, we were processed in and we exited the intake building individually rather than with officers escorting us in groups. It felt fantastic to walk alone toward my assigned housing without an officer leading the way.

The biggest difference was the attitude of the prisoners. Instead of convicts ogling us and buying and selling us as sex pawns like the convicts did at UCI, the inmates at this prison welcomed and greeted us with dignity, as if we had just arrived at a free college in the woods.

As we came out of the intake building, they gathered around for introductions. They not only shook our hands, but they told us they were there for us if we had any problems or special needs.

This unexpected friendliness shocked me. All of us new arrivals stood there speechless. We looked at each other with quizzical grins and raised our palms, as if to ask, "Can you believe this?"

The men in blue at Baker chuckled at our body language as if they understood our quiet emotional reaction. Then they told us about the various Christian services being held at the chapel.

As I looked at the radiant faces of our new friends, I thought of Moe, who would have broken the silence with a song at that moment. I stepped forward. "I see you guys have quite a lot of freedom here. Is it really okay for us to congregate like this?"

The Baker bunch laughed like choir members who were asked if they knew how to sing. A bright-eyed young man moved toward me and announced. "I'm George Roberts. And this ain't heaven, brother, but it's the sweetest joint we've seen this side of the Jordan."

We all laughed, and he nodded. "Yes, we can gather to have church on the compound as long as we're in eyesight of an officer."

I said, "Well then, let's pray right now."

George said, "That's a great idea. Why don't you lead us, brother?" He checked the name tag on my shirt. "Cooper," he added.

With a grateful heart, I lifted my voice toward heaven and prayed, "Oh, Father, I thank You for Your kindness in sending us from the Rock to this sweet camp. I'm deeply grateful for these brothers who have welcomed us. And in this moment we dedicate ourselves to serve You with them while we are here at this place . . . that sure doesn't feel like prison."

The residents laughed and said, "Amen!" and then directed us to our assigned dorms. I was housed in D-Dorm, along with 71 other men. There I was led to an upper bunk near the middle of a room that must have been fifty by eighty feet. Like a hound dog going around in circles, to feel more comfortable, I looked around and took the place in. It was empty except for the officer assisting me in locating my bed, another one behind the glass of the guard station, and the eight of us from the Rock.

Pushing my earthly belongings up on the bunk, I noticed two inmate housemen seated in front of the dayroom. They were very subdued, but it seemed to me they watched our every move as if we were from outer space.

They were right, in my case. My heart was in my throat since I was in culture shock from the Rock. The atmosphere at Baker seemed free. The place smelled so much cleaner and everything about it seemed to be open. One thing was the same, though. Like my former "home," it did not have air-conditioning. I was used to living without it in the humid Florida climate and smiled when I noticed battery-operated fans attached to the iron framework of many bunks. I would be comfortable.

I excused myself to go use the bathroom. The freedom to do that pleased me, and I liked the looks of the toilets. Everything was spotless, so one could use the bathroom without worrying about picking up a disease.

The restrooms contained urinals, commodes and the expected group showers. All were within view of the officers but out of sight of our sleeping area. For the first time in three years, I would have limited privacy.

Baker appeared to be the top of the line, but what I liked most about it was the mobility the prison staff granted the inmates. I could go anywhere on the compound without a pass, except at count time or lockdown.

That evening just before count, a black man introduced himself. "My name's Zap." He said his nickname with a smile as bright as the prison floor. His name tag told me his real name was Samuel Simmons.

We had only a moment before positioning ourselves on our bunks to be counted. "I'm glad to have you as my bunk mate," he said. "I promise I won't snore or bore you to death."

I laughed, gave him a three-step prison-style handshake and climbed up on my house to wait for the officer to stop by to hear my number. Once seated in an upright position with my legs dangling off the edge of the bed, I looked down on the top of my bunkie's head and whispered, "Zap, I'm happy to meet you. My name is Pops, and you'd better treat me with respect." I thanked God that I was no longer Ninety-nine to anyone.

I couldn't see his face, but I heard him laugh as he replied, "I'm not going to be suckered and call you Pops. They tell me you're as young as you want to be on the court. I already got the word 'bout you."

I was surprised that my hoops reputation had preceded me, and I countered by telling him my real name. "Most people call me Brother Ken, but not on the basketball court."

"No matter," he said, "I'll zap you one-on-one." As he spoke, count time was announced over the PA system, so

I couldn't answer his challenge. We had to sit in absolute silence and at attention.

I knew even at this relaxed camp, I couldn't talk and was not supposed to move during count, but I could not resist responding in some way. On a scrap of paper I wrote, "You're on, Zap. Now I know why you call yourself Zap. But watch out. I might just zip your zap." Before the officers came by, I dropped the note down to land on his shoulder.

During count, as the officers went from bunk to bunk to make sure we were all accounted for, I thanked God again for closing the Rock and transferring me to Baker Correctional Institution, where I could meet a friend like Zap. In comparison, this was freedom. Here I was able to feel a sense of joy. The new reality was almost too much to absorb. Yet, it was real, and I was gaining ground on true freedom.

When count cleared, I took a hot shower without worrying about being raped. Then I returned to the dayroom to mix with the guys who came over with me. There I met new dorm mates. After a few minutes, I excused myself and slipped over to my bed. I propped up and leaned back on my pillow. I recited Psalm 23, thanking God for being my Shepherd and leading me to this green pasture. I slid down under the clean sheet before lights-out and slept like a lamb in the Shepherd's arms.

At five o'clock I awoke, eased out of bed, washed my face with cold water, dressed and by six sauntered to chow on my own. Traipsing along the one hundred yards of sidewalk that connected the dorm and chow hall, I looked up to the eastern sky toward Jacksonville. I told my heavenly Father that it sure would be good if the Christian volunteers from the city who visited us at Union would come to the woods to minister. It was important to maintain a sense of family.

Following an unbelievable breakfast of scrambled eggs with fried potatoes, sausage, toast and coffee, I visited the chaplain's office. Don Williams, one of the inmate chapel workers, smiled when I asked him about Prison Fellowship volunteers. He showed me a calendar of events.

"They'll be here next week."

Don grinned. "They come in every three months to do a three-day seminar, and this is their time."

"I did Prison Fellowship at Union. Who are their leaders here?"

He nodded and said, "Don Weston and Pat Bloodworth are the mainstays, and Sandi Woods comes in from time to time." He said it with such a calm voice.

I was so excited. "That's fantastic! They ministered to me at the Rock, and I can hardly wait to see them. They're like my family."

I guess I was more than animated; I was ecstatic.

The following Thursday, the first day of the seminar, I wanted to visit with all three of my heroes but sought out Sandi Woods, Mister Magoo's adopting mother. I just had to find out how my little feline buddy was doing. I felt like a kid. "How's Magoo?" I inquired, before asking about her and husband, Lou.

"Magoo is the delight of our lives. Lou and I thank God for him all the time. He's become like our kid, and such an important part of our family."

My thoughts ran together. "I feel like I'm his godfather, so please tell Lou how much I appreciate both of you for loving my little godson. Please cuddle him for me."

Miss Sandi's eyes sparkled. "That will be our pleasure. He is stunted from the broken back, but he romps and plays like any normal ten-inch-long cat with tunnel vision."

I laughed and noticed Don Weston sidling up to my elbow. We shook hands.

Don said, "God sent you to the right place, Ken. We were praying that you and some of the other guys would be sent to Baker when you left Union."

I touched his arm. "Our time together at UCI made us family. Thanks for loving me while I was there and for praying me into Baker."

33

The Chuck Colson seminar got me off to a great start at the new prison. It dealt with God's plan for my life. I decided on Friday of the three-day event to make Jeremiah 29:11 and 14 the benchmark Scripture for my stint at Baker and for the future. I wrote it in the back of a New Testament supplied by the Gideons: "For I know the thoughts that I think toward you, saith the Lord, Thoughts of peace, and not of evil, to give you an expected end . . . and I will be found of you, saith the Lord: and I will turn away your captivity. . . ."

I was still incarcerated, and the future seemed unsure, but when they moved me to Baker, I knew God had ransomed me from the Rock. I was no longer a slave held hostage. Apparently the ransom had been paid for my release to this prison in the woods. The trees, the ponds beyond the fences and the red birds flying overhead reminded me of my home country, made me feel free and cleared my mind. Truly, my captivity at the Rock was one phase of God's plan for my life, and now a new phase of freedom had begun. It began to take shape sooner than I thought it would.

In early January, Neal Stavely, my classification specialist, called me into his office. "I'm recommending that your custody be changed from maximum to minimum. This will give you a chance to prove to the Parole Commission that you can be trusted outside the fence."

"You mean I'll be able to go outside the gate before my hearing in April?"

"That's right."

I know I must have had the dumbest look on my face. I was flabbergasted. Six months earlier when the Rock closed, I was expected by prison officials to die in prison, and now this kind man was talking about my walking out the gate to work. Everything was happening so fast I couldn't take it all in and sort through it. My mind just couldn't process all that was pushing me toward freedom.

I never believed I would die in lockup and always said I'd do three to five years, but now that the moment might arrive after just three years, it was difficult to believe that I would be given the opportunity to high step it through the main gate on my own.

I was assigned work as the clerk for Mr. McVey, the outside maintenance supervisor. The first day, as I approached the front gate, it was a beautiful spring morning. The sun was shining just for me. A dream was coming true. I had visualized it hundreds of times, and now I actually stood at the gate waiting for the control room officer to hit the electronic switch that would unlock it. I heard the lock click.

After a moment's hesitation, I pushed through the opening in the metal barrier that separated me from the outside world. My feet floated over the concrete. After a few steps, I heard the gate lock behind me. Incredibly, I was actually outside the prison and walking toward the maintenance building. About five paces along the sidewalk, I glanced back to make sure they weren't coming after me to cuff and shackle me and drag me off to solitary confinement to await my new charge of attempted escape. I smiled and skipped along for a few steps. The child in me had come out to play.

After that initial experience of freedom, I became accustomed to being able to pass through the gate every morning and walk to work at the maintenance building. Even so, I never lost my childlike attitude of gratitude, and my boss treated me just like a free man.

In March, when the parole examiner came to interview me, I had been working outside the fence for two months without one slip. He looked me straight in the eyes, extended his hand and introduced himself. "I'm Franklin Davenport."

His hand was warm and his grip firm. That encouraged me. I said, "Inmate Cooper." I was careful to stay within that no-man's land that separates staff and inmate.

He got right to the point. "Mr. Stavely has recommended that we take sixty years off your date . . ."

My heart skipped a beat. I didn't hear the rest of his declaration. "Ah, I'm sorry. Would you say that again, please?" I snorted through my nose self-consciously. "Just the last part."

He smiled and said, "If the Parole Board will go along with Mr. Stavely's report, that would take sixty years off your projected release date." He glanced down at the paperwork in his hands. "That would put you out the gate and into a work release center the first week of June."

"This year?" I asked. "You mean June of this year?"

He checked the paperwork again, then looked up at me with a smile. "That's right. June coming up. This year."

I almost fainted but managed to clear my head. "Sir," I blurted, "I don't know what to say. I know I'm ready, but good things are happening very quickly."

"Don't get your hopes too high, Cooper. I'll make my assessment and report my findings to the Commission. The Board will consider my recommendation along with Mr. Stavely's."

"I don't know what to say, sir. But I can assure you that if you support my parole, you will not be disappointed."

His eyes narrowed. "What do you mean by that?"

"Well, two years of hard time at the Rock convinced me that prison is not the place for me, and I'm determined to never do anything again to get myself locked up. I won't even spit on the sidewalk, much less look at a bank."

The examiner laughed with me.

Following the interview, I had no idea what he would recommend, and I felt guarded about my chances. The run of good fortune was snowballing, and being released by June seemed too good to be true. The first person I talked to was Mr. McVey. "I haven't done a thing to make this happen. Maybe I just don't have enough faith that God will do it, but this scares me."

"I understand. You've been through a lot."

I sighed. "I feel like I'm going to wake up and this will all have been a dream."

He looked at me, pointed his finger at my chest and said, "That's typical of inmates who have been put down so low. When they see themselves coming back to the top of the heap, their self-worth has been so shattered that they can't receive it."

I laughed and said, "You're absolutely right. I feel unworthy. I think of the hostages and all the hurt I caused. I'm afraid to believe the good report for fear it won't come true."

"That's an understandable defense you put up to protect yourself. But in your case it's clear to me that you're on your way, not only up, but out."

I believed him and praised God for His plan to release me from prison on the first week of June. Undoubtedly my anticipation of getting out, combined with the coming of spring, caused me to stay on the mountaintop day and night. I wanted to hug everybody on the compound and skipped once more when I went back out the gate to work that glorious day.

34

Being assured of getting out at God's appointed time, that night I dreamed that one day I would be in a position to help men who, like me, were coming out of prison. For some time it was in my mind to develop a ministry bridging the gap from prison to society. The dream was in living color and surrounded by sound. When I awoke the name that kept coming to me was *Adam*, an acronym for *Adopt a Man*. It was perfect. I wanted to give every man a chance to live as a new creation in the Lord. Each man needed the opportunity to express his new beginning through living the changed life in normal society.

In the coming weeks, I didn't share my dream with many Christian brothers. Instead, I harbored and nurtured it. I sensed that God had dropped the thought into my heart, and He would make a way for me to fulfill it in His perfect time.

On Sunday mornings another inmate, Floyd Foster, who was my good friend, though young enough to be my son, came to the chapel service with his mother. She was a striking woman who appeared to be my age or a little younger. From the first moment I saw June in that worship service, I was attracted to her. Her son was a fine young man, so I knew she had to be someone very special. She carried herself with dignity and displayed a spirit of peace and joy radiating from her smile. When I looked at her, I wondered what had gone through Adam's mind the first time he saw Eve.

There was a separation between the inmates with visiting guests from the rest of us inmates in that chapel service. I could see June and Floyd over in the visitors' section and forced a bold prayer. "I want to meet her, Lord. Please send someone to visit me so I can be in the visiting park when she visits Floyd."

I hadn't had a visit for months, and it took awhile for my prayer to be answered. Then I received a visit from Jim Whyte. It was a grand occasion. He not only came to see me for the fellowship. He came to discuss the parole plan that he and Raymond Duncan would present to the Commission in April. As important as that visit was, my desire to meet Floyd's mother distracted me. When I walked into the visiting park, Jim greeted me.

As we made our way to the picnic table, I saw June seated with Floyd and other family members. They were visiting near the sandbox where children played. I glanced at June from time to time but managed to listen to Jim. "Ken, we have a definite plan we believe the Parole Board will favor. You'll live at the work release center, and I'll be your sponsor. I'll help you find work. If we can't get you something quickly, we'll work out something at the newspaper."

"That's great!"

Mr. Whyte nodded and smiled as we continued our conversation.

I leaned over and touched my friend on the shoulder. "With all the loose ends, it's hard for me to relax and let others do things for me, but I really do appreciate it."

We talked out all the plans, and after about an hour, I pointed to Floyd and his family. I asked Jim if it would be all right to invite June over to talk with us. Jim approved, so I sauntered over and stood across the table from Floyd, behind his mom. I pointed to her and then back to myself. Floyd smiled, but to tease me, he shook his head a little as though he was not going to introduce us. She started to turn around so Floyd said, "Mom, I want you to meet a good friend of mine. This is Ken Cooper. Ken, this is my mother, June."

I looked into her soft blue eyes and said, "Good to meet you, June."

Her face beamed as she nodded. "Nice to meet you, too."

Floyd said, "This is my wife, Cherrie, and"—he pointed to a beautiful little girl playing in the sandbox—"that's my daughter, June Carlene."

I was impressed and let them know it. "What a beautiful family."

June and I hit it off from the start. She was articulate, displayed a keen sense of humor and didn't look down on me. I loved her spirit, and I was spellbound by her gorgeous blue eyes sparkling under the most beautiful gray hair accented with waves of white.

We really enjoyed our visit. In fact, she appeared to be as happy to know me as I was to meet her. We barely noticed anyone else as we talked and laughed.

She looked me in the eyes and said, "I have a vision of helping men as they come out of prison."

I could feel my eyebrows shoot up.

She added, "I want to adopt men and help them adjust to society."

I burst out laughing so loud Jim, Floyd and Cherrie stopped talking and stared at me. I said, "June, that's the exact vision God has given me. What do you call yours?"

She said, "I call my vision *Adam*, which is short for *Adopt an Inmate*."

Goose bumps ran the length of my body. That's when I knew God brought us together. I touched her hand and exclaimed, "That's amazing. I call mine *Adam*! It stands for *Adopt a Man*."

We laughed and looked at each other but didn't know what to say. I was smitten and wanted to get to know her better, but I knew it would be difficult since Jim had already told me I might be released before he could visit again.

When visiting time was over, Floyd and I stood side by side and watched Jim, June and Cherrie, with the little girl in her arms, walk toward the gate. They grew small in the distance as they passed through. I thanked Floyd for introducing me to his family, but I didn't tell him that something special had happened. I would cherish the visit with his mother for a long time.

From that windy day in March, June and I corresponded and developed a relationship that brought me thankful laughter. June was there for me during sorrow as well. On April 9, my brother Jim died in an automobile accident.

I was devastated. His warnings during my bank robbery days came alive, and I felt a great love for him. It comforted me that he had gone to heaven, but I knew that I couldn't go to the memorial service. The sense of his loss was deepened. In my agony Floyd reached out to me. He got word to June the day it happened, and it was comforting to know she was praying for me.

Ironically, the day after Jim's release to heaven, the Florida Parole Commission met to consider my release from prison. Facing the two cataclysms at the same time clashed like meteorites in my mind. Overwhelmed, I "met" with my long-time friend Robert Schuller through his devotional writing, early the next morning. I arose at 4:30. When I opened the little booklet to the devotional for April 10, my mind refused to believe what my eyes read. The theme for the week was "Unlock the Gate," and the Scripture text for the day was Romans 7:25, which read, "Thank God! It has been done by Jesus Christ our Lord. He has set me free."

I read the words over and over, crying uncontrollably. I knew Jim had been set free and I would be soon. In between gasps, I sobbed, "We're free! We're free!" The inmates around me woke up and looked around in confusion. Zap roused and stood up. He touched my arm and said, "Brother Ken, you cry all you want. It'll help you deal with your brother's death."

Through the fog surrounding me, I realized the men would think I was just mourning my brother's death. That sobered me enough that my gasping for breath was not so deep. I stared at my bunkie. "Zap, that's only part of it. Take a look at my devotional study for today."

He took the book, read the caption and smiled at me.

I said, "You see, brother, it's not just about Jim's release from the prison of his body, it's about my being released from prison by the Parole Board today."

The young man was speechless, so he hugged me with all his might.

That afternoon, Chaplain Roy Morrison called me to his office. I can't remember how I got there from my workplace, but I must have walked. Even so, I'm also sure I could have floated. When I entered his office, he was as excited as I was and exclaimed, "The Parole Board voted to release you!" He stood and stepped around his desk with his arms open.

I hugged him as if he were my benefactor, thanked him for the good news, glanced toward heaven and thanked God for His unbelievable blessings. Then I danced a jig that would have put Lil' Abner of old to shame. As I was whirling around in a circle, I shouted over and over, "God has set me free. God has set me free. I'm free!"

Word got out about what God had done, so I carried "Schuller" with me and showed inmate after inmate the caption, "Unlock the Gate."

Two days later, God sent me a helpful word through a Helen Steiner Rice poem on a sympathy card from June. The mixed news had taken me on an emotional roller coaster, mourning Jim's death in one breath and praising God for my freedom in the next. From one moment to the next I didn't know if I'd be up or down. Schuller's words were echoed in June's card. I was reminded that God had set Jim free as surely as He was about to set me free. That message, June's thoughtfulness and the love of the brothers opened my spiritual eyes. I grieved Jim's death in a new light. He was free indeed.

Chaplain Morrison continued to minister to me, and June's encouraging words helped me through one of the hardest and most confusing times of my life. I wrote in a letter to her, "June, this is the first time a loved one's death hasn't sent me reeling into a state of anger and rage. I know for certain God has done a real work in me. I believe the Bible refers to it as deliverance."

She understood what I was going through better than anyone else. June had lost two sons to death, one at two months of age and one when he was twenty, but God helped her through the time.

June wrote, "Floyd and Andrew were inseparable, but due to an accident resulting in Andrew's death and Floyd's imprisonment, I lost one son to death and the other to prison." She added, "One night as I was sitting alone, I cried out to God and told Him I felt utterly alone. I asked Him to comfort me with His presence. The prayer no more than left my lips when I felt two big strong arms embrace me. I thanked God for loving me that much. Since that time I have never doubted He is there for me when I need Him and when I ask for His help."

Six weeks later, on May 23, an officer woke me at 4:30 in the morning and told me to pack my belongings. He didn't tell me the purpose of my early wake up, but I knew I was bound for Dinsmore Work Release in Jacksonville—freedom's final gate.

As my feet hit the cool floor, my adrenal gland woke up and squirted joy juice into my system. I could hardly restrain myself from shouting and jumping, but I held back and got busy gathering my personal things. My books and writings went into a larger box. Dr. Schuller's little devotional ended up on top of the rest of the treasures, so I sneaked a peek at his word for the day. Under the caption, "Prayer Is the Key," he quoted a portion from Psalm 116. I read it twice to stamp it on my mind. When I finished and put it back on the stack, I caught a glimpse of Zap moving around. He got up and stood beside our bunks, so I laid my hand on his shoulder and said, "Later, Gator."

He flashed a beautiful set of white teeth. "Thanks, Ken. You've been like a father to me."

I hugged him and challenged, "You know, prayer is the key." I lifted a finger. "Talk to God every chance you get."

"I will, Pops, and your hoops game will be at the top of my prayer list."

"At my age I need all the prayer I can get, especially for my ball game." We laughed. But the next few hours were like days to me.

Finally, an officer escorted me to the gatehouse, where I sat and waited until a ride came for those being transferred that day. No one joined me, so I waited alone. At about 9:15, another officer came for me, and we passed through the gate. I thought about the significance of the nine o'clock hour. That was the time of day Jennie died, and it was the hour I chose to rob banks. I smiled at the irony if not providence of it, and thanked the Lord that my appointment with freedom was scheduled at the ninth hour.

I boarded the bus. It didn't matter that the guards reminded me of the two grumps who had brought me there a year earlier. I was happy that these men were assigned to transport me to my destination. I loved the officers, the bus and the other men already on the bus when it got there. More than that, I loved the realization that I was making my final giant step to independence. Glancing down at the cuffs that held me, I smiled. My wry grin reflected my attitude. Not even the discomfort of the steel on my wrists and ankles could spoil the euphoria I felt. I knew God opened the gate for me. I was outward bound.

Across the aisle a prisoner I didn't know motioned to me, put his palms together under his chin and silently mouthed, "Thank God." I wondered if he was an angel sent to remind me that I was being released through God's forgiveness and grace. I couldn't stop the instant tears and silently put my hands together in the fashion of prayer and raised them toward heaven. The man saw that I, too, was exceedingly grateful for being set free. He smiled and gave me a thumbs-up.

Turning to face the window, I slid down into the seat and closed my eyes. As I worshiped God, I asked Him to clothe me with His presence in that radiant moment. In the next breath, I praised Him for embracing June in her darkest hours. Opening my eyes, I gazed out the window and remembered the Schuller nugget for the day based on Psalm 116. It was a passage I went to many times in the darkest days at the Rock. The devotional appeared in my mind, and I read it from the screen of my remembrance. *Prayer is the Key. I love the Lord because He hears my prayers and answers them. Because He bends down and listens, I will pray as long as I breathe.*

Just then the bus jerked as the driver missed a gear. This sudden jolt made me laugh as I prayed, "Lord, please help us make it to work release safely."

A half hour later the DOC chariot pulled into Lawtey Correctional Institution. I frowned when it stopped. After thinking about it a moment, I figured they were stopping to pick up another man destined for work release. Then one of the officers poked his head in the open door and shouted, "Cooper, oh-eight-seven-eight-six-eight!"

"Yes, sir!" I shouted back.

He stepped up into the bus and made his way back to me. Staring at my name tag he said, "Get off the bus." He allowed room for me to get out of my seat as he pointed the way.

I was flabbergasted. Something was wrong. I wondered if the state had changed its mind. No, that couldn't be it. I was on my way out. God ordained it, so this was a mistake. Finally, I found my voice and protested, "This is not my destination. I'm headed to Dinsmore Work Release Center."

His eyes turned to steel. He snorted and without a word pushed me toward the door. I felt the restriction of the shackles as I tripped along the aisle. My body was as unwilling as my mind, and I nearly fell. The officer grabbed my arm to steady me, and I managed to make it down the steps. I checked the gray block buildings and choked, "Just another prison." I felt utterly hopeless. Stiffening my chin, I muttered, "I can't believe this is happening to me."

I followed the commands of the officer and was quickly processed into LCI. The only consolation was that the perimeter was lined with a common six-foot fence without security wire. It was a minimum-custody camp. That brought a wry grin. If God's will was for me to remain in prison, at least it would be at a mini camp. During processing, I asked the officer, "Why have I landed here?"

He smirked at me and said, "How should I know? All I do is process inmates in. I don't call Tallahassee to find out what they're up to."

In less than an hour I walked out of the processing building into this new joint. Unlike Baker, there was no welcoming committee. An officer with a drawl routinely pointed the way across the compound toward my new dorm and said, "Over yonder past the multipurpose building, that's your new home."

It was all I could do to drag my body through the gate and onto the sidewalk leading to the housing area. I felt totally alone and forsaken. My mind told me to walk tall, but my shoulders slumped. I couldn't remember ever feeling so let down. I wanted to die right there but knew I had to keep going. As I passed the medical building on my left and headed for what appeared to be the multipurpose complex, I heard music from under some trees between the two buildings. It was a familiar country gospel sound of strumming guitar, and I wanted to see who was playing it.

I was still squeamish, so I glanced over my shoulder to see who was watching me. Seeing no officer in sight, I eased my way toward the guitar music. Something about it was lifting the dark cloud hanging over me. As I approached the shade from a huge oak, I heard, "Brother Ken, step across the Jordan."

My heart leaped and I gasped, "Moe!" When I stepped into the shade I couldn't believe it was really him.

He stopped playing and gave me his familiar grin.

"It is you, Moe! How in the world did you get here?"

"On a big gray bus, just like you."

"What's this place about?"

"It's a transition camp for men on their way out," he said. "Where are you headed?"

"Dinsmore," I said.

"That's good." His voice became singsong as he said, "A big gray goose will fly outta here for Dinsmore in a couple of weeks."

35

As usual, Moe sang the right song. On the fourth day of June, I boarded what I hoped would be the last prison bus I would ever ride. I was allowed to board without shackles or cuffs for this trip. I was elated.

When the "gray goose" took off, I checked out what was happening through the window. We headed north on 301. As the little prison community became small behind us, I thought about the stopover at Lawtey and wondered if God arranged it so Moe and I could see each other one more time. It was a puzzle to me, and I asked Him to show me how the pieces fit together. Instinctively, I knew that would come later, since I was too engrossed in this trip and couldn't focus on everything at once.

Eighteen miles north, the bus turned onto I-10 and headed east toward Dinsmore. It seemed the cars were tiny as they flew by. All I had to compare them to was the '70s gas guzzlers I drove before my fall. The little convertibles reminded me of my dream of flying down the beach in an MGB. As the traffic streamed by, I tried to imagine who the people were, where they were going in such a hurry and if any of them were a part of God's plan for my new life. It was odd, but I now looked at everyone as a person of worth in God's hands. That thought calmed me.

Before I realized it, we had arrived at Dinsmore Work Release Center in northwest Jacksonville. As I stepped off the bus, I felt truly free. I gave the place a once-over. Though I would still be locked up at night, the authorities would release me during the day to go to work somewhere in the city. That flash raised chill bumps, and I thanked God for my new life outside the prison fences.

While waiting my turn to be admitted, I took in the design of the structure. It rose from a slight man-made knoll in the middle of a natural swamp. Plate-glass doors and windows replaced the concrete walls and steel bars of prison, and there were no fences or guard towers. The work release center looked like a college dormitory designed by Frank Lloyd Wright. Standing there reflecting on my free-man image in the looking glass, I thanked God that this place was a part of the grand design of the Master. My life was included when the Architect drew up the divine blueprint. It was a great feeling to be in God's will.

After my housing assignment, I dressed in civilian clothes June brought to the center. Everything fit perfectly. Those clothes let me know that, without a doubt, I was freedom-bound. Following a short orientation, I was taken out to look for work. The interviews that first week brought nothing but turndowns for a former bank robber looking to land a public relations job.

But Dinsmore turned out to be exactly what I needed.

I wasn't pressured to find immediate employment, and I was allowed to ease back into society rather than hitting the road running.

After a few days, it was clear to me I was still doing time. I had one foot in lockup at night and the other on the street during the day. Jim Whyte served as my sponsor, taking me to job interviews, parole office appointments—and more importantly to me, my first meal outside the prison gate. He took me to Casa Molina for Mexican food and called it my freedom meal. Then he took me shopping and bought a black suit I told him was fit for the former gentleman bank robber, but not for a journalist.

Jim ignored my sense of humor and my horrible typing speed, and hired me to write for the *Florida Times-Union* newspaper.

I enjoyed the workweek immensely despite typing just seventeen words a minute. I wrote human-interest stories for *The Neighbor*, the community news and features section of the paper.

It was a perfect job for me, an ex-offender who was finding my way in a strange world that had changed dramatically during my four-year absence. Working as a staff writer, I was able to get acquainted with many of the movers and shakers of the community. I could relate to them in a positive way as a reporter and fellow citizen rather than as an ex-convict. It amazed me that this was God's plan.

June visited me on Saturdays and brought the most delicious food I had eaten in years: homemade potato salad, garden-fresh green beans, buttermilk fried chicken and heavenly coconut cream pie for dessert. We held hands as I said grace over the food, got acquainted eating our picnic lunch while sharing our life stories, our hopes for the present and our visions for the future. Each visit lasted an hour, but seemed like thirty minutes. I felt God was using these times to put us together for His purposes. We would someday organize the Adam ministries and adopt men coming out of prison.

On Sundays, as June was visiting Floyd at Baker, I attended Shiloh Free Will Baptist Church with Barry Myers, a volunteer chaplain at Baker. It was a little country church five miles down the road, but Pastor Leonard Owens and his family made it seem like I was back home in Kentucky each Sunday.

A few weeks into my experience at Dinsmore, an important page of God's blueprint was placed on the table. Major Hardy, the man who ran the facility, called me to his office. I was nervous though he came across as a friendly man. Yet there was something about him that made me realize he was aware of the power he wielded. Maybe it was his tone of voice, or possibly his body language telling me to be cautious when he said, "Sit down, Cooper. I see from your file you have considerable experience as a public speaker."

I fidgeted, wondering what he might be getting at, and took care to downplay my skills. "That's right, sir. I'm a rusty hack, but I enjoy trying."

He rubbed his chin before expressing his plan. "I want you to speak to a group of businessmen Friday night."

I was astounded but managed, "Thank you, sir, but I can't do that."

"What do you mean you can't do it?" he demanded.

"I know you know what's best, sir, but I'm—"

Major Hardy interrupted me. "It's right down your alley, Cooper."

"Oh. How so?"

He grinned. "It's a group of bankers."

I almost fainted. "Oh, n-no, sir. You've got the wrong man. I couldn't . . ."

His gaze narrowed and he put both hands flat on his desk. "Oh, yes, you can, inmate."

My mind whirled. There was that display of authority. Doing what he told me to do was a no-brainer. "Yes, sir. Of course, I'll do as you say." Finally, I admitted, "It's just that I'm overwhelmed at the thought of facing a group of bankers."

His lips moved into a slight smile.

I got control of myself and asked, "What's the topic they want me to speak on?"

"The criminal mind, especially as it relates to robbing banks. They're interested in how you chose the various banks and how you planned the robberies . . . Basically, how the criminal mind works, what you thought and what triggered that sort of thinking."

I thought about it and said, "Hmm. This Friday?"

"This Friday."

I rubbed my forehead and considered the audience. "A group of bankers?"

"Bankers."

I grimaced. "May I be dismissed?"

"Work on it and make it interesting."

"I promise you it will be that."

He nodded, and I left in a daze. In my job with the State of Kentucky I spoke to heads of state, dignitaries and celebrities, but never had I been as apprehensive as I was in that moment. I headed back to my room to clear my head.

Lindsay, a hardworking and bright young man, was one of my two roommates. He had quickly become a good friend. When I told him my plight, he said, "Old Gray, you can do it hands-down."

"Easy for you to say, kid. You've never faced one of your victims, much less a hundred of them at the same time."

My young roomy was elated and teased me further. "Tell you what I'll do, Mr. Bank Robber. I'll beat you at pinochle tonight, and then you'll be humble enough to do the job."

I smirked. "Yeah, well, how about going with me and driving the getaway car? And while I'm in that meeting, leave the engine running."

Lindsay simply smiled, but later in the evening, as promised, he beat me at pinochle.

At my request, the major allowed June to transport me to and from the Friday evening event. When June and I walked into the grand ballroom of the downtown hotel, I laughed, called her Bonnie and whispered in my most gangster-like slur, "C'mon, let's go case another joint."

Hundreds of people were milling around talking and laughing. It was a mix of an equal number of men and women. I said to June, "Well, it appears these bankers brought their wives." I seemed to be relaxed, but cringed when our host escorted us to the head table and seated me next to John G. Hollingsworth, president of the North Florida Board of Bankers. The thought of how I'd always wanted to be seated next to money ran through my mind, but I kept myself from trying to be funny. Instead, I smiled, shook his hand with enthusiasm and introduced June. On the outside, I was animated and happy to be there, but on the inside, my gut was telling me to abort, run and get out while there was still a chance.

Mr. Hollingsworth was as cordial as his expensive suit

was smart. I complimented him on his tie, but I was actually feeling self-conscious that I was wearing the only suit I owned. I apologized to God and asked His forgiveness for my feelings. Jim Whyte had purchased the suit, and I really was grateful for it.

I needed psychological help when I said to Mr. Hollingsworth, "Please tell me about this huge crowd." I swirled my hand around at the people. "I assume the couples are bankers and their spouses." I flipped my hand toward a separate section. "But who are all those women over there?"

He nodded. "Those are mainly tellers from this region."

I gulped and almost spilled my water. I faced at least two hundred tellers and it made me look down and mutter, "Oh, God, please forgive me."

Mr. Hollingsworth coughed and told me he couldn't understand what I just said. I laughed and said, "Oh, I was just talking to God about this pickle He placed me in."

My host didn't seem to understand my statement or appreciate my predicament. "Yes, I hadn't thought about it, but this may be a night you will long remember."

I laughed self-consciously, "Yeah, if I get through it."

Then I turned to June and touched her arm. "I'm glad you're here with me. This is a lot worse than I thought it would be."

She smiled.

"Did you hear Mr. Hollingsworth? I'm facing two hundred tellers!"

"You'll do fine, Clyde. It's better than two hundred years."

"Thanks, Bonnie, I needed that."

Within the hour I was introduced. My stomach tightened into a knot. When I stood up to speak and got into the seven-point outline on the printed pages before me, I was doing fine until the second point about the criminal mind.

I intended to tell my audience how I had cased the various banks and devised a master plan before robbing them. The face of my last hostage flashed before me and my throat constricted. I continued forcing my words to come out, but I knew that wouldn't work. Sweat popped out on my forehead as adrenaline flowed.

To give myself a moment to figure out what to do, I took a drink of water, picked up the papers and laid them down before saying, "I don't know if any of you have ever had this experience—when, right in the middle of speaking, you feel you are choking up. I learned in prison, when this happens it is God telling me to change the subject." The people moaned and rolled their eyes. I knew I was on shaky ground if not in quicksand. "So with your kind indulgence, I will deviate a little from the script." I had no earthly idea what I would say next. They moaned again, and several smirked at the dignitaries at the head table. The knot in my throat became a stone.

I glanced at June, took another drink of water and said, "Yes, I learned when this choking comes, God is telling me to talk about something else. I just wish He would tell me what to say."

There were a few laughs, but a restless wave washed across the crowd as I watched and waited for what would pop into my head. My limited experience with God taught me to start the process by opening my mouth in faith before He would fill it. So to get things rolling I said, "I've got . . ." A thought came to mind and I voiced it. "I've got two questions I want to ask."

There were more disgruntled looks, and I didn't know

how long it would be before I got the dreaded hook from the head table. "How many of you have been in a bank when it was robbed?"

The vast audience seemed much happier with the question than I was, so I instructed them. "Raise your hand if you have personally witnessed a bank holdup."

Across the crowd hand after hand shot up. I was dismayed and momentarily dumbfounded. I counted at least twenty hands and prayed none of the people had been *my* targets. Then I said, "I'm sorry. I don't know what to say. But it grieves me deeply that so many of you have been victimized and suffered trauma. I'm truly sorry."

The unhappy crowd groaned. I heard a few hisses and what sounded like derisive laughter. I attempted to ignore it. "Now, the second question." My heart beat in my throat but I finally got the words out. "Will you please forgive me?"

A belligerent woman down in the front leaped up and screamed, "How dare you ask us to forgive you!"

She was weeping. My heart sank into my stomach. I looked at June and hoped she knew I was asking her to pray.

Then the woman blurted, "I was in a bank when a man died at my feet."

"I'm so sorry," I muttered.

"You should be. The bank robber shot a customer! He bled all over my shoes and died at my feet."

My legs trembled. I was stunned and felt absolutely helpless, so I prayed as I continued to look at the woman.

About that time a woman to my left seated in the mix of tellers slowly rose and said, "I've been in three robberies, but *I* forgive you."

She paused, but I couldn't say anything. During the silence, several women around her let her know they were very unhappy with her. Some made fists and stared at her. Others held up open hands in dismay while still others simply gaped.

She elaborated. "Yes, sir, I forgive you. I can see you have truly repented."

An impulse to run to her shook my body, but I stifled it, gulped and said, "Thank you."

She was nearly crying when she whispered, "Go and sin no more."

The picture of Christ and the adulterous woman in the chapel at UCI lit up my mind, and in that moment, I knew what she must have felt when the crowd was ready to stone her and the Lord said, "Neither do I condemn thee."

After the meeting, I sought her out and thanked her for coming to my rescue. She touched my arm, looked at June standing beside me and said, "I'm Alberta Schultz, sister of Sergeant Ben Johnson."

I teetered for a moment and tried to regain my composure. Ben Johnson was the corrections officer murdered by an inmate at the Rock a few weeks before I landed in that hell hole. I finally managed to say, "I'm truly sorry for your loss."

"That's okay, Mr. Cooper," she interrupted. "I'll never get over it, but in order to go forward with my life, I have to work at forgiving the man who killed Ben."

We stood there weeping unashamedly for what seemed like a minute. Then I held my arms open and gathered her in like an older brother, whispering in her ear, "Prayer is the key, and I will pray for you as long as I breathe."

The trauma of Friday night left me in a daze on Saturday morning. But my mood brightened when I saw June come roaring up the drive to the work release center. I was stunned as I watched her approach. She was picking me up for my first four-hour furlough in the car of my dreams, an MGB convertible. I couldn't believe it. She knew nothing of my vision of flying down the beach in one, and I didn't know she owned a sports car, much less an MGB. As I realized I was about to take a joyride set up by the Lord, the teenage boy in me jumped up and down and I shouted, "Wow, Father, You've done it again!"

June and I laughed and reveled in God's grace all the way to the beach where my dream came true. We roared down the sandy shore in her miniature chariot with the top down. As if God had timed it, at that moment the sun ascended from the Atlantic and cast its light across the shimmering waters. The orb of light grew brighter, and its outer circle formed a golden band. Thankful that the lovely creature across the car wore no wedding ring, I turned and gazed at June, wondering if this was how Adam felt sharing the first morning with Eve.

Captivated, I attempted to see into the future, where she would fit into my new life. I focused on her outward beauty, taken in by her radiant smile, sky-blue eyes and gray-white hair blowing in the wind. Eve could not have been more attractive.

And, in that fleeting moment, my heart told me June and I had a spiritual connection that would carry us far. Who but June, a victim of crime who met me in prison, could understand and share my overwhelming feelings of freedom?

I looked toward the sky and silently thanked my heavenly Father for her and praised Him for the joy He had given us. Then, unable to hold back, I stood up, raised my hands toward heaven and praised God with all my might.

As we chased a three-tiered cloud with a white train across the blue sky, I bellowed, "I'm free! I'm free! I'm free!" I plopped back down, beaming from ear to ear as I looked at my lady.

"And, you're forgiven," she said.

EPILOGUE

God's ransom for Ken Cooper is complete. Upon his release from prison, he married June and together in Christ, they began to lead others held hostage to addictions along the road to redemption.

Co-founders of Prisoners of Christ, Jacksonville, Florida, and House of Hope, Gainesville, Florida, they have been involved in the ransom of hundreds of prisoners with addiction problems. Both of these independently operated faith-based transition ministries offer short-term care. They are directed by recovering addicts and report a 90 percent success rate.

The Ken Cooper Prison Ministry, founded in 2000, provides long-term transition services to selected inmate addicts. Those in the program are housed in three Jacksonville-based aftercare facilities directed by ex-offenders once held hostage by addictions.

Using Integreality as the primary approach to overcoming addictions, the Coopers have developed a team of fourteen men and women who lead discipleship and recovery education classes for males and females in two major prisons. Graduates report a remarkable 80 percent success rate.

The KCPM evangelism and discipleship teams share the good news of freedom through Jesus Christ with thousands of men and women in prison. For more on this organization, go to kencooperprisonministry.org or write to Ken Cooper Prison Ministry, P.O. Box 77160, Jacksonville, FL 32226.